# SICK & TIRED OF BEING SICK & TIRED

This book belongs to Howard Edwards. May it not roam far from home. Please return this book when you're done reading it.

**Previous books by Neil Solomon, M.D., Ph.D.**

The Truth About Weight Control

Doctor Solomon's Easy No-Risk Diet

Doctor Solomon's Proven Master Plan
for Total Body Fitness and Maintenance

Doctor Solomon's High-Health Diet

Stop Smoking, Lose Weight

# SICK & TIRED OF BEING SICK & TIRED

NEIL SOLOMON, M.D., Ph.D.
MARC LIPTON, Ph.D., M.P.A.

WYNWOOD™ Press
New York, New York

The names and identities of patients have been changed to protect their confidentiality.

**Library of Congress Cataloging-in-Publication Data**

Solomon, Neil, 1932–
Sick and tired of being sick and tired / Neil Solomon, Marc Lipton.
p. cm.
Bibliography: p.
Includes index.
ISBN 0-922066-02-7 : $18.95
1. Chronic fatigue syndrome—Psychosomatic aspects. 2. Mind and body. 3. Neuroimmunology. I. Lipton, Marc. II. Title.
RB 150.F37S65 1989
616'.047—dc19 89-5395
CIP



Published by WYNWOOD™ Press
New York, New York
Printed in the United States of America

To my loving wife, Frema
and our great sons, Ted, Scott, and Cliff
and their families

NEIL SOLOMON

In loving memory of my father, Albert I. Lipton
and to my mother, Helen
and daughters, Laura and Ellen

MARC LIPTON

# Acknowledgments

We would like to express our sincere appreciation and respect for several people without whose help this book would never have been written.

Gary Sledge, Editor in Chief, and now with *Reader's Digest*, had the vision to accept our proposal and to help us develop a presentation that would permit us to communicate our findings to our readers.

Ann McMath, Associate Editor, was our project manager. Without question, if it were not for Ann and her personal commitment to and belief in our work, this book would never have found its way to your bookstore. She is a superb writer and brilliant thinker.

Evalee Harrison, Executive Director of the Health and Movement Institute and one of the very best physical fitness specialists in the United States, worked directly with us to tailor our unique exercise and movement program to combat $PS^2$. She did a superb job that will benefit millions of $PS^2$ sufferers.

Kathleen Roberts worked with us from the first word put on paper. Her research capabilities and writing skills permitted us to find new studies before they were even in print. She has the capacity to translate them into understandable language.

Mildred Sindell's accumulated journalistic skills helped us say what we wanted. She was an invaluable and creative sounding board whose contributions were significant.

My extraordinary wife, Frema, a Medical Psychotherapist

trained at the Johns Hopkins School of Medicine, contributed her invaluable psychological insights and was a superb editor. Her love and support mean everything to me.

Our brilliant colleague Dr. Richard E. Layton shared with us his expertise on allergy, candidiasis, chronic fatigue syndrome, and environmental illnesses.

Dr. Marco Clayton contributed his knowledgeable support and his expertise in otolaryngology.

Thanks to Julie Cummings, Margie Aronow, Carole Moussalli, and Jorge Ferrer, medical student at the Johns Hopkins School of Medicine, for reviewing our book.

Most important, we want to thank our wonderful patients, who have been our partners in practice for many years. It is their patience and confidence that helped us be successful. The success and the very hard work are really theirs.

We would like to extend a special acknowledgment to William Barnhill whose skill as a writer made this book possible.

# Contents

Note: No doctor can practice medicine in a book for patients he has never examined. And no book can replace the skills and personal attention of a competent physician. This one, then, contains only my clinical observations and reports of the treatments Dr. Lipton and I have used successfully; it is intended to be neither a diagnosis nor a treatment of your medical problems. If you have undiagnosed symptoms, you should see a physician.

# Preface: You Do Hurt! We Believe You!

Sick and tired of being sick and tired. If you have ever felt this way, you are not alone. Perhaps you have struggled with physical symptoms for a long time. Perhaps you do not know what is causing your problems, only that something is wrong. And perhaps you have been told by a physician, "There's nothing I can do to help you" or "I can't find a thing wrong with you" or, more disheartening, "It's all in your head."

If so, it is understandable that you may have become disillusioned, even more tired and depressed as time goes on. Take heart! Believe that Dr. Lipton and I want to help you, because we believe we can.

Through consultation with each other and our patients, Dr. Lipton and I have created a carefully conceived program designed to meet our patients' special needs. What we have learned can help you, too. Our program treats a physical problem called Profound Sensitivity Syndrome, and chances are better than half that it might be the origin of your ailments. Let me explain.

Within the last decade a remarkable discovery has been intriguing progressive-minded physicians and their patients in search of healing. It is known by various names, such as psycho-physiology, neuro-immuno-modulation, and, the most elaborate, psycho-neuro-immunology. All of that is fancy medical terminology meaning simply that your health and well-being depend upon a close interaction between your mind and body. In fact, mind and body should be considered one entity.

I want to make two clarifications, however, about what I've just said. First, this discovery is not really new; it was known to ancient cultures. In India, one of the oldest centers of the study of health, *aryuveda,* was concerned with the intricate balance between body and mind, and the ancient Greeks sent their sick to healing temples where the ill looked for help in their dreams.

Second, though I used the word *simply* above, there is nothing simple about the mind-body connection. It is a complex natural network of interdependent systems—more complex than anything mankind could ever devise. What we've actually been discovering is how it works and, the most exciting part, how you can help make it work more efficiently for *you*.

Dr. Lipton and I are visible testimony to the complementary workings of mind and body, a coupling of two formerly separate disciplines of medicine. I am an endocrinologist and physiologist; he is a clinical psychologist.

Our teaming up, Dr. Mind and Dr. Body, began accidentally on a cold day in January 1977. At that time I was heading the Maryland State Department of Health and Mental Hygiene, and was waiting to testify before the state senate on a bill to improve health care for Maryland residents. My thoughts at the moment were with some patients in the private practice I maintained on nights and weekends.

A young man (I called anybody more than eight years younger than myself a "young man" then) sat down beside me and introduced himself as Marc Lipton. "I'm glad to have this opportunity to meet you," he said. "I have heard a great deal about you."

I in turn had heard that Dr. Lipton was coming to Baltimore to head the city's Mental Health, Addiction and Retardation Services. I had been impressed by his credentials and enjoyed chatting with him. Soon it became evident that individual patient care was of great interest to us both, in addition to working to improve medical care for the groups that were our prime concern at that time.

In a few minutes I was called to testify before the legislature and made a mental note to keep him in mind for any of my patients who might need a psychologist.

Several months later, we collaborated on treatment for four patients in rapid succession and were pleased that in each instance—the problems ranged from a severe rash to sexual dysfunction—the patient was completely cured.

During the months that followed we continued to collaborate on cases for which a mind-body approach seemed most beneficial. Good results with patients suffering from a variety of conditions that affect millions abounded as we combined our fields of interest.

It was through this joint treatment and research that we began to recognize a biochemical phenomenon. We named it Profound Sensitivity Syndrome or $PS^2$.

This syndrome, examined through the course of this book, can cause a wide diversity of otherwise unrelated symptoms; perhaps you have endured several of them. As you employ the specific techniques detailed here to combat it, we think you will find there are new avenues of relief.

And for those of you not now suffering from physical maladies, this information has tremendous implications for your capacity to sustain good health and control over your life.

We begin by understanding that physical distress can be triggered by the mind and vice versa.

*Gregg's Vomiting.* Gregg, for instance, was one of our first joint patients. A 38-year-old male, Gregg was referred to me by a noted gastroenterologist who, along with two other specialists in his field, had evaluated Gregg's severe vomiting. Gregg threw up intermittently on a daily basis and was terrified at night, fearing vomiting involuntarily and choking in his sleep. No medication had ever provided him relief.

When tested, Gregg proved to be allergic to several foods. I placed him on allergy-medication therapy for two months. Although he reported some reduction in his vomiting and gastric distress, his symptoms had not been reduced as much as I would have liked.

I suggested to Dr. Lipton that we collaborate on Gregg's case. I would continue his allergy treatments, and Dr. Lipton would provide psychotherapy and hypnotherapy.

Dr. Lipton soon ascertained that Gregg had several emotional problems, especially an inability to express anger. He suppressed most of his emotions, and they appeared to have converted into his intense gastrointestinal reaction.

Success came slowly, but we did succeed. He was cured after just three months of our joint therapy. Dr. Lipton attributed our success primarily to my allergy treatment; I felt he had been most instrumental in the patient's recovery. In any event, the three of us were gratified by Gregg's improvement, and the understanding of $PS^2$ was under way.

Since I left my state position in 1979 and Dr. Lipton left his city position in 1983, we have referred many patients to each other and it has been exciting to see the positive results. This has not been accidental. Clearly, our combined mind-body treatment has made a difference.

My prescribed medication, diet plans, and exercise regimens, specifically tailored for the individual's problems, facilitated but were not sufficiently complete cures for Profound Sensitivity Syndrome. The desired outcome was enhanced by Dr. Lipton's employment of behavioral techniques such as biofeedback, psychotherapy, and clinical hypnosis.

To date we have treated hundreds of patients with $PS^2$ and have explored and documented the scientific relationship between troubling thoughts or feelings and biochemical explosions in the body.

In this book we share with you our medical findings and tell you of the research and clinical experiences of other practitioners, as well as some of the insights gained from my lifelong study of the psycho-neuro-endocrine and immunologic interactions—how the mind affects the body and vice versa.

Dr. Lipton and I have tried to encourage our patients to be our partners in these explorations. In fact, we have been working on three levels simultaneously in an effort to bring all the cofactors of health into harmony.

First, we consult together as medical doctor and clinical psychologist, creating a unique team to treat the mind and the body as one; second, we each consult with our partners (patients) about their particular problems and what, as partners, we consider the best mode of treatment; and, third, we help our partners/patients "consult" with their own minds and bodies to understand how they feel and to learn what treatments will make them feel better.

Dr. Lipton and I would like to help you learn the "secrets" of treatment for conditions from which, to date, you may have been unable to get relief.

But you don't have to come into our offices to learn about and benefit from our findings. By examining the case studies of patients with $PS^2$, patients who previously could find no medical cause or cure for their physical maladies, we have developed a program to treat all who suffer from Profound Sensitivity Syndrome.

Throughout this book, we will teach you the same principles and techniques that we teach our patients. You, too, can actually learn to control the biochemical interrelationships between your body and your brain. You can learn to read your body's signals and take charge of your own healing and maintenance for optimal health.

Come join us. Nothing in the treatment of $PS^2$ is hard or painful. In fact, we have learned much of what we share from our patients themselves. It could make a substantial difference in the quality of the rest of your life.

# 1

# Why It's Not All in Your Head...

"Dr. Solomon, I'm sick and tired of being sick and tired."

Those words were spoken to me one morning by a new patient named Margaret, whom I will tell you about in a minute. They symbolize the frustration felt by many patients who come to me with various complaints and a history of previously unsuccessful treatment.

These patients have been to one doctor after another with a curious assemblage of physical problems. The symptoms vary, but occur simultaneously. Since no one disease can manifest that particular grouping of symptoms, doctors are left baffled, their patients worried.

One patient may complain of fluid retention, increased mucus, and a sensitivity to milk. Another may develop headaches while battling irritable bowel syndrome. Still another may suffer from fatigue and a strong intolerance of light, while being afflicted with sensitivity to chemicals.

And, further, these patients have received a consistently negative message from their doctors. Whether or not this is stated or implied, the physicians' reactions are unmistakable: "No one disease can cause all of this. It's got to be in your head."

In one sense, it *is* all in the patient's head because, as my colleague Dr. Marc Lipton and I have discovered, that's where the biochemical phenomenon Profound Sensitivity Syndrome ($PS^2$) begins.

Anyone can have $PS^2$. If you do, then your very thoughts and emotions are causing physical changes in your body—that is, symptoms of sickness that may have been hanging on for some time or seem to have no medical cause. This reaction is direct and immediate, and is likely an inherited and possibly learned response.

Our clinical experience and research suggest $PS^2$ occurs when the natural, healthy balance of functions in the brain, endocrine system, and immune system breaks down. In short, we believe that thoughts and emotions affect the limbic and hypothalamic systems of the brain, triggering an outpouring of biochemicals that can have a profoundly harmful impact on the entire body.

This situation is typified by Margaret.

*Margaret's Arthritis.* A 44-year-old mother of two, Margaret spoke in a throaty monotone. Her complaints included insomnia, chronic fatigue, headaches, irritable bowel syndrome, and the beginnings of rheumatoid arthritis.

"But I have to be honest with you, Dr. Solomon," she said as we talked. "My doctor thinks that this is in my head. Nobody really listens to me anymore."

Compiling a detailed evaluation of her background, I learned that Margaret's difficulties had started five years before, just after a house fire destroyed everything her family owned. About two weeks later, she developed migraine headaches and fatigue, followed by numerous other physical problems. They assaulted her, one on top of another, until she felt as if her "entire body was hurting." The death of her father and an episode involving her son and drugs added to her misery—mental and physical.

From Margaret's complete physical examination, I found evidence to support her complaints. Her blood pressure was high. Her skin was dry. Joints in her fingers were swollen and sensitive. Blood work confirmed early-stage rheumatoid arthritis. Her eyes and nose ran and her nasal mucous membranes were pale—a sign typical of allergy. I had suspected $PS^2$ at work and now there was little doubt.

After the examination I asked Margaret to join me in my office.

"Margaret," I began, taking a seat beside her, "you're suffering from Profound Sensitivity Syndrome."

She looked at me, her eyes alert for the first time. "You mean there really is something the matter with me?"

"There are definitely a number of things the matter with you."

She relaxed a bit as I went on to summarize the direct pipeline effect between her thoughts and feelings and the biochemistry of her body. Her mind did play a role in her illness. I explained further that while I would be treating her to help reduce the physical symptoms I also wanted her to see Dr. Lipton.

"He's a colleague of mine, a clinical psychologist who will show you ways to help you gain control of some of the physiological difficulties you're experiencing."

Margaret's shoulders slumped a little. "So—in other words—I really am crazy."

"Absolutely not, Margaret," I countered. "You are certainly not crazy! You see, most people don't understand that the brain is a biological organ that has an impact on, and control over, the entire body. You happen to be wired in such a way that you get an exaggerated translation of what is going on in your mental processes. This stresses your entire body. It does not mean you are crazy; it means that you have Profound Sensitivity Syndrome and there are specific techniques that can help you overcome that sensitivity."

Margaret agreed to the plan. While I treated her arthritis, anemia, gastrointestinal distress, and fatigue, Dr. Lipton helped her identify a number of learned patterns of thinking that were aggravating her predisposition to $PS^2$.

Primarily she had a tendency to worry about things over which she had no control. It was almost a form of magical thinking on her part: If she worried about a problem long and hard enough, perhaps she could influence its outcome. This chronic pattern of worrying, and the emotional impact it had, apparently triggered the limbic-hypothalamic system in her brain. This, in turn, caused her pituitary and adrenal glands to overproduce hormones, and the overreaction affected her immune system—all resulting in increased stress to her entire body.

Dr. Lipton taught her a new way to think beginning with the Serenity Prayer, which was of particular utility for Margaret's magical thinking. The prayer, attributed to Reinhold Niebuhr, states: "God, grant me the serenity to accept the things I cannot change, the courage to change the things I can, and the wisdom to know the difference."

Margaret also came to learn that things will either get better or worse regardless of how hard she worries. If they get better, she has worried too soon. If they get worse, the worry did not help.

Dr. Lipton told her to write down all the things bothering her. Then she was to think about and write beside them what steps she could take to effect change. If she could not change them she was told to repeat to herself, "I cannot change it, I can only change my reaction to it," whenever she started to worry.

Then Margaret learned how to use biofeedback, self-hypnosis, and other relaxation techniques, all of which have proven to be most effective in the treatment of $PS^2$. You will be learning more about them later.

After a few more consultations and several months of home practice, Margaret came into my office practically beaming.

"Dr. Solomon," she said, "I feel like a new person." Indeed, her fatigue was almost completely gone and she could sleep for at least five hours every night without awakening. Her arthritic joints were much less painful, and her stomachaches and headaches had "gone away." Lab tests confirmed the physical improvement.

Margaret's case is not, as I have stated, an isolated one. And while the difficulties that bombarded her were intense ones, we have found that even mild occurrences, the kind we face every day at home or on the job, can lead to $PS^2$. Understanding that the way we handle our emotions can cause physical reactions offers a clearer perspective on how to control our bodies' responses.

When you consider that, according to epidemiological researchers, roughly 42 percent of all patients who visit family doctors have emotional components to their complaints, you can see the scope of the problem. These people are medically ill, but their illnesses were probably caused or made worse by their emotions.

Then, there are many patients who suffer from medical conditions that, for no apparent reason, fail to respond to treatment; and there are patients who have pain much more severe than would normally be expected. Unfortunately, as with Margaret, too many physicians assume that these people suffer nonexistent, imaginary disorders. $PS^2$, a very real medical malady, is in my opinion widespread in the United States. Whatever name we give it, it can be both treatable and preventable, and its absence adds a happier dimension to living.

*Bob's Fatigue.* I might mention here something that occurred to me while treating a patient named Bob. He had complaints of lightheadedness, fever, and swollen glands. He had been to a number of physicians and as I checked his records I saw that several of them had noted the same symptoms I had seen. The one thing all the doctors agreed upon was Bob's unusual level of fatigue; but in no case was a diagnosis offered.

I found that last point intriguing. From my experience I would have predicted that a patient's chart would include at least two or three diagnoses from the different doctors consulted. "Nerves," "anxiety," "stress," or "psychological issues" are often listed as the source of an otherwise unexplained illness.

But then it came to me: Most of those types of diagnoses had been handed only to my female patients. I could not remember any male patient of mine being handed a diagnosis of "nerves"—even if another more medical-sounding diagnosis could not be given.

There seemed to be a bias here: some physicians did not perceive their male patients as having an illness that was really "all in their heads." Male patients appeared to have more credibility. If they said they were sick, they were sick, even if the cause was unknown. I wondered if any articles on this subject had appeared in the major medical journals or if any studies had been conducted.

As I learned later, popular health magazines were aware of this trend, as were many of my understandably frustrated female patients. Interestingly, when I questioned some of them I found that if a male doctor admitted to a female patient that he could not discern the cause of her ailments, she tended to trust and respect him more for his honesty. I do not have enough feedback on the way female doctors perceive their female patients to speculate on their responses in this situation.

In any event, for too long some medical treatments have been developed in the mistaken belief that all illnesses—in women *and* men—can be compartmentalized into separate, mutually exclusive physical and mental realms. But the more Dr. Lipton and I work together on cases and the more $PS^2$ patients we encounter, the more certain we become in agreeing with the growing number of medical scientists who assert that there are no diseases that are wholly unrelated to the mind and its impact on the body.

The mind-body connection is intricate and fascinating. Let's take a quick look at the one system within it that is most affected by $PS^2$: your immune system.

## Your Immune System

Since the immune system takes the knocks of Profound Sensitivity Syndrome, I would like to give you a very simple understanding of how that system works. This will be helpful as you learn to read your body's signals properly to make your body work better for you.

I have to confess that it is not easy to visualize the immune system. Unlike the nervous or cardiovascular systems, which clearly trace their way through plastic models of the human body in biology class, the immune system is all over the place.

It is partly composed of body cells that make up the skin, blood, and lymph system. For example, part of it is one strand of a three-strand pipeline connecting the mind with the rest of the body. The two other strands are the nervous system (brain, spinal cord, and nerves) and the endocrine system (hormones).

Think of that pipeline as open and operative at all times. The rate of biochemicals flowing through it is controlled like the spigot on a faucet. Constantly relayed messages generated by your thoughts and feelings turn the flow up or down.

Your body reacts in one of two ways. In most people the brain reads the body's signals correctly and knows to turn down the faucet. This results in a normal effect on the immune system.

Other people, however, millions, in fact, have an exaggerated outpouring of these biochemicals and are "profoundly sensitive" to them. They are poorly insulated against them and cannot alert the brain to stop the flow. Thus, the body is flooded with abnormal amounts and reacts with a variety of physical symptoms that cannot be traced to any other source.

*Lee's Swelling.* Lee is a case in point. She was a 32-year-old, 170-pound woman plagued with excessive weight shifts every month. Each month about ten days before her menstrual period, she would gain five to ten pounds, some of which she then lost after her period. Prior to her period she was tense and irritable, snapping at everyone. Everything took such effort.

She needed two wardrobes because of her size changes. Her thinking "felt fuzzy."

Laboratory tests revealed that Lee's "faucet" poured out an excessive amount of a hormone called aldosterone secreted by the adrenal glands. This was a direct result of overstimulation from the pituitary gland in the brain and caused sodium retention, resulting in excess fluid. She was given medication to correct the fluid retention, was placed on a well-balanced diet and exercise program, and was taught stress-reduction techniques, which will be discussed in later chapters. Within four months she lost 44 excess pounds of fluid and fat. Soon her aldosterone level returned to normal and with it her former sunny disposition.

Science has known for a decade that severe emotional situations (bereavement, for instance, or social isolation) can affect immune function. The discovery of $PS^2$ shows us that not just intense mental strain, but every thought and emotion—good or bad—can have a direct bearing on health.

Now we can teach you to modulate the abnormal amounts of biochemicals released as a result of $PS^2$ and show you how to train your brain to pick up on the signals, and turn down the faucet.

This allows you to control the effects between your thinking and feeling and, therefore, what happens to you physically. In fact, the sensitivity that produces these physical problems and diseases is exactly the same sensitivity we can capitalize on to help you reverse the reactions that have caused the problems in the first place.

Ever since Dr. Lipton and I became aware of this syndrome about five years ago, we have been able to help hundreds of patients who complain of various "inexplicable" maladies—even patients with serious autoimmune components to their diseases such as rheumatoid arthritis, pernicious anemia, diabetes mellitus, colitis, systemic lupus erythematosus, and myasthenia gravis.

Another distinguished colleague of mine, Dr. Richard E.

Layton, a pediatrician, found that children also are susceptible to $PS^2$. It may be manifested by allergies, recurrent colds, and ear infections, as well as attention-deficit disorder. As is true with most medical conditions, early treatment can prevent problems later in life.

Every person experiences a bodily release of biochemical substances in response to thoughts and emotions—even happy thoughts and feelings. The key to healing for those who have $PS^2$, and continued good health for those who do not, is in the mind's ability to perceive the problem accurately and control the flow. Because everyone is affected, everyone can benefit from the techniques we will be discussing. And although the biological process is complex, the ability to regulate it is easily acquired.

## A Fanciful Picture of the Immune System

The immune system's function is to protect you. It works like a barrage of patrolmen let loose, constantly on the alert for any foreign substance that tries to invade the body. When the immune system recognizes any material as foreign, various patrolmen mobilize to destroy that alien substance, which we call an antigen or foreign invader.

The patrolmen mobilized by the immune system include various types of white blood cells called lymphocytes. These are divided into two types. B-cells, derived from bone marrow, concentrate on dealing with alien cells in the bloodstream before they have infiltrated cell tissue. They swarm about like a front line of defense. T-cells, from the thymus gland, lie in wait like a reserve force. They attack those cells that have already become infected with germs. It is the T-cell that decides whether or not a transplanted tissue or organ will "take" because it determines what belongs to your body (which it does not attack) and what does not belong to your body (which it does attack).

These patrolmen cells subdivide into other cells that enhance immune function, stop the immune attack after the battle is over, destroy foreign invader antigens, plus perform numerous other jobs.

Antibodies are also components of the immune system. These highly specific defense forces are formed in response to individual antigens to help protect the body against future attacks by the same invader.

The immune system never sleeps. It is always on the alert to categorize the millions of substances that enter our bodies as either harmless or foreign.

**Immunological Overreaction: Allergy**
**Immunological Underreaction: AIDS**

Yet mistakes do occur. Sometimes the immune system overreacts and decides that a harmless substance, such as cornstarch or ragweed, is an invading antigen and attacks it. This gives rise to allergic symptoms.

At other times the immune system fails to attack a true invading antigen successfully, such as with the virus that causes AIDS, acquired immunodeficiency syndrome. This is because the AIDS virus itself cripples the immune system. Thus, the body can no longer make sufficient antibodies to destroy the invading AIDS virus.

Most of the time when a virus punctures the cell membrane, it looks something like a tack stuck into a grapefruit. It can be seen. The AIDS virus, however, manages somehow to find its way *inside* the cell. It is no longer observable. Thus, to the body itself, the cell looks normal. The AIDS virus is not detected until the cell explodes. At that point, the immune system cannot fight the enormous level of degeneration.

**Autoimmune Disease**

Sometimes our patrolmen make another mistake and attack our own forces—our own body organs—mistaking them for an alien invader antigen. This results in damage to our own organs and is called autoimmune disease.

How could this happen? What causes the body, in effect, to attack itself?

Imagine some of your body's cells, the memory cells, going around with a camera and taking pictures of every single membrane of every single cell in your body. Those pictures are then stored in a filing system, available for comparison studies.

Now, the memory cells go around your body again taking a whole new set of pictures. They carry these new pictures to the chief memory inspector. He looks at each new picture and compares it to old pictures of the same membrane. If he finds an exact duplicate in the files, all is well. If, however, the new picture is not located in the memory files, the chief memory inspector sends antibodies, like bullets, to destroy that invader. This process is repeated again and again.

Now suppose that a virus has attacked a membrane and the cells did not heal to the exact specifications of the originally pictured membrane. When the memory cells take a photo and send it back, there will be no comparable picture in the memory bank. The chief memory inspector will give orders to attack and the body will make antibodies against that cell membrane. The attack will damage it further, and that organ may not be able to heal under the self-propagating attack.

## How PS$^2$ Affects Your Immune System

This relatively new concept of psycho-physiology (to choose one of its names) is a revolutionary happening in the history of medicine. The most recent revolution began with the discovery that nearly all of our bodily systems are intricately involved in protecting us against such invaders as viruses, toxic bacteria and fungi, parasites, and cancerous cells. Researchers found that the never-ending battle goes far beyond, is far more exciting than the pursuit we just described. It's more like an intergalactic battle.

Dr. Lipton and I have chosen to call this more complex immune system model the neuro-endocrine-immunological link. This term refers to the crucial role that the neurological (brain and nerves) and the endocrinological (hormonal) systems play in influencing, and being influenced by, the immune system, and, thus, how all three are all linked together.

Of particular importance to me has been the inclusion of the endocrine system in the link between the brain and the immune system. In fact, I first became interested in the study of the interreaction of hormones with the nervous and immune systems while still in medical school.

Through the years I was able to study with such notables as Dr. George Sayers, who was my mentor in physiology; Dr. Robert Ebert, from whom I learned how hormones interact with the immunological system; Dr. A. McGhee Harvey, an expert on autoimmune disease; Dr. William Blake, who taught me the complex interrelationships between hormones and kidney function; and Dr. Nathan Shock, regarding nutrition and the neuro-endocrine-immunological functions as they pertain to the aging process. Through Dr. Hans Selye I got insight into the broad relationships between the psycho-endocrine and immunological functions.

Putting my experience with the endocrine and immune systems together with Dr. Lipton's psychological training has brought my interests full circle and revealed the link through which $PS^2$ operates.

We are all familiar with stress, and most if not all of us are aware that newspapers, magazines, and television are carrying more and more stories about how environmental contamination further taxes our bodies. This is bad for us. It can make us sick. We all have to learn to relax.

First, we need to understand when we use the word *stress* in the above context (as it's usually used) we are actually referring to our response to certain events. Dr. Lipton and I prefer the word *sensitizer* to connote those factors, either chemical or emotional, that can elicit a stress response.

Remember, stress is an internal reaction, most often individually idiosyncratic. A stress-inducing event for you may not be a stress-inducing event for your neighbor.

For example, one person may be sensitive to the way her spouse is responding to their child. The interaction of that husband and child can be conceptualized as a sensitizer—a factor that has the ability to bring an internal stress response in the wife.

On a different level, from a chemical perspective, if an individual has an allergic predisposition to a particular antigen, this, too, can be conceptualized as a sensitizer.

Second, we need to understand that sensitizers do not occur only in response to negative events. No one can avoid all sensitizers; stress comes in all forms. As the late Dr. Hans Selye put it in his landmark treatise, *The Stress of Life:* "No one can live without experiencing some degree of stress all the time. You may think that only serious disease or intensive physical or mental injury can cause stress. This is false. Crossing a busy intersection, exposure to a draft, or even sheer joy are enough to activate the body's stress mechanism to some extent."

The next step is to understand how these sensitizers affect the three body systems we are discussing, the neurological, endocrinological, and immunological. In other words, this is how thoughts and feelings can make you sick.

First the neural component. The autonomic nervous system (ANS) is made up of part of the central nervous system (the brain and spinal cord) and part of the peripheral nervous system (the nerves running from the brain and spinal cord to all parts of the body).

The brain is a master controller, some 500 million times more complicated than our most advanced computer. It controls all *voluntary* activity, from tugging stubbornly at the zipper of your tight pants one morning, to grimacing in horror at the sound of fabric ripping as you bend over that afternoon. And it computes the information that the brain sends through the five senses, such as your eyes confirming that everyone is now staring at you.

The brain also unconsciously controls all involuntary activity in your body, using some of the same routes through the nervous system. Examples of this include heartbeat, gastrointestinal secretion, release of some hormones, and regulation of blood flow—the last of which is confirmed by the blush you feel rising to your face.

The ANS is the fastest-acting component of your response to sensitizers. You've probably heard of the "fight-or-flight" response. This sudden, overwhelming anxiety that spurs us to attack, physically or verbally, or to run away from the stress-provoking situation, is initiated by the sympathetic nervous system (SNS), the brain's command center for excitement. Whether or not you are actually blushing, it is likely that the sympathetic nervous system is inducing internal responses such as starting your heart pounding, causing you to perspire, and changing the flow in your blood vessels.

Your responses now move into the endocrine (hormone) system; the ANS has stimulated the neurons (brain cells) of the hypothalamus, a brain center controlling glands such as the pituitary. The hypothalamus is, in turn, signaling the ANS to react further to stress, thus creating a looplike interdependent feedback system. By combating $PS^2$ you will be inhibiting the stress response before the feedback system "kicks in." This means you will be stopping the hypothalamus from alerting the ANS to the need for a hyperstress response. You can enhance this control, depending on how accurately you are reporting to yourself what is happening to you.

Now, let's assume that $PS^2$ is interfering and you have not been able to stop the sensitizers charged by the sound of that rip. Anxiety has the upper hand. The stimulated hypothalamus and, in turn, the pituitary gland release neuropeptides. These are strings of amino acids produced not only in the brain, but by immune cells (including the lymphocytes) circulating in the blood that we discussed earlier. At the same time, these glands and immune cells have receptors for neuropeptides so that these systems are in constant communication with each other.

The neuropeptides from the stress-excited hypothalamus can inhibit the manufacture of lymphocytes, thus undermining the immune system. These neuropeptides, when released by sensitizers, can also encourage inflammatory action in tissue as well as growth of malignant (abnormal) tissue. When the endocrine system behaves normally, it helps to maintain healthy lymphocyte function and normal tissue growth.

When it does not behave normally, such as when $PS^2$ enters the picture, the endocrine system throws the immune system off balance. In this case, for instance, you may have a hyperactive immune response to ripping your pants. Those B- and T-cells may go overboard in trying to enhance immune function, resulting perhaps in an allergic reaction.

So several episodes like the one suggested here may exacerbate your existing allergy to strawberries, making your hives that much worse. Or your B-cells may be inhibited from producing antibodies, thus leaving you exposed to infection by viruses or bacteria. These are just two out of many, many possible immune-compromised scenarios.

As hypothesized here, we believe $PS^2$ is the inability to restabilize your system when the need for the fight-or-flight response has passed, thereby reducing the biochemical outpouring before it harms you.

When this biochemical hyper-response occurs over and over for a prolonged period, the body's systems become confused, erratic, and unstable. The endocrine system misinterprets normal signals, cutting off its supply of some substances, releasing massive supplies of others. The organs, blood, muscles—all of which also release hormones—follow suit. The immune system then exhausts itself trying to respond to these erratic and jumbled hormonal signals. The result: an immune malfunction that leads inevitably to illness. In fact, a sensitizer such as the Epstein-Barr virus is capable of setting off this cascade of chemical reactions, resulting in Heather's problems.

*Heather's Epstein-Barr Virus.* Heather felt out of control of her health—and her life. She was from Florida; her deep tan made her appear—at first glance—robust. But as she said, "I know I look healthy, Dr. Solomon, but believe me I'm pale under this tan. I lie out on the beach because I don't have the strength to do much else."

Heather was in her mid-twenties, unemployed, and living with her family. In fact, coming to see me was her parents' idea. She seemed to think there was no point. She told me that she had been close to completing a graduate degree in commercial art when "it" struck her down.

"What was 'it'?" I asked her.

"Oh, you know," she answered. "CEBV—that thing going around."

I told her that we did not know for sure whether or not she had CEBV—chronic Epstein-Barr virus—and that we should hold off on a diagnosis for now. She gave me a disappointed response, seeming apathetic about everything we discussed as I examined her, as if she did not have the energy to care one way or the other. I wanted her to care, to work with me to make her better.

Chronic Epstein-Barr virus is often difficult to diagnose because the agent causing the symptoms is not really known. At first it was thought that finding high levels of antibodies to Epstein-Barr virus in a patient's blood clinched it. Many patients, however, have no, or normal, levels of CEBV antibodies in their blood. Still, an unusually high number of CEBV antibodies is a good indication of CEBV *if* the patient's symptoms and medical history back this up. If the antibody count does not suggest CEBV, the symptoms and medical history alone must indicate the illness.

One complaint all CEBV sufferers seem to share is an overwhelming, often disabling fatigue. Clustered around fatigue are symptoms that vary greatly from person to person and may include muscle aches and tenderness, joint pain, swollen glands (particularly in the neck), low-grade fevers, mild to extreme weakness, mild to severe depression, and anxiety. The symptoms appear to get worse when a person is experiencing tension.

I had Heather's blood tested, and her high levels of antibodies to Epstein-Barr virus combined with her symptoms and history were indicative of CEBV.

When I told her, she replied gloomily, "Yeah, I figured. Well, that's that."

"That's what?"

"That's it for the rest of my life. I can forget about school, my career, getting married. . . ." Her voice trailed off. Her head was bowed and she seemed to be falling asleep. But when she lifted her head I saw tears running down her face.

I handed her a tissue, asking her to tell me what she was feeling. At first she was crying too hard to talk. When she could I realized I had been in error: Heather was far from apathetic. That was just her way of defending herself against her fear that she would never get well again.

She told me she had pretended that she was anemic or suffering from mononucleosis. She also pretended that she was lying on the beach day after day as a sort of extended vacation, that someday she would go back to school.

When I asked her about friends, her answer brought a fresh batch of tears.

"I don't have any friends anymore. People don't want to deal with you when you're in bed half the time, when you can't go out or make plans, when you're too tired to have a conversation. At first they're nice about it, but they expect you to get better. And when you don't your whole life just kind of drifts away." She wiped at her eyes. "It's better to be alone. It's better not to be reminded of how much you have lost."

She looked at me to see if I understood. I did understand. I had many CEBV patients who were suffering from the same fears, the same sense of loss and hopelessness. I had wanted her to explain herself to me, to talk about it. I hoped that this would be her first step in coping—admitting that she had an illness. She had to do this before she could try to get better.

"Heather, things are not hopeless. You haven't lost everything. You've been rejecting the people who might help you," I reminded her. "You wouldn't even go to a doctor until now."

She nodded, seemed calmer, more receptive to what I was saying.

I continued, "There are a number of treatments we can try to alleviate your symptoms. I've had good results with many patients. Treating your body, however, is only half the battle. The other half is treating your mind."

Heather listened as I outlined the joint mind-body approach Dr. Lipton and I often used. "I'm not saying there is a cure for this condition yet. But I think, with your help, we can make you better so you can live a relatively normal life with it."

Heather arranged to stay with a friend ("I guess I forgot about Sharon," she said sheepishly) and came to see us regularly over the next few months. She seemed to enjoy the two-part cooperation treating her mind and her body at the same time.

This approach was impressing upon her the unhealthy ways she handled stress, and how they affected the intensity of her symptoms and her response to treatment. It was also helping her achieve a feeling of control over her life.

She regained much of her strength, though she still had to be wary of too much tension. Plus, she needed to practice relaxation techniques when life got hectic. Most of her muscle aches and weakness went away. They reappeared only when she pushed herself too hard over several days.

She had learned how to keep CEBV in check much of the time. She knew we would monitor her illness for as long as she needed us. But there was still some unfinished business.

Dr. Lipton and I both felt she had artistic talent. We encouraged her to go back to school. "You need more than a reason to be healthy, Heather," I told her. "You need a reason to live. Your immune system needs it." I was telling her what she already knew.

Dr. Lipton suggested she think about going back part-time. She was hesitant at first, afraid of a relapse. As we impressed upon her the importance of getting back into life, to feel that she was doing something useful, she agreed to try.

Heather did finish her schooling, going part-time, and is now working part-time as a commercial artist. She hopes one day to be able to take on a fuller schedule, but for now concentrates on coping with the days she doesn't feel good, and congratulating herself on those she does.

As you see, our patients have very real physical conditions that require medical attention. Recovery begins, however, when the mental or emotional factors surrounding the illnesses are looked into as well. Heather, by influencing how she reacts to her sensitizers, can influence the way she reacts to the biochemicals they produce.

A phenomenon called Sudden Death Syndrome (SDS) is one of the most dramatic examples of the power of the mind over body, the most extreme effect of $PS^2$.

In some cases of SDS, a hyper-response to sensitizers causes a massive, overwhelming release of biochemicals that results in collapse of the heart and blood vessels. This can happen when someone who has never had signs or symptoms of heart disease suddenly suffers a fatal heart attack. This is the case of the person who dies upon hearing that a child has been arrested, or that a spouse has had an accident. People have also been known to suffer SDS after receiving a citation for heroism.

We will teach you, in subsequent chapters, how to regain control of your health by dealing effectively with your sensitizers.

## Profound Sensitivity Syndrome Profile

I have observed patients over the years, studying their case histories in search of similarities, clues that would lead us to predictors for $PS^2$. Defined broadly, $PS^2$ is a hyper-reactivity of the body to any stressor, or sensitizer, that results in illness that may not seem at first glance to have a clear-cut medical cause.

We were looking for some way of knowing who might be most susceptible. Prevention, after all, is the best medicine. Slowly, as the number of $PS^2$ patients mounted, Dr. Lipton and I began to detect certain revealing signs and characteristics.

The typical patient suffering this syndrome usually complains of several of the following physical problems:

1. Insomnia
2. Gastrointestinal problems that can include: ulcers, colitis, irritable bowel syndrome, chronic constipation or diarrhea
3. Chronic back or neck pain and/or joint and muscle pain
4. Allergies (extreme sensitivity to foods, pollens, or chemicals)
5. Recurring yeast infections
6. Chronic fatigue of unknown origin now called chronic fatigue syndrome
7. Epstein-Barr virus
8. Cerebral symptoms, including either problems with concentration and thinking or hyperactivity
9. Excessive loss of hair, dry skin, and/or brittle nails not due to hypothyroidism
10. Tension, migraine, or mixed headaches
11. Autoimmune disorders, including diabetes mellitus (sugar diabetes), rheumatoid arthritis, systemic lupus erythematosus, pernicious anemia, ulcerative colitis, and Addison's disease (adrenal insufficiency)
12. Hypothyroidism
13. Intolerance of heat, cold, and/or light
14. Excessive fluid retention
15. Skin problems, including rashes, hives, and vasculitis
16. Premenstrual syndrome

Further:

- Patients suffering from $PS^2$ tend to be creative. They daydream and have vivid nighttime dreams. They are sensitive to the feelings of others.

- They have a hyperactive hormonal response that can often be traced to a single severely traumatic event. This is what first led me to believe there may be a genetic predisposition to PS$^2$. That belief was reinforced by the fact that nearly all patients suffering this syndrome seem to be both physically and emotionally supersensitive. They react swiftly and dramatically to both emotional and physical stimuli.
- There is what appears to be a direct hyperactive flow of biochemicals going both ways through the pipeline between the mind and all the organs and systems of the body. Physiological reactions relate to thoughts and emotions, and profound emotional responses relate, in turn, to physical distress.
- For some reason we do not understand, PS$^2$ patients are often overly sensitive to medication. They respond quickly and dramatically, frequently experiencing side effects and adverse reactions, even when drugs are prescribed at the lowest possible effective doses. This may lead to lack of compliance on the part of some patients, leaving physicians feeling frustrated.

  Dr. Michael Weintraub of the University of Rochester School of Medicine gave me an amazing depiction of a patient who fit this description. He had a patient with allergic reactions triggered by increased histamine levels from a cold. She would break open a Contac capsule and take three of the tiny little balls. Two did not help her; four were too many.
- Symptoms are often more pronounced. The patient with arthritis feels greater pain than a physician might expect him to after assessing the severity of the disease. Or someone with allergies reacts more quickly, more dramatically to allergens. This characteristic often lends itself to the inclination to label this patient a "hypochondriac" or "malingerer."
- The most obvious trait of the PS$^2$ sufferer is his or her poor response to traditional medical treatment, or susceptibility to recurrence of the condition despite what appears to be a total response to first-occurrence treatment.

  This is very apparent with PS$^2$ sufferers particularly as

it relates to recurrent viral infections. For example, one patient of mine, Florence, age 39, was treated repeatedly for strep throat. During each occurrence her physician would give her an antibiotic. Her strep would clear completely, only to recur about two months later. It was interesting that the strep was actually gone at the time the antibiotic was terminated, but because of her $PS^2$ and the impact it was having on her immune system, the bacteria would reattack—continually. After her last treatment with antibiotics and our treatment for $PS^2$ her strep infections disappeared completely.

Another example was Harriet, a 51-year-old businesswoman who experienced recurring mononucleosis. Her mono returned repeatedly for several years, even with prolonged periods of rest. Her problem cleared slowly after treatment for $PS^2$.

- Finally, I find patients with Profound Sensitivity Syndrome admit almost unanimously to feeling they cannot control the external life events that distress them or their internal reactions to those events. Often, they complain of feeling helpless in the face of life and their medical problems.

Perhaps you see yourself in this profile. Perhaps you have not understood why you have certain physical problems making you sick and tired. Or perhaps you are healthy and want to do all you can to stay that way.

Then this book can help you. And we'll start by taking a quick look at the all-important last point in the $PS^2$ profile—a feeling of lack of control.

## Taking Control

In *Helplessness,* his landmark work on uncontrolled stress, Dr. Martin Seligman, a psychologist at the University of Pennsylvania, declared that helplessness is "learned," that coping unsuccessfully with stressful events actually teaches some individuals to remain helpless against the onslaught of future events. This helplessness takes a physiological toll: Your brain fails to produce the chemicals needed to stimulate desirable responses elsewhere in the body—in the endocrine system or the immune system—and you become predisposed to any malady that comes along, from colds to cancer.

In her book, *Minding the Body, Mending the Mind,* Dr. Joan Borysenko writes:

"Most of us eventually will feel that life is out of control in some way. Whether we see this as a temporary situation whose resolution will add to our store of knowledge and experiences or as one more threat demonstrating life's dangers is the most crucial question both for the quality of our life and our physical health. . . . Without the conviction that we have some control, we have no way to negotiate the tides of life."

Look at the recent findings of the National Institute of Occupational Safety and Health (NIOSH) regarding "pink-collar workers," of which there are around eighteen million in the United States. NIOSH reports that these female office workers, with children, married to blue-collar workers, suffer great stress. They are at three times greater risk of developing cardiovascular disease than other women, and fifty percent greater risk than men.

Consider: Most women in pink-collar jobs work because their families need the extra money; they have little option of quitting if they are unhappy. Since most employers today are still reluctant to promote women from clerical to managerial positions, these women often perform monotonous, routine tasks with little real meaning or satisfaction. They have no control over anything that happens in the office.

Contrast them with the men who run America's largest corporations, who have great stress but equally great control over their work environments. In a Metropolitan Life Insurance Company study of corporate stress a few years ago, the death rate of corporate executives was 35 percent lower than that of similar men in less powerful jobs.

The obvious conclusion: If we can control our environments, the experiences that produce a biochemical stress response, we can avoid the harmful effects of that internal chain reaction.

Unfortunately, we cannot always control external events. But a large body of research has been amassed over the years to prove we can control our *reactions* to those events; we can use certain behavioral techniques to gain *inner* control.

As Benjamin Disraeli said in 1832, one hundred years before I was born, "Circumstances are beyond the control of man; but his conduct is in his own power."

And this is the way to overcome the wearying symptoms that undoubtedly make you sick and tired of being sick and tired.

# 2

# ...And What to Do About It

How severely is $PS^2$ affecting you? A little? A lot? Can you consistently control your body's biochemical reactions, or do you feel overwhelmed by the health problems plaguing you?

Probably you fall somewhere in the middle: You are frustrated with symptoms that have been hanging on too long and you've reached the point where you want to do something about it.

This is just one area we will be discussing in this chapter. After determining the extent that $PS^2$ affects you physically and emotionally, we help you establish a plan of control. We also show you how to work with your doctor so that you may benefit the most. And, finally, we'll show you how you can check your compatibility with the traits of other $PS^2$ sufferers who were helped.

## $PS^2$ Evaluations

Let's start by analyzing some important signs that could pinpoint how much $PS^2$ is affecting you, signs that will reveal what we might call your "helplessness" level. By evaluating your responses to these questions we can then devise a plan to help you regain control over some currently out-of-control areas.

It is important first to emphasize that people fall into two general categories based on their own psychological makeup and defensiveness. One category is composed of individuals who are aware of, and can evaluate, the extent to which they experience negative effects of the interplay between mind and body. The second category is composed of individuals who cannot determine accurately those ill effects. This second group includes the person who is apparently distraught, but insists, "No, I'm not upset. Honestly, I feel fine." This person is probably not purposely misrepresenting the truth; rather, his coping mechanisms prevent him from recognizing his negative responses.

Thus, the following evaluations offer a dual approach. The first is a self-assessment and the second is to be given to a family member or close friend for his or her observations of you. You will need both for an accurate appraisal.

**Self-Evaluation**

Put the number of the most appropriate response in the box to the left of the following statements. If the answer is "Never," write "0" in the box, and so on.

0 Never
1 Sometimes
2 Often
3 Frequently

☐ 1. I have difficulty controlling my emotions.
☐ 2. I give in to bursts of anger or tears, or snarl at those around me.
☐ 3. I have trouble concentrating, often slipping into daydreams instead of zeroing in on the problems at hand.
☐ 4. I feel sad for no apparent reason.
☐ 5. I feel tired, even after I've had a full night's sleep.
☐ 6. I experience free-floating anxiety—apprehension, fear, the feeling of impending calamity—without knowing what is causing those feelings.
☐ 7. I am uptight, tense, feeling all strung out.
☐ 8. My mouth and throat are dry, parched.
☐ 9. I am startled easily. Even small sounds make me flinch.

- ☐ 10. I grind my teeth without realizing it.
- ☐ 11. I have trouble getting to sleep, or staying asleep.
- ☐ 12. I tap my fingers or move my feet as though listening to music.
- ☐ 13. I have stomach problems—for example, diarrhea, indigestion, nausea.
- ☐ 14. I have recurring headaches, more often than once a month.
- ☐ 15. I suffer chronic pain in my neck or lower back for which my doctor can find no medical cause.
- ☐ 16. I lose my appetite for no apparent reason. Or, on the reverse side of the same coin, I find food comforting when I am upset and I overeat.
- ☐ 17. I smoke cigarettes.
- ☐ 18. I seem to be having more small accidents than I once did, dropping things, tripping, denting a fender on the family car.
- ☐ 19. I experience muscle tension in my neck and and/or shoulders.
- ☐ 20. I feel like withdrawing from people and the world.
- ☐ 21. I feel as if things are very hopeless.
- ☐ 22. I am afraid of that with which I am not familiar.
- ☐ 23. I find myself complaining more than I feel I should.
- ☐ 24. I am aware that I lack the capacity to sympathize with other people's problems.
- ☐ 25. I have many allergies.
- ☐ 26. I generally feel very frustrated with my life.
- ☐ 27. I have bad dreams.
- ☐ 28. My alcohol consumption is greater than it should be.
- ☐ 29. I drink too much coffee.
- ☐ 30. I feel extremely fatigued and lifeless.
- ☐ 31. I experience ringing in my ears.
- ☐ 32. I find myself stuttering.
- ☐ 33. I get lumps or the feeling that something is stuck in my throat.
- ☐ 34. I feel alone and abandoned.
- ☐ 35. I feel like throwing things or striking out at people physically.
- ☐ 36. I find myself depressed.
- ☐ 37. I am unable to relax.
- ☐ 38. I feel a lack of interest in my life.

☐ 39. I procrastinate.
☐ 40. I feel indecisive, unable to make a decision.
☐ 41. My thoughts become jumbled and I am unable to express myself in a coherent fashion.
☐ 42. Once in a while I find that my mind is completely blank.
☐ 43. I feel guilty.
☐ 44. I feel like killing myself.

Now add the scores from each of the 44 boxes. If you scored between 14 and 20, it is likely that you are at low risk of suffering physical problems. If you scored between 21 and 44, you are at moderate risk and need to take some decisive steps to reduce your risk status. If you scored more than 45, you are at high risk of suffering severe physical consequences from your hyper-reaction to sensitizers.

Remember, too, before you conclude that you are at low risk, it is essential to give the Observer's Evaluation to a family member or close friend. The scoring system for this questionnaire is the same as that used in the Self-Evaluation.

**Observer's Evaluation**

Put the number of the most appropriate response in the box to the left of the following statements:

0 Never
1 Sometimes
2 Often
3 Frequently

☐ 1. He/she laughs in a somewhat inappropriate fashion.
☐ 2. He/she doesn't really seem tuned in to other people and appears to lack empathy.
☐ 3. He/she is irritable and grouchy.
☐ 4. He/she gets angry easily.
☐ 5. He/she complains too much.
☐ 6. He/she pouts and appears moody.
☐ 7. He/she cries too often.
☐ 8. He/she appears to have a lot of anger.

☐ 9. He/she seems depressed.
☐ 10. He/she seems to lack energy.
☐ 11. He/she shows a number of nervous habits, such as constantly chewing gum or pencils or tapping fingers or cracking knuckles.
☐ 12. He/she bites his/her nails or lips.
☐ 13. He/she talks "a mile a minute."
☐ 14. He/she perspires a great deal.
☐ 15. He/she breathes quickly.
☐ 16. He/she frowns and grimaces.
☐ 17. He/she fidgets.
☐ 18. He/she has rashes and/or itchy skin.
☐ 19. He/she often just stares into space.
☐ 20. He/she drinks too much alcohol.
☐ 21. He/she smokes too many cigarettes.
☐ 22. He/she drinks too much coffee.

Now total the score. If the rating is between 5 and 10, then you are perceived to be at low risk. If the score is between 11 and 22, then you are perceived at moderate risk. And if your score is more than 22, then you are perceived to be at high risk.

If you find that your Self-Evaluation falls into the low-risk group and the other evaluation is in the moderate or high range, then give the Observer's Evaluation to a second friend or family member and take a look at those scores. If the second observer's scores are also moderate or high, then most likely you are unable to appreciate your own risk state.

If this is the case with your scores, try to assume a nondefensive, exploratory posture and take a careful look at the evaluations. Talk to the person who filled out the questionnaire and listen to what he or she has to say. Accept the fact that we all have our blind spots, and that our capacity to evaluate ourselves tends to be far less objective and accurate than the perceptions of others, particularly those who are closest to us and who care about us.

If your self-evaluation is in the moderate or high range, but others evaluate you in the low range, go on the basis of your own evaluation. You are probably able to present yourself in a calm, controlled fashion, showing few outward signs of stress yet suffering all the same.

*Anthony's Deaf Ear and Chronic Fatigue.* Anthony, age 29, had multiple complaints including headaches, sinus problems, chronic fatigue, stiff neck, and recurrent colds and sore throats. I treated him for several of his symptoms and, because he impressed me as being extremely stressed and emotionally constricted, referred him to Dr. Lipton.

Dr. Lipton gave him the self-evaluation form and asked him to have his wife fill out the same form with her perceptions of Anthony's state. When Anthony returned the forms, Dr. Lipton saw that Anthony had rated himself with 9 while his wife had rated him with 40! Subsequent discussions convinced Dr. Lipton that Anthony was denying all of his problems and taking a totally defensive stance.

Dr. Lipton helped him reconceptualize his notion of manhood (Anthony said it was being "able to take it") by suggesting that a man was someone who had enough strength and courage to look at himself honestly.

Before long, with new understanding, Anthony took the test again and rated himself with 46. Psychotherapy helped transform him from an angry and defensive type-A personality into someone who was calmer, more objective, and healthier—both mentally and physically. Every one of his physical symptoms, including his lifelong sinus problems, disappeared.

## A Plan of Control

The information you have just recorded can be used as a diagnostic aid as you begin to assess your life in terms of helplessness.

Take a look at the questions you or your friend marked 2 or 3. Analyze the question to discover what the problem is. For instance, if you indicated that you often feel guilty, be honest and write down what you feel guilty about. Repeat this with other questions. Is there one particular problem causing a number of stressful responses? Are there several out-of-control areas of your life?

Now, take each problem area one by one and think about all of the possible actions you can take to resolve or reduce it. For instance, suppose you have determined that you are not sleeping well. You have rated yourself as being anxious and angry as well as depressed. You have also rated yourself as feeling guilty quite often.

As you examine your responses, you become aware that one of the major issues behind them is the fact that your former spouse has moved a thousand miles away with your two children. That has so upset you that you felt the best way to deal with it was to put it out of your mind.

You are aware now that this is not the best way to cope. Instead, try this: Write down a statement of the problem, an action plan, and a timetable. Here is an example:

1. *Statement of the problem:* I am divorced and feeling guilty, upset, and agitated over lack of involvement with my children.
2. *Action plan:* Call the children on the telephone once a week. Write a letter every two weeks. Join a local self-help group to find out how to cope better with the situation.
3. *Timetable:* Call the children within the next 48 hours. Write within the next 7 days. Arrange a meeting within the next 30 days.

Here is an important part. You must discuss this statement of the problem, plan of action, and timetable with a friend or family member or trusted advisor such as your clergyman or doctor. Why is this important? Because our capacity to judge ourselves is, at best, limited. Remember, if you had been handling this problem correctly in the first place, it wouldn't have become a problem.

Getting the objective assessment and suggestions from a

concerned party will do two things: First, it will provide you valuable input as to the workability of your plan; and second, it will give you some incentive and monitoring help to ensure your own follow-through.

This plan can help you start to feel in control of some events that may have affected you more than you realized. *And once you are in control you are not helpless.*

You cannot always escape from your problems, but you'd be surprised to discover just how many steps you can take to rid yourself of the trauma of helplessness.

## Working with Your Doctor

We have stressed the importance of discussing your emotional—not just physical—concerns with your doctor. Too often, when a patient neglects to tell a physician what is troubling him or her, it undermines the doctor's ability to diagnose the problem and prescribe a successful plan of treatment. Let's look at your responsibilities toward your doctor and yourself.

Perhaps I can best illustrate the importance of a good working relationship by telling you about Bill, whom I call my mystery patient. His case shows how treatment can be adversely affected by a patient's reluctance to share important emotional components of his or her life with a physician.

It also points up the larger issue of admitting the causes and realities of emotional turmoil to oneself. This is not always easy; often the problems you would prefer to block out are the most important with which to deal. The deep emotions surrounding them are the very catalysts for those physical symptoms you want to shake. It is true that denial can at times be healthy, such as when we truly cannot do anything about a situation. But most often, as with Bill, denial can prevent us from addressing and resolving our problems.

### Opening Up

*Bill's Denial and Increased Stress Hormones.* When I saw Bill for the first time he walked slowly, hesitantly, in the manner of one very old and very tired. His medical records told me he was only 55. As he lowered himself onto the sofa in my office, I noticed his eyes were creased by lines of pain.

He merely stared at me as I introduced myself, and his answers to my questions were monosyllabic. The information he offered was minimal. He told me he and his wife had been separated four years. He lived alone; his three grown children lived elsewhere in the country. He worked part-time as an office clerk, having left his full-time job because of incapacitating pain in his hands, feet, and knees.

Though I suspected that his silence was indicative of some deeper problem, I was able to find out little beyond the symptoms that brought him to me: chronic fatigue, sleeplessness, frequent colds, lack of appetite, and severe pain in his joints. I learned later from the laboratory tests that Bill also had incredibly elevated levels of stress hormones and that his immune function was very low. He was a prime candidate for any hostile bug around and definitely had little ability to stop the internal assaults on his body.

I continued probing with questions.

"When did the pain start, Bill?"

"Oh, about two years ago."

"Can you describe it?"

"Well, it's worse in the morning. I can hardly bend my knees."

I nodded. "Go on."

"It's hard to do much with my hands, and my feet don't feel comfortable in anything but house slippers."

"Did this pain come on you suddenly, or did it begin slowly?"

Bill rubbed his knees. "Sort of both. That is, the pain came on pretty suddenly in my knees and traveled slowly to my hands and feet."

I asked if he had gotten a diagnosis, since he brought no medical records with him.

"No," he said. "I know what's wrong with me. It's the

rheumatism. I just promised my daughter, Ellie, that I'd have it looked at."

"You do have a bad case of rheumatoid arthritis. I wish you'd talked with your daughter about it sooner."

Then Bill surprised me. He seemed to come to life for a moment. "Dr. Solomon," he said, "would you like to see a picture of my Ellie?"

Quickly he took out his wallet. I was pleased at his interest. "Yes, I would. Your other two children are sons, is that right?"

He nodded as he brought out a photo. I looked at the frayed picture and saw an attractive young woman with a winning smile. "She's pretty."

Bill took back the photo and said in a slightly trembling voice, "Like her mother. She looks like her mother." Then his face became sad and wistful again. He would say no more. I returned to the subject of his arthritis.

"Bill, do you take any medication for the pain?"

He shook his head. "I don't believe in it."

"But I'm sure you'd like to do without some of that pain."

"Well, yes, but that's just the way it is with rheumatism. I know other people who have it, and they say you just have to live with it."

Then Bill surprised me again by asking suddenly, "Do you have a family?"

I nodded.

"Wife and kids?"

"Yes, that's right."

"Any daughters?"

"No," I said with a laugh, "all boys. Just like 'My Three Sons.' "

"Wife still alive? You still together?"

"Yes, Bill," I said. "Tell me, why do you ask?"

"No reason. Just wondering."

Once more we returned to strictly medical topics. "Bill, I have to disagree with those folks who told you there's nothing you can do about your arthritis. Some medications may help, but they work with varying degrees of success for different people. The one thing we've found that seems to help just about all patients with arthritis is exercise to help keep the joints mobile. We suggest, as well, certain pain-reducing techniques."

Bill rubbed his knees again. "Techniques?"

"That's right. Not pills. *Mental* exercises that can lower your perception of the pain."

He didn't seem interested. "I guess I'd better try it. Ellie would want me to."

He listened as I outlined his course of treatment. First, I showed him a series of morning exercises I recommend to patients with arthritis, simple stretching maneuvers done while in bed to loosen and relax the muscles and joints. Then I discussed with him my stress-correction plan, designed specifically to combat the physiological effects of stress and $PS^2$ (which I'll be discussing later), and he promised to give it all a try.

Drugs to combat the arthritis did pose a medical problem. I felt that Bill's already-high levels of cortisol ruled out the use of corticosteroid medications, which can be effective. Because of their many side effects, these should not be used unless the benefits far outweigh the risks.

Instead, I persuaded him to undergo a carefully monitored three-month course of a powerful nonsteroidal anti-inflammatory drug. I believed it might reduce the inflammation, swelling, and pain. Then I encouraged him to work with Dr. Lipton, who would train him in techniques like relaxation and biofeedback. Bill agreed.

As he was leaving, I told him that I admired his bravery in the face of all that pain. He said something strange in reply: "Oh, that's not the worst pain."

I was puzzled. "Do you have any other pain?"

He looked away. "No, not like that. Just like I told you."

I still had the feeling I was missing something, but Bill would not talk anymore. I could not force him to open up; he would have to decide to do that himself.

Every time Bill came to see me he had the same listless look on his face. He did say that the exercises and training with Dr. Lipton were helping quite a bit. He was also getting some benefit from one of the medications we had tried. Still, I had hoped for more progress. I had expected him to be experiencing much less pain by then.

Then, one day, when Bill walked into my office he seemed like a different person. It took a moment for it to hit me. He had been chatting away ever since he had come through the door! He was telling me about his job, his children, his daughter's visit, the "nice old lady" he'd talked to in the waiting room. I didn't know what had happened, but, whatever it was, I couldn't have been more pleased.

He no longer had much pain. He could now move his legs and fingers freely. He still had some pain in the mornings, but the exercises and pain-reduction techniques were keeping it at a manageable level. He also told me he had gone back to his full-time job. Before he left he said with a smile, "I told Dr. Lipton he could talk about it with you."

Mystified, I talked with Marc at the first opportunity. "Bill would hardly talk before," I said. "What happened?"

"Oh," Marc said with a laugh, "I just showed him that I was as stubborn as he was. I kept after him to talk about himself until he just got tired of my persistence."

Then he grew serious. "That man has been in mourning for years with no relief."

"Mourning? Mourning what?"

"The death of his wife. That, combined with his daughter's move, seemed to set the stage for a flare-up of his arthritis."

"But Bill told me they were separated."

"I know. That threw me, too. You see, he didn't want to admit to himself that she had died suddenly—it was a car accident. They were very close and the grief overwhelmed him.

Saying they were separated was his way of not admitting to his wife's death without actually having to lie about it."

So Bill's arthritis had been made much worse by his inability to deal emotionally with the sensitizers besieging him. His devastation at losing his wife was compounded when his daughter left town. As his pain became worse and he was forced to change his job, his stress built to an almost intolerable level.

Bill was unable to stop the effects of Profound Sensitivity Syndrome, specifically as it related to his arthritis, until Dr. Lipton broke through his wall of silence. As soon as Bill overcame his reluctance to discuss his emotions, we were able to help him help himself. Once he began talking out his loss, recognizing the need for a change in the way he controlled his grief and loneliness, his arthritis pain and joint function finally began to improve.

The latest lab tests confirmed what we were seeing: His stress-hormone levels and immune function were now both normal. While he still had some pain he was handling it better.

## Positive Feelings

Can you express your feelings? Do you feel comfortable enough with your doctor to talk about what may be bothering you? Dr. Lipton and I believe that the way you feel about your doctor actually has a great bearing on his or her ability to help you.

You will find that not every physician feels your relationship with him or her is that vital to your healing. In fact, many feel that studying the psychological factors of an illness demeans their skills and contributions in some way, as if positive emotions on the part of the patient were meant to take the place of competent medical care.

Norman Cousins, whose role in his own treatment and against-the-odds recovery was described in his book *Anatomy of an Illness,* addresses this very concern in the September 1988 issue of the *Journal of the American Medical Association.* While stating that such reactions on the part of physicians are understandable, Cousins also calls for a balance, "one that recognizes that attitudes such as a strong will to live, high purpose, a capacity for festivity, and a reasonable degree of confidence are not an alternative to competent medical attention but a way of enhancing the environment of treatment. The wise physician favors a spirit of responsible participation by the patients in a total strategy of medical care." He adds, "The physician has a prime resource at his disposal in the form of the patient's own apothecary, especially when combined with the prescription pad."

While reviewing records and speaking with patients, Dr. Lipton and I realized that those who experienced substantial improvement were the same ones with a positive feeling for us. All of this was admittedly very subjective, based on our combined clinical impressions. Yet as we started to look at the results in more detail we found three interesting factors that seemed to contribute to our patients' successes. These are factors that could relate to your relationship with your doctor as well.

It became apparent, first, that the successful patients liked us initially, not as a result of having been helped. They also related well to the personal treatment approaches that Dr. Lipton and I used. This was a particularly interesting clue. Some of the patients either liked Dr. Lipton's approach and disliked mine, or vice versa. It became clear, also, that our common patients who liked *both* of our approaches did much better than those who liked just one.

A second factor related to success seemed to be the patient's confidence in the particular medical treatment we recommended. For instance, when the patients liked us but did not feel particularly confident about the treatment approach, they seemed not to respond as well.

Third, we both identified an element that, for lack of a better term, we called "trust." Those patients who seemed to have a high trust level toward us did better than those who did not have that feeling. For example, suppose I said to a patient, "These drops won't make you nauseated." The person who responded by saying, "Maybe they won't nauseate me, but they'll probably make me sick," had a lower trust level than someone who said, "I'm certainly glad to hear that."

The combination of these three elements—liking our personal and treatment approaches and having trust—all of which we call the "receptivity quotient," related directly to the degree to which our patients improved.

Do *you* feel good about your relationship with your doctor? Is it comfortable and open? The following questions will help you determine just how high your receptivity quotient is with your doctor, and whether or not it might be advisable to find another. It will also assist you in finding a doctor if you don't have one.

**Your Receptivity Quotient**

Answer each of the following questions with "1" for true and "0" for false:

____ 1. My doctor is the type of person who would never admit that he/she doesn't know the answer.
____ 2. I need to understand the reason for everything my doctor is doing.
____ 3. My doctor, although quite competent, is in business primarily to make money.
____ 4. My doctor is very competent but a real s.o.b.
____ 5. If he/she weren't my doctor, he/she is the type of person I'd really enjoy being friends with.
____ 6. My doctor is extremely thorough and when he/she tells me something, I am quite sure it is right.
____ 7. He's/she's a great doctor but I surely wouldn't want to be his/her relative.
____ 8. Most people I know would really like my doctor as a person.
____ 9. I feel quite secure and confident after meeting with my doctor.

____10. Each time my doctor has treated me, what he/she has done has made a great deal of sense to me.

Scoring: To compute your receptivity quotient, add your total score for questions 5, 6, 8, 9, and 10. Subtract from that number the total of your scores from questions 1, 2, 3, 4, and 7. The highest (best) score is 5. If your receptivity quotient is 3, you might want to think about looking around for another doctor. If it is under 3, don't think about it, just find one.

## Healthy Traits

As an extension of the doctor/patient quiz, I also analyzed the voluminous case histories Dr. Lipton and I have compiled on our hundreds of patients who were able to reprogram their biochemical responses. I wanted to determine whether or not there were any characteristics shared among them, any personality traits or health habits that could actually predict the outcome of their treatment.

My curiosity was well-rewarded. There are indeed certain traits these patients shared. Along with their susceptibility to $PS^2$, all possessed at least nine of the following healthy attitudes, characteristics, and actions.

These health-regaining patients

- Were willing to take control. They accepted responsibility for their own lives and health. They believed they could change and improve their lives and did not give up. (Patients who felt helpless responded the poorest.)
- Became actively involved in their treatment programs. In other words, when they had input into the specifics of their treatment program, and where choices could be made, they helped in the decision-making process. They accepted the concept of doctor and patient working together as partners.
- Were patient. A certain amount of impatience is understandable in anyone who is ill. But without exception, these patients maintained a calm and watchful attitude during the time it took to achieve results.

- Had positive attitudes. They liked to learn new things and set new goals to achieve. They were happy and had enthusiasm for life.
- Loved themselves and had high self-esteem. They cared for others, had good family and personal relationships, and tended not to feel lonely.
- Used their creativity, I suspect, to better visualize the hoped-for results of their treatment and, therefore, to participate more enthusiastically.
- Laughed and smiled often. Psychologically, laughter can put life's burdens in perspective, making it more likely that the next one will roll off your back. Physically, laughter is a fair physical workout for your diaphragm and lungs and fills the bloodstream with immunoglobulins (disease fighters) and possibly endorphins (the body's natural painkillers).
- Enjoyed music and listened to some every day. Many also read poetry or books regularly.
- Maintained good posture. I believe two things might account for this shared trait. Good posture often suggests high self-esteem, and patients who like themselves respond better to treatment. Also, an erect bearing allows a better blood flow and more oxygen into the lungs, both of which, as you will see, combat the effects of $PS^2$.
- Did not smoke, or had stopped smoking.
- Exercised, ate properly, and got adequate sleep.
- Ate at least 20 grams of protein for breakfast.
- Did not suppress crying or groaning when they felt like expressing themselves.
- Took vacations.
- Did not rush to effect a change. (It can take up to 21 days to accept new behavior.)
- Breathed slowly to help them regain control when they started to get angry.
- Forgave themselves for not being perfect.

All of these positive traits can be acquired. Perhaps you see yourself in most of them already. Perhaps you see some you would like to incorporate into your life-style. Why not start with a few that you feel comfortable tackling and give yourself

21 days to try them out? Soon you will start to do them subconsciously and will find that you are rewarded—physically and mentally—for your efforts.

Dr. Lipton and I believe that this listing, along with the evaluations and control plan regarding $PS^2$, as well as the doctor/patient partnership information, can help you to know yourself and your environment better. That knowledge, combined with a desire to take control of your health, could mean positive changes for you in ways you may never have considered.

With this as background, you will find yourself approaching the techniques in the chapters that follow with newly gained insight. Each chapter offers specific advice on a subject designed expressly to help you overcome Profound Sensitivity Syndrome. We have taught many hundreds of patients these techniques. We think you will find them equally effective.

# 3

# Changing Faulty Thinking

We have seen that the brain is the control center for every part of the body. The brain has a direct and major impact on our health and our capacity to fight off disease.

Unfortunately, not all people who suffer from Profound Sensitivity Syndrome understand the brain's role in their illnesses. These patients may find relief from the physical symptoms, but you can see that help often needs to go deeper.

If you have suppressed immune function, for instance, you can be helped by medicines that build immune response, but you can also try to find the reason for the suppressed immunity in the first place. More often than not, the reason for a variety of illnesses relates to faulty thinking patterns.

*Irene, the Perfect Wife, with a Bad Back.* Irene was obviously in a lot of pain, though she was trying hard not to show it. Her records indicated that Irene was 31, married, and had two children. Her husband was an executive in a large company and, Irene assured me, "a very busy man."

I began to question her about her pain.

"It's really nothing, Dr. Solomon. Just a bad back, you know. I wonder, though, if you could prescribe some pills for when it gets too bad." I examined Irene's back and from shoulders to hips her back muscles were bunched-up and hard with tension.

"How bad does it get?"

Irene hesitated for a moment, then said, "Well, pretty bad. I can hardly do my housework without feeling like my whole back is just a pincushion of needles."

As I pressed upon different areas of her back, Irene winced. "You're really hurting, aren't you?"

"Oh, well," she said, "I'm not one to complain. Everybody has problems. It's just that it gets hard for me to function, with the gardening and the record-keeping and all."

"You seem to have a pretty full schedule. Irene, your back needs a lot of rest. What would you say to cutting back on some of those chores, to begin with?"

Irene looked alarmed. "Cut back? Oh, no, I could never do that! I have to keep up the house. My husband, John, says we have to keep up the property value. And keeping a garden cuts down on costs. John is very frugal with finances."

I thought to myself that while the house might be holding up, Irene's back wouldn't for much longer. "Irene, you said that this problem began with a fall back in—" I looked in her chart "—September, is that right?"

"Yes, about eight months ago. I was putting up wallpaper, and I fell off the stepladder. I think I sort of twisted my back as I was falling."

"Wallpaper? So you know how to hang wallpaper. That's quite a skill."

"Actually, I'd never hung wallpaper before. In fact, I made a few mistakes and had to do it over. But it's so much more economical if you do it yourself."

I was beginning to understand. "I suppose your husband preferred you do it?"

Irene replied, "Oh, yes. He says I do such a good job." Irene's expression was earnest and straightforward. Apparently she never thought of the possibility of outside help.

"And your children. You said you have two boys, eleven and four years old?"

"Oh, yes. They're wonderful boys, Dr. Solomon. Tommy,

the younger, is just beginning school and Eric, well, he's very bright but a bit of a discipline problem. I've been giving him some extra tutoring in math at home."

Even though I knew the answer to the next question, I asked anyway. "Wouldn't it be easier to arrange for a math tutor to help Eric?"

Irene looked at me in surprise. "My goodness," she said. "I couldn't think of it! Do you know what some of these tutors charge? And besides, John says I do such a good job."

I continued, "So what has been happening the last eight months with your back—after you fell?"

"After I fell, my back hurt so badly that our doctor said I must stay in bed for at least a couple of weeks. Poor John had to handle all the housework and chores himself. It was very hard on him and—well, I'm sure you can see that it was just an impossible situation. That house falls apart without me."

"And after the two weeks—"

Irene interrupted me, "Dr. Solomon, I didn't stay in bed for two whole weeks! John got some pain pills from one of his friends at the office, and I managed to get back on my feet after a week. I couldn't have done it without those pills, though."

"And your back has gotten better or worse since then?"

"Oh, sometimes it's worse, sometimes it's better. When it gets so painful I can't stand it, I just take some more of those pills. John gets them for me."

"And what did your doctor have to say about all this?"

"Oh, well, I didn't bother him again about it. He seems to think I should take the time to nurse my back. No offense, but some doctors just don't realize the responsibilities their patients have."

I wasn't offended, I was amazed at both John's and Irene's nonchalant attitudes toward her physical pain. I decided that I would have to be blunt. "Irene," I said, "if you don't get some help for all your work you'll be spending a lot more than two weeks in bed in a hospital." Irene flinched a little.

"Not only that," I continued, "but I see no reason why John

cannot take on some of the responsibility while your back heals. Surely he can help with the gardening and the housecleaning or hire someone who can. You should not be bending and twisting. Your back needs rest, relaxation, and proper exercise. And that doesn't include hanging wallpaper!" I expected Irene to put up a fight. Instead, she just sat there looking stunned.

I was afraid I had been too harsh, but after a moment Irene said slowly, "You mean my back might go out on me?" I nodded. Irene was thoughtful. I felt sure she was thinking about all the things she wouldn't be able to take care of if she were incapacitated.

We talked some more and I asked Irene if she would be willing to see Dr. Lipton for counseling related to faulty thinking. I was surprised when she replied that it might be good for John to attend, too. I said I thought that was an excellent idea. I then taught Irene some back exercises and instructed her to do them twice daily. I stressed the importance of keeping her back strong and supple. Before she left, I advised Irene to make an appointment with Dr. Lipton as soon as possible.

Irene canceled her follow-up appointment with me and I didn't see her again for a few months. I thought, with disappointment, that John had gotten the upper hand after all. But when I saw Irene again she was walking straighter and her face was not pinched and drawn with pain. And her husband, John, was beside her—and shaking my hand.

"Dr. Solomon," he said, "I almost barged in on you a few months ago to tell you not to interfere with my marriage. I just canceled Irene's appointment instead. But then I found I had trouble on my hands. She started to fight back!" I didn't comment but was pleased to see that John seemed to be in a good humor about it. He went on, "I thought our marriage was over when she kept dragging me in to see Dr. Lipton. Once he recommended that she follow up on her idea of finishing college. I objected at first, but she showed me a stubborn side

I'd never seen before." Irene was smiling and looking rather pleased about this.

"So, were you able to work things out?" I asked.

John said, "Well, it took a while. Dr. Lipton made me eat a lot of crow and I sure didn't appreciate that. But I began to see how much I was taking Irene for granted. You see, my mother was one of those women who tried to be perfect for my father. She took care of *everything* for him. I expected no less from Irene—and she used to want to do everything perfectly for me. I see now that was hurting her in the long run."

Irene said that her back still gave her some trouble, but the exercises along with the relaxation training and counseling she had gotten from Dr. Lipton had helped. "I finally realized how my negative thinking patterns were affecting my body," she said. "That's made a tremendous difference, that and the cleaning woman John hired to do the housework!"

John broke in. "It may sound silly, but I do the relaxation exercises with her. I never realized before how tense I was! I was taking medicine for a stomach ulcer, but with the exercises, Irene and I are *both* off medication."

John had certainly surprised me—as had Irene. More than her back had been mended. She had even decided to study to become a physical therapist and help other people with back problems. Her whole life had taken a new turn—something that might never have happened had she not changed her faulty thinking.

Remember that in relation to $PS^2$ the way we think about things determines how we feel. Our feelings are then manifest in the limbic area of the brain, which, in turn, stimulates the neuro-endocrine-immunological link. In other words, to turn the process around, physical difficulties can signal ongoing destructive thought patterns.

Thus, Dr. Lipton and I believe that it is possible, by understanding your underlying emotions, to treat the cause of your problem. When people are helped to restructure their thinking, the disease process is often reduced dramatically.

In working together with our patients we have discovered that combining traditional medication with training to tap into their own internal pharmacies socks a tremendous one-two punch, knocking out disease most effectively. In other words, medication administered from *outside* the body can join forces with medication administered from *inside* the body—by the mind from the body's own drugstore.

These drugs, actually chemicals called biotherapeutics, are substances produced naturally by your body. Your mind can tell your brain to release them to fight your disease.

From the pharmacopoeia of the body's drugstore comes alpha interferon, which has the capability to fight against hairy cell leukemia. Insulin is a well-known "drug" that helps regulate normal carbohydrate metabolism and prevent diabetes. Cortisone counteracts inflammation, allergies, and arthritis. Growth hormone can actually help a person grow taller. Chemotactic agents allow the body's white cells to gobble up and destroy invading bacteria or viruses.

These miracles of medicine and others (some have been recognized for generations and others are being discovered at a remarkable rate) can be more at your disposal as you learn to change harmful thought patterns into healthful ones.

In this sense, all medical treatment should be considered and practiced as "behavioral medicine." We should not treat in this manner only the few cases easily recognized as relating to life-styles and attitudes.

*Tom's Do-It-Yourself Doctoring and Hypoglycemia.* Tom, a 53-year-old truck driver, had never been sick a day in his life—until he learned that his wife had been unfaithful while he was out on the road. Soon he started to get headaches and took large doses of aspirin to relieve the pain. Sometimes he would be overcome by waves of anxiety; he would start to sweat and become excessively hungry. Then he began drinking to combat the anxiety. If a headache hit when he was driving, he experienced confusion and difficulty with his vision. He would pull off the road, try to sleep it off, and go to a doctor in whatever city he happened to be near.

Invariably, blood tests appeared normal, including those for blood sugar levels. His puzzled family physician referred him to me for diagnosis and treatment.

As Tom related the times his symptoms seemed most severe, a suspicious pattern emerged: The symptoms always seemed to begin after he took aspirin or had a few drinks. Laboratory tests proved he was allergic to neither alcohol nor aspirin (salicylates), so I tried another test. I gave Tom two aspirins and had him wait in my office until symptoms began, then I gave him a small amount of sugar mixed in orange juice. The symptoms vanished as if by magic. Tom had hypoglycemia, a condition in which the body is unable to produce enough sugar. Since both alcohol and aspirin reduce sugar production, either was enough to generate a hypoglycemic reaction. An aspirin-and-alcohol-free diet would end the symptoms, I concluded.

Emotionally, Tom's problems with his wife were resolved through psychotherapy. The inner message Tom was telling himself about his situation was causing him anxiety and stress-induced headaches. Self-medicating his anxiety with alcohol and his headaches with aspirin was interrupting the normal production of sugar by his liver. It could not access correctly the supplies in his body's own drugstore.

Now that he has gotten to the bottom of his problems and corrected his faulty thinking he is no longer abusing his body, his mind is clear, and he is doing well.

Later in this chapter we will define two forms of faulty thinking—problems in philosophical perspective and irrational thought patterns—and ways to restructure them. This will not only order your emotions, but will command your brain to administer the natural drugs available to help the body. As Alfred Adler wrote in 1939, "Man knows much more than he understands." Perhaps we can begin to put to use a little of what our minds and bodies already know.

## The Power of Our Thoughts

Dr. Albert Ellis, noted psychologist, is heralded as the initiator of the study of the interconnection between thoughts and emotions. It was he who first stressed—three decades ago—the idea that our seemingly natural tendency to think self-defeating thoughts is a major contributor to our emotional upsets.

This means that our emotions exist within the realm of our control. Emotions and feelings can, therefore, be dissected and understood more easily when we recognize how we think.

Research shows further that most of us develop our thought patterns—positive or negative—by adolescence. We continue with those, regardless of the harm they do, throughout our lives—unless we realize it and do something to change them.

This was the case with a patient of ours.

*Carol's Defeatist Thinking and Asthma.* I met Carol in an unlikely manner. I was strolling down a street in Philadelphia when I noticed a crowd of people a short distance ahead of me. As I reached the crowd I heard someone say, "Has anyone called for an ambulance?"

Realizing someone needed help, I made my way through the crowd to see a young woman crouching beside a wall. A glance was all it took to see she was in trouble. Her face shone with perspiration and the skin around her mouth had a faintly blue cast. There were traces of froth on her lips. Her breathing was rapid and labored, each exhalation accompanying a deep-throated wheeze. Her hands clutched at her chest as if it were a source of pain.

Fear and pleading were in her eyes. I knelt beside her, told her my name, and said that I was a doctor. It was obvious she was having a severe asthma attack, but there seemed to be more symptoms. Constriction of her bronchial passages would account for the difficulty in breathing, but not for severe chest pain. I felt for her pulse to check the regularity of her heartbeat; it was racing furiously. Suddenly I realized the hand I was holding was wet with sweat and trembling. Along with the asthma she was having a classic panic attack.

I tried to calm her. I explained what was happening to her and eased her into a sitting position against the building. That gave her lungs a better chance to draw in oxygen. I murmured a stream of reassurances: "Try to breathe slowly and deeply. Don't worry about anything. Try to make your mind blank—or, better yet, think about something pleasant. There's nothing to be afraid of; I'm here and an ambulance is on the way. You're going to be just fine."

In a few moments I could hear the approaching ambulance and soon the crew had strapped her onto the stretcher. I rose, dusted off my knees, and prepared to leave, but she grabbed my hand and pleaded, "Please come with me to the hospital. I'm so afraid."

I nodded and climbed into the ambulance with her. Within minutes she was being wheeled into an emergency treatment area, still clutching my hand, and given the drugs she needed to calm her asthmatic spasms. When she had finally calmed down enough to regain control, I felt free to be on my way.

While I had told her my name, it never occurred to me that she would remember it. I was surprised one morning a few weeks later when she turned out to be my next patient. She smiled shyly, holding out her hand as she approached my desk. "I know you don't remember me," she said. "I'm the woman whose life you saved in Philadelphia."

Flattering as that was, it was not accurate. "I do remember you, Carol," I said. "How have you been?"

"Well, not so good, I guess. I need your help again. There's no one else I can turn to."

Her medical questionnaire listed one complaint: asthma.

"You understand I am not a specialist in the treatment of asthma," I said. "But I would be happy to refer you to my associate, Dr. Layton, who is."

Even before I had finished speaking she was shaking her head. "You don't understand," she said, beginning to look frightened. "It's more than the asthma. Something else is happening to me. My doctor says it's just overwork, that a vacation will straighten me out. But I don't dare take one now."

During the next fifteen minutes as we talked, a picture emerged of a driven, talented, frightened person who always expected the worst from life. Her problems revolved around her perceptions and thoughts more than any medical ailment. Her negative attitudes had grown so that she suffered constant anxiety and beyond, into the realm of panic disorder.

At age 34 she had been offered a full professorship at a major university in the Midwest—but was afraid to resign from her current position because she was "sure the offer would be withdrawn." Her boyfriend was planning a job transfer to the new city as well because their relationship was too important to him to abandon—but she was "sure he would change his mind." And on it went.

Other than the asthma, she was in good physical health. But, judging from the sky-high levels of stress hormones in her blood, I knew this could change at any time. I concurred with the treatment given by her regular physician for the asthma and talked with her about her negative thought patterns. I was confident that, if she was willing, she could learn how to change that defeatist pattern of thinking.

She agreed and went to work with Dr. Lipton right away. When I saw her again six months later, she had made some major decisions in relation to her pessimistic thought patterns—and her future. "I just wanted to say thanks before I left for my new job," she said. "I've learned a lot about the negative way I looked at life, the way I automatically thought the worst. I haven't had a panic attack in more than a month."

Because Carol was able to overcome her negative thinking, her health benefited. Her thoughts now, rather than creating physical distress, were helping her body heal itself.

Negative thoughts, if not redirected, will escalate. The fear that "I am not sure I can do this" soon becomes "I cannot do this." That may lead to the idea, "I am a complete failure." As the thought intensifies, we become more nervous, our emotions get the better of us, and our health suffers.

In 1985 researchers sponsored by the National Institute of Mental Health classified anxiety disorders as the number one psychiatric problem in the United States. They estimated some thirteen million Americans suffer anxiety disorders and need treatment. But everyday cognitive distortion, such as the preceding example, causes needless jitters and pain for countless millions more. Obviously, there is too much negative thinking going on in too many of us.

Here is a useful example to illustrate how you can make yourself change. Without moving any other part of your body, raise your right pinkie until it is pointing upward. You have just changed—not drastically, but still, you have changed. The physiological process was complicated, involving the brain, body chemicals, nerves, tendons, and muscles, but the change was made and your mind caused it. You thought it and it happened.

Realizing that the body depends on the mind and the mind on the body, we begin to understand how some people are able to perform amazing feats. By their belief in "mind over matter" some can walk on fire or stop pain and bleeding. They have voluntary control over their autonomic processes—those involuntary functions over which we supposedly have no control.

In a demonstration in 1970, for instance, an Indian named Swami Rama calmly stopped his heart from beating for seventeen seconds. Others have been known to make the heart skip a beat when given a certain hand signal or to stick needles through their arms with no signs of pain or bleeding.

These show phenomenal belief systems. It's important to keep in mind, however, that belief is a two-edged sword. The belief that you are *not* in control of your mind-body's "involuntary" behavior, that you are a victim of it, can harm rather than heal. Simply being unaware that the will is a powerful healer can leave you open to the onslaught of disease. So can ignorance of the fact that your most powerful enemies may well be faulty thoughts.

*Jody's Bulimia Plus.* As a potentially life-threatening example of faulty thinking taken to an extreme, we have Jody. She was a 21-year-old college student who would binge on foods, particularly on sweets, and then go into the bathroom and make herself vomit. In the four months before seeing me she had lost 52 pounds. At five feet four inches and 86 pounds she was emaciated and her menstrual periods had stopped.

Pitting of the enamel of her teeth clued me in to her vomiting. (Pitting comes from hydrochloric acid in the stomach.) After we talked for a while she admitted that she did, indeed, do this. I found further that she had a metabolic defect as well as allergies to certain foods.

Jody was afraid to stop her binging/vomiting behavior for fear of becoming fat. If she gained part of a pound she saw her body as "grotesque." Her mother tried to help her understand that "thin is in—but not too thin" but Jody was repelled by the idea of gaining weight and they fought constantly. Jody insisted that she alone knew what was right for her frame size. She felt she "must" achieve her "ideal" weight. She wanted to measure herself against her thinnest girl friend and be thinner.

I treated her metabolism and allergy problems and referred her to Dr. Lipton, who helped her with her thinking errors, her distorted perception of her body's size. He included her mother in several sessions. Eventually, after quite some time, Jody's perceptions became more realistic and her eating patterns became healthier. Now she is slowly gaining back lost pounds, her periods have returned, and I have assured her I won't allow her to go over her ideal weight.

With the understanding that changing faulty thinking changes our lives, let's see how we can recognize the two groups of negative thought processes we are all susceptible to, problems in philosophical perspective and irrational thought patterns, and ways we can learn to correct them.

## How People Make Themselves Unhappy

One evening while having a late dinner with Dr. Lipton I asked him this question: "Marc, based on your twenty years experience as a psychotherapist what do you feel are the most common reasons that people create their own unhappiness?"

I asked him this because earlier in the day I had seen two patients who were literally "making themselves sick"—to the point that I could not cure their ailments as fast as they seemed to develop them.

His response, an outline of the three major problems in philosophical perspective, with further emphases from case studies of our work with patients, will provide you with a useful box of thinking tools to help you examine any anger, depression, fear, or other feelings that may be creating problems for you.

### Loss of Perspective

The first, strongest belief that perpetuates emotional and physical debilitation is loss of perspective. We get upset about minor issues. We fail to see the bigger picture.

*A Couple Find Their Way—After Husband's Depression.* For instance, a couple came to see Dr. Lipton because financial problems were supposedly ruining their marriage. It had started when the husband invested $50,000 in a "sure bet" opportunity. His wife advised against it, but he went ahead with the deal.

Before long he realized that the deal was fraudulent and his money was gone. His "partner" had absconded.

His wife exploded with anger. She berated her husband, who was doing a fine job of that himself without any help from her. She complained that all she had ever wanted was a nice, quiet life with her husband and to be happy. But that wasn't enough for him. No, he wanted to be rich and had lost their hard-earned money. While their initial reactions were understandable, the problem came when they held onto their placement of blame, constantly reminding each other and themselves.

She could not forgive him, and he could not forgive himself. He started working twice as many hours a week at his sales job and had a major heart attack six months later. As a result of "his failure," his wife's chronic anger, and his heart attack, he was in a major depression; their marriage was near collapse.

This couple had made themselves miserable almost to the point of destroying their marriage and ruining their physical health. Was it because they needed $50,000 to be happy and healthy? No, this was past history, irretrievable. They had simply lost perspective on what was really important in their lives.

It took time and understanding before they could reassess their values and start to put their marriage back together.

This loss of perspective occurs day in and day out. It contributes perhaps more than any other issue to self-generated unhappiness and poor physical health. Our philosophies and perspectives on life have a direct link not only to the biochemistry and physical health of our bodies, but to the subjective state of happiness itself.

You can help yourself gain perspective on a problem by asking: "If I knew I were to die five years from now, would I still be upset about this? If the answer is no, why be upset now?"

These questions can jar you back to a more lucid perspective because we generally have difficulty believing that we will die someday. On an emotional level we tend to feel that we will live forever.

This is why a school of philosophy and later a school of psychotherapy, called existentialism, suggested that we accept our *daesin* or "being"—our mortality. Such contemplation helps us keep priorities in order. Instead of thinking, "In the future when I get 'this,' then I will be happy and enjoy life," we set about changing the present for the better. Too often, the implication in waiting for future fulfillment is that what we desire never comes, and we are kept from enjoying ourselves now.

The clearest sign of emotional maturity and adjustment is the capacity to savor and to enjoy our lives on a moment-to-moment basis. To be truly living in the "here and now." This does not preclude rational planning for the future; it develops a sense of contentment and satisfaction rather than fostering a chronic and insidious sense of dissatisfaction, discontent, and never-ending futuristic focus. Living only for tomorrow never allows us to enjoy today and, from a biochemical perspective, keeps a level of destructive secretion of substances in the blood that erodes our health.

**Chronic Powerlessness**

The second negative philosophy relating to the happiness-misery continuum is a sense of helplessness. We talked about this earlier—and will talk about it again, so crucial is a sense of control to the workings of the mind-body connection. Those people who feel that they are not helpless have the highest levels of emotional and physical well-being. When one of my patients says, "I will leave it to God," I usually reply with my mother's favorite saying: "God helps those who help themselves."

*Martha's New Sense of Power After Physical Deterioration.* Martha, a 51-year-old happily married saleswoman with two grown children, was referred to me by an internist friend who could not help her chronically deteriorating physical condition. She had lost thirty pounds in the past year and was much too thin, had had a series of pulmonary, urinary, and vaginal infections, had clearly suppressed immune function, and appeared as if she were "dying" in front of my eyes.

Upon examination I found no apparent source, or etiology, for these problems. I placed her on a high-calorie diet and treated her for her infections. Then I referred her to Dr. Lipton to see if he could come up with any ideas as to what was going on with Martha. In the interim I ordered an MRI (magnetic resonance imaging) scan to determine whether or not she might have an undetected tumor.

After three sessions with Marc the problem became clear. Martha had worked as a saleswoman for 25 years. When her boss passed away, the store closed and she took another sales job at a well-known women's clothing store. She had been in that position for eighteen months.

Her new boss had a true "sadistic personality disorder." He berated her constantly in the most bizarre and hostile fashion. Because Martha had been reared by a tyrannical father and, after holding her previous job for so long, considered quitting a job as personal failure, she found herself "helpless" to do anything about her predicament.

These factors contributed to her adopting a posture of learned helplessness. Her only way out was to destroy her health so that she would become so sick she would be unable to work.

After ten sessions with Marc she was able to free herself from this sense of helplessness. She finally quit her job and began to look elsewhere. Within a week she looked as though she had just returned from an extended vacation in Hawaii.

Martha's bout with helplessness was fairly circumscribed by one situation. Many of us view ourselves and our entire lives from this philosophical perspective—a perspective that can destroy us from the inside out.

**Enough Is Enough**

The third major negative philosophy is the failure to distinguish what is within our capacity to change from that which is not. We neglect to work on the things we can do something about, and we expend enormous energy on things over which we have no control. In other words, we try to change the unchangeable. Here is an example, one that Dr. Lipton calls the "Mothers-Never-Say-Die Syndrome."

*Erma's Problem with Her Child.* Erma was a 55-year-old married mother of three sons. One was a doctor, one a lawyer, and one long known as a "sick jerk." The sick jerk had been in trouble since he was a child, first with poor behavior in school, petty thievery, dropping out of college, three divorces, car accidents, expressed hate of his immediate family, and a few problems too bad to mention here.

Erma, as I am sure you have gathered by now, spent at least half of her waking life trying to "fix him up," even though she had been told by everyone for thirty years that the only thing that would "fix him up" would be a brain transplant.

But that did not discourage Erma. Undaunted by the misery she was causing her husband, the sense of neglect and resentment she had generated in her other two sons, and her own chronic upset and constant level of hyperarousal, Erma marched on into one physical illness after another.

A turning point came one day when she admitted to Dr. Lipton—and herself: "Maybe I've been acting like a bigger jerk than my son." Dr. Lipton replied, "I think that's a very astute insight," and helped her understand further the difference between changes we can and cannot make.

Another symptomatic syndrome falls into this category, one that Dr. Lipton has labeled the "If-Only Syndrome": If only I had gone to college; if only my husband were a kind, sweet, considerate man; if only I had loving and supportive parents; if only my child weren't an insensitive, spoiled person; if only I had been born rich; if only, if only, if only.

As Marc says, "At some point in therapy with my 'If only' patients I usually respond at an opportune moment by saying, 'If only I were a chicken I could lay an egg.' If the patient says, 'What do you mean?' I know he or she needs more therapy."

When focusing on that which we cannot change, and making ourselves miserable and physically ill in the process, we have too little time or energy left for those aspects of our lives that we *can* change and thereby improve our happiness and satisfaction.

Expending thought and emotional energy is similar to making financial investments: You look for areas with the greatest likelihood of generating a safe and predictable profit. This takes a lot of wisdom and sensitivity to techniques that strengthen our resolves.

## Irrational Thought Patterns

An irrational thought pattern is one not appropriate to the facts. Psychologists call this kind of thinking "cognitive distortion." Challenges become menacing monsters, small problems become insurmountable obstacles—and it all happens in the mind.

Cognitive distortion may cause you, for example, to imagine a mildly critical comment from the boss as a forerunner to disaster. Instead of accepting the criticism as it was intended, to correct some small inadequacy in your performance, you brood about it in constant fear. You feel out of control in the situation, helpless, and, in severe cases of thought distortion, hopeless. Thus, the response to that particular sensitizer, which should have subsided in a matter of minutes, now goes on and on for days, months, and too often, for years. These chronic distortions of thinking can cause you to be in a chronic state of stress and end up triggering your biochemistry to erode your physical health. Here are nine irrational thought patterns:

### 1. Black-and-White Thinking

A young working mother comes home an hour late, after a hectic day at the office. The babysitter is irritable at her tardiness. The children are screaming as a result of being unfed. Looking at the havoc the woman tells herself, "I'm a terrible mother and a failure as well."

This woman habitually makes the error of thinking in extremes. She is either completely good or completely bad, never in-between. This type of thinking occurs often in perfectionist people. They tend to be hard on themselves, especially when a mistake has been made. They then find it hard to forgive themselves.

### 2. Know-It-All Thinking

A wealthy older gentleman is seen spending time with a beautiful young woman. Rumors spread that the young woman is a "golddigger," interested only in the man's fortune.

Know-it-all thinkers are sure that they can determine the motives or reasoning of others. The inherent danger in this attitude lies in the fact that, without sufficient information, snap judgments stand a good chance of being wrong.

Not many enjoy the company of an obvious know-it-all. Know-it-all thinking, however, can take on a more subtle form when a person assumes that she knows what another person is thinking about *her*. An insecure person may assume that because a friend passes her in the hall without so much as a "hello," this friend is ignoring her. The friend, however, absorbed in her own thoughts, may have failed even to see her.

It is possible for two people who engage in know-it-all thinking to have bitter arguments, each reading more into a sentence or situation than was ever intended.

### 3. Expecting the Worst

A news report warns that a dangerous disease has been discovered, causing symptoms such as headache, high fever, itching, and irritability. Lillian turns off her set before learning that the disease has been confined to European countries. The next morning she awakens with a headache and concludes that she has contracted the new disease.

We sometimes label people who expect the worst as people with overactive imaginations. Often they spend so much time worrying about what terrible thing *might* happen that they neglect to enjoy the present. These people need to stop and smell the proverbial roses.

### 4. Measuring Up

Susan and Beth are best friends and juniors in high school. Susan is secretly proud that she has always gotten better grades than Beth. One day both girls receive their SAT scores and Susan scores a little lower than Beth does. Susan chides herself and thinks, *I must be getting dumber.* The next day, on a math test, Susan gets an A and Beth a B. Susan breathes a sigh of relief.

People who measure themselves against others may find themselves on an emotional seesaw. They can never feel good about themselves based on their own merits; they feel satisfied only when they are better than someone else. Like Susan, when someone else surpasses them they tend to feel depressed and inadequate. Relief comes only when they emerge as comparatively superior. Insecure people can often be heard saying, "Well, I'm better than she is, anyway." Competitive people tend to do a lot of comparing.

### 5. Mother Hen Thinking

Mr. Brady, a first-year college instructor, feels it is his job to be everything to his students—outstanding teacher, good friend, sage counselor. Consequently, he gives his students his home address and telephone number. He sets aside several hours per week for students to drop in, and he works until three in the morning three nights a week in order to prepare interesting lectures and study aids.

As the year wears on, Mr. Brady realizes that his time and efforts are not appreciated. In fact, his students are actually taking advantage of his good nature. Disillusioned, he decides not to work so hard. Two days later, however, he feels so guilty and irresponsible that he returns to his compulsive style of working, in spite of his unappreciative students.

Many parents engage in Mother Hen Thinking. They must do everything and have all the answers for their children. Human beings, however, are not omniscient, nor are they omnipotent. We were not meant to be everything to everybody. Although Mother Hen Thinking is seen in people who are sensitive and compassionate, such people have unrealistic goals. Their disappointment is heightened when they realize that they cannot meet everyone's needs. They are further disillusioned when others fail to appreciate their efforts.

### 6. "I-Know-You" Thinking

Barbara comes home from work one evening to find her husband, Frank, watching television. Without a word she passes by him and goes into the kitchen to cook supper. She thinks to herself, *If Frank really cared about me he would know that I'm tired and would offer to cook dinner.*

What's wrong with this kind of thinking? The problem is that Barbara is making herself angrier and angrier at Frank because she expects him to be able to read her mind. Meanwhile, unsuspecting Frank sits in the other room not realizing that Barbara is angry. It is a good bet that Barbara will be irritable for the rest of the evening but, rather than confront Frank by asking him to help out once in a while, she will suffer in silence.

### 7. Heart-Over-Head Thinking

John gets laid off from his job and he feels like a failure. After applying for several positions and receiving two don't-call-us, we'll-call-you letters, John feels even more insecure. Finally, he receives an invitation to a job interview, but his spirit is so broken the interview is a disaster.

This type of thinking, in which a person allows his or her negative emotions to replace rational thought, acts much like a rolling, ever-growing snowball. Negative emotions affect the way a person acts, which results in negative feedback, which, in turn, reinforces even deeper negative emotions.

## 8. Rehabilitation Thinking

Carrie and Paul are planning to be married. Since the engagement, Carrie notices that Paul has several bad habits that she has never been aware of before. *Oh, well,* she tells herself, *once we're married I'll change all that.*

Thinking that others should change to make you happy overlooks the obvious fact that the world does not revolve around any one person. We can control only our own behavior, not the behavior of others. A person may change "for you" but no one will change unless he *wants* to. Trying to induce change in another's behavior will eventually lead to resentment and may reinforce actions in the opposite direction.

## 9. I Must, You Should, They Ought, Thinking

Diane is disillusioned with her boyfriend, Ted. He just doesn't understand her needs.

Here are samples of her needs: "He should want to be with me all the time. He should recognize my need to be with my friends and not just with him. He should bring me flowers and take me to a nice restaurant every time we go out. He should be more spontaneous. He shouldn't be jealous when I spend time with my old boyfriend because we're just friends. He should know that it drives me crazy when he even looks at another woman."

Diane has made a set of rules that she expects Ted to follow. Of course, it is impossible for Ted to meet her standards. He has no way of knowing what they are at any given moment and Diane demands the impossible.

People who expect others to follow their rules find themselves intolerant of others. Likewise, these people may place high standards on their own behavior: "I should be a perfect mother." "I should always be independent." "I should always be selfless." This necessarily leads to disappointment in self and others.

* * *

Perhaps you have had one or more of these irrational types of thoughts. This is not unusual. If you find, however, that the way you are thinking is disrupting your own peace, then some changes may be in order.

Indulging in faulty thought patterns can result in symptoms that range from depression to irritability, from insomnia to anxiety. Let's examine various ways of eliminating faulty thinking. Remember, until it is cleared up, $PS^2$ will continue to bombard your body.

## Making Changes

In order to change your own patterns of faulty thinking, it is important to understand what they are, remember them, and then decide what a more appropriate alternative would have been. Here are three methods our patients have found to be successful:

### Keeping a Journal

Probably the surest way to identify your own negative thought patterns—philosophical and irrational—is to keep a record in a journal. This is not difficult or excessively time-consuming.

Even if you find it hard to discipline yourself to write down all of the elements at first, you will find that using pencil and paper makes the process more objective. It is difficult to recognize our own faulty thinking because we feel uncomfortable criticizing ourselves. It may help to look at what's written on the paper as if you are looking at someone else's problems.

Here is a sample of a journal page kept by one patient on the day she was to be interviewed for a new job. Marie was afraid of cutting loose from the security of her old job, even though she hated it. The never-ending criticism of her surly boss created so much stress for her that she was becoming ill—colds, flu, migraine headaches, back pain. But on the day of her interview, she was filled with negative thoughts. Her journal looked like this:

**Thought Journal**

| What I'm Doing | How I Feel | What I'm Thinking | What Else Could I Think? |
|---|---|---|---|
| Waking Up | Anxious | I'm so nervous I'll never get the job. They won't like me because I'm a blathering idiot. | I'm nervous because I'm going for an interview. That's perfectly natural. |
| Sitting in waiting room | Anxious | That other applicant looks so smart and polished. If only I looked better. | I look fine. If I'm right for the job I'll be hired. I can only do what is within my ability. It doesn't matter what others do. |
| Having interview | Depressed | He says he's impressed with my qualifications but thinks I should relax. He must think I'm terribly uptight. Why did I ever come? | He was being nice and only wanted me to be less nervous. He's actually very complimentary. I'm making a big deal over nothing. |
| Evaluating interview | Depressed | I blew it completely. | I did okay. I was just a little nervous. |

The final entries in column four were not made on the day of the interview; Marie was unable to sort those out, to select and accept rational counterparts for her negative thoughts, until later. I hope that reading her entries will help clarify the process for you. (By the way, she got the job!)

Getting feelings down on paper makes them more tangible and harder to forget and, thus, easier to combat. We recommend using a full-sized notebook with lined pages. Divide each page into four vertical columns. Label the headings What I'm

Doing, How I Feel, What I'm Thinking, and What Else Could I Think?

To get you started, think about a recent experience in which you felt a strong negative emotion or recognized an unhealthy thought pattern. In the space provided below, fill in each of the columns. Give particular thought to column four. What would have been a more appropriate, more rational thought?

**Thought Journal**

| What I'm Doing | How I Feel | What I'm Thinking | What Else Could I Think? |
|---|---|---|---|
| | | | |

Whenever you find yourself feeling a self-defeating emotion, take out your notebook and jot down responses in the appropriate columns. Don't worry about proper grammar or sentence structure; the important thing is to get honest information down fast. If you have trouble filling in column four, set the journal aside for a few hours. The extra time will give your emotions a chance to settle down and your thoughts to clear.

## Interrupting Faulty Thinking

A study in the *Journal of Personality and Social Psychology* (December 1988) suggests that a major cause of depression is the inability to distract oneself from distressing thoughts.

Whereas those more in control of their thoughts can make the shift away from negativity, depression-prone people cannot. Furthermore, when volunteers were given several topics to think about in place of a negative one, depressed people tended to choose another upsetting subject.

If you, too, have a tendency toward dwelling on the negative, this exercise will help you erase a negative thought once it has entered your mind.

When you have a little spare time—and some privacy—take a pad and pen and make a list of the negative thoughts that seem to be causing you the most problems.

Now, set the kitchen timer for two minutes and look at the first thought on your list. Close your eyes and focus on it. Let it fill your mind: "I'm a terrible mother because I didn't buy my son a new car for Christmas. . . ."

When the timer sounds, open your eyes, take a sharp, deep breath, and stand up quickly. Try to wipe the thought from your mind, as if it had been frightened away by the timer bell. If it tries to sneak back into your thoughts, try bursting into song, humming, or making ridiculous noises—a chicken clucking, a cow mooing, a train whistling. The funnier the better; few things can chase away self-disparaging thoughts as well as laughing at ourselves.

Practice this until you can lick those intruding negative thoughts.

### Replacing Faulty Thoughts

This exercise will help you nip self-defeating thoughts in the bud.

It is fairly simple: When you are aware that a negative thought is forming, replace it with one that is positive. Actually, though the idea is simple, the level of self-control it requires can be surprisingly demanding.

Think of six *positive* thoughts relevant to you. Here are some examples:

1. Life is really great!
2. I'm a fortunate person to have such a wonderful family!
3. My family loves me very much!
4. I am good at my job!
5. I can do [fill in] better than anyone else I know!
6. This new approach to thoughts is really going to help me be healthier and happier!

Write your selections down. Fix them in your mind. Now, whenever you begin to have a distorted thought, you should recognize it and replace it *immediately* with one of these positive thoughts. Repeat the positive thought over and over again in your mind.

If you are faithful—and determined—you will succeed. You will be able to replace a negative thought almost before you realize it is a negative thought.

And you will have acquired an extremely valuable tool: the ability to control your own mind. It is something that few people ever learn. Indeed, most people feel they are at the mercy of their own minds, that any thought good or bad that springs to mind must be indulged. But you know better now. You have learned a great secret: Your mind can think about only one thing at a time.

## Thinking Ahead

Changing faulty thinking is much more difficult than changing behavior for the simple reason that modifying the way we think requires total honesty about ourselves. Complete truth is difficult because we like to imagine ourselves as perfect beings. Plus, it is hard to imagine ourselves any other way than the way we are.

But now that you understand how faulty thought patterns and emotions can lead to immune suppression, which, in turn, causes physical illnesses, you are probably ready to take that step of honest self-evaluation.

And as you banish faulty thinking, you will find that you have more control over your bodily destiny than you probably ever believed you could. You can cause your brain to change the pattern that leads to Profound Sensitivity Syndrome and play a different role, the healing role you desire.

# 4

# How God Helps Those Who Help Themselves

That, as I said, was my mother's credo. She lived by it and passed it on to me. Now, more than half a century later, I can validate it. In some of the case studies that follow, you will see the part I have been privileged to play in this area with several patients, and why I can say without hesitation that we have certain responsibilities in our search for health and healing.

You have learned how to get a handle on control in your life and you will be learning physical and mental techniques later. But this mind-body discussion would not be complete without a look at an often-ignored dimension of every human, the part of you that monitors and can even direct the relationship between your mind and your body. That dimension is the spirit, joining mind and body in an inseparable bond.

What does it mean to consider the "spiritual" side of health and healing? Mostly it raises a lot of questions and too few answers. But we do know that this amazing connection of mind, body, and spirit is real and that you can strengthen it.

The spirit and its capacity for faith can be the mind's most powerful ally in healing the body. In fact, the role of the mind is so vital to the health of the body that we could even say that some diseases appear to "seek out" certain states of mind, and that health "selects" attitudes and beliefs that are quite different. Particularly if you have $PS^2$ it is vital that you nurture attitudes and beliefs that attract health. Strong religious or spiritual beliefs generate enormous emotional impact and the capacity, at times, to produce startling biochemical reversals.

The story of Theresa is the story of faith in a higher spirit that literally helped save her life.

*Theresa's Heart Problem and Faith in a Higher Spirit.* When Theresa came in for her first appointment, she looked at me with an odd expression, as if there were some special significance in this meeting for her. As we talked she apologized for being so absorbed with her thoughts and began to tell me an amazing story.

At age fifty Theresa had a valve problem in her heart. During an operation to replace her aortic valve, she developed serious complications and hemorrhaging. Later she was taken to her room. Just as she slipped into a coma she heard doctors telling her husband and two children that she was going to die.

She lost touch with the outside world, but her spirit could communicate with God easily. She prayed, asking Him to help her, and deep in her spirit she believed she heard His reply. He told her that she would not die. Furthermore, she had to believe that she could help herself. And she could help herself most by believing in His healing power. From that moment on, even in her unconscious state, Theresa knew she would make it.

Four days later she awoke from the coma, and shortly thereafter she returned home from the hospital.

One afternoon she had a sudden impulse to watch television, something she rarely did. She heard a doctor speaking about ways people can use their minds to help heal their bodies. She did not catch his name but the idea intrigued her.

Several months went by and one day while she and her husband were visiting in Baltimore she felt she should see a doctor. For no particular reason, she chose my name from the ones listed in the phone book.

She made an appointment and was surprised to find that she recognized me; I was the doctor she had seen on TV. After telling me this story she said she feared I would think she was crazy. Of course, I didn't. I believe too firmly in the dimension of the spirit and do not doubt that God would use it to heal mind and body.

Theresa turned out to have hidden allergies. They were triggering an outpouring of adrenaline and histamine in response to her stress and causing a fast heartbeat. She was desensitized to the allergies, taught to de-stress, and with her continuing faith in a Supreme Being has sustained herself in continuing good health.

Let me say at the outset that a story like this does not indicate any special qualification on my part. It is only because Theresa was willing to do all she could to help herself, and shared her story with me, that I even played a role in it. I am sure that many other physicians who believe in the power of the spirit have equally inspiring stories of healing being aided by this important dimension.

In fact, based upon documented cures from Christian as well as non-Christian sources, there is absolutely no question that a strong faith in cure, along with cognition or imagery specifying the type of cure desired, does on many occasions produce the biochemical changes required to correct the condition.

It may seem incongruous that empirical knowledge can actually enhance faith, but science and religion need not be adversaries. Each can tell us something about the nature of reality; each can help us understand our lives more fully. We are physical beings, but we are also spiritual beings; the two cannot be separated so easily. Nor can many things affect the mind-body connection as much as faith can.

There is inherent power in faith; it indicates an intensity of action not present in simply thinking happy and good thoughts. Faith means belief *in* something to do you good. It includes the dimensions of the personal, interpersonal, and religious.

We probably think most often of faith in relation to God, though the idea of God means many things to many people.

Whether or not there is an energizing capacity that comes from the divine Spirit, I will leave to the theologians' speculations. But I do conclude that nothing on this earth can produce in human beings the intensity of focused emotional impact for potential cure and healing that faith in God has been documented to do.

Actually, as far as Profound Sensitivity Syndrome is concerned, it is not important what your belief is. Your faith-filled beliefs and your neighbor's may be poles apart but, from a purely medical standpoint, there is no right or wrong position for your immune system.

For instance, many of our patients are convinced that they are not working alone, but in cooperation with God. Many others believe that their own power of suggestion is running the whole show. Still others fall somewhere in the middle. Whatever the case, we have seen a mighty health-enhancing force at work in strong systems of faith. And the greater the faith, the better it helps the immune system heal the body.

*Janet's Prayers Are Answered—Thyroid Problem Helped.* About two years before she came to see me, Janet, age 27, felt as if she was choking whenever she swallowed food. This was enough to terrify her, but she developed other troubling symptoms as well. Soon she was feeling tired most of the time, she had increased forgetfulness, increased menstrual bleeding, her voice became hoarse, and her sex drive decreased.

She told me she was scared and did not know where to turn for help. She only knew she felt terrible all the time.

Just as she was about to give up all hope, her mother, who had a strong belief in God, prevailed upon her to go to church and pray. Janet said that her faith had sustained her in past crises, but she had not been to church since long before her illness. So with her mother's help she "dragged herself" to church, hoping for an answer to her prayers.

Certain words the priest spoke seemed to have special meaning for her: "Listen for His signals. God will guide you."

She and her mother prayed and each lit a candle. Then she went home, lay down, and opened the newspaper. In a few moments, she noticed my health column printed there. It dealt that day with a problem similar to hers. She took this as the sign she was looking for. She got my address, made an appointment, and came to see me.

After evaluation and lab work we discovered Hashimoto's thyroiditis. This meant she had a firm, enlarged thyroid gland with circulating antithyroid antibodies. In other words, antibodies from her immune system were attacking her own thyroid gland and causing hypothyroidism (underactive thyroid).

She was relieved to find the source of the problem. Having a name for it was the breakthrough she needed. With the appropriate mixture of thyroid hormone and her renewed faith, her thyroid gland was brought under control within a year.

Norman Vincent Peale is a familiar name long connected with the importance of a positive belief system. In his recent book *The Power of the Plus Factor,* Dr. Peale suggests the importance of "feeding" the spirit with spiritual food—and the healthful rewards. He writes:

> Peace of mind is important to well-being, to successful achievement and happiness. How is it attained? One of the greatest passages in the Bible says, "Thou wilt keep him in perfect peace, whose mind is stayed on thee . . ." (Isaiah 26:3). The word *stayed* is a reference to the ropes and stays that hold a ship's mast upright, even in the worst of storms. So it means that if your mind is braced on God—the vast, immovable, unchanging, everlasting God—the anxieties and confusions and tensions that surround you will not penetrate the peace that enfolds you. You will be quiet and controlled, without strain or stress.

Remember that people with $PS^2$ generally have no insulation against the negative effects of sensitizers. For you more than others, as a prophylactic measure against the continuation of $PS^2$ maladies, it is essential that you foster the kind of "spiritual climate" in which good health can thrive. "Feeding" the spirit with peace is the answer.

It may sound strange to you, but we have patients who actually express gratitude for getting sick. They tell us of a greater "spiritual understanding" they have achieved through struggling with their illnesses. Some say it has brought them closer to God, some attest to feeling closer to some "divine force" they cannot name. Others say they have come to feel a deeper love for themselves and others. No matter what they attribute this new experience to, they all seem to agree that they have become more *spiritual* people. This is the word we hear over and over.

*Raymond's Fateful Heart Attack.* Raymond, 53 years old, came to me three months after having a myocardial infarction (heart attack). He had headaches, elevated stress hormones, and gastrointestinal problems, particularly diarrhea. He was depressed, fatigued, developing allergies, and very frightened. He was trying to do too much too soon in the office he supervised. He was a prime candidate for biofeedback and psychotherapy. Dr. Lipton and I began working with him.

Three months later I was surprised when Raymond made an appointment just to tell me that that heart attack was the best thing that had ever happened to him. He explained that he had never known how miserable he was until he had been forced to reassess his values and priorities. He said that for the first time in his life he was appreciating his wife and children, felt for the first time ever that there was a God, and would never go back to the blind ignorance of his pre-heart attack mentality.

This turn of faith is not limited to conversations in the offices of medical or clerical professionals. We are witnessing a powerful upsurge of faith all over the world. Evangelical organizations are smuggling huge numbers of Bibles into Iron Curtain countries. Televangelists are flooding the airwaves (and some of them *making* waves). Eastern religious beliefs and practices are continuing to grow through meditation and prayer groups.

Medicine is also catching up with this trend: Books and articles professing the healing power of the mind are prominent in bookstores and on magazine stands. Meanwhile, scientists keep discovering the powerful effects of belief on immune function, while physicians note "miraculous" cures directed by the faith of their patients.

Of course, those who have continued over the centuries to flock to faith healers or to sites of miraculous cures have not lost sight of that sacred connection. Nor have the tribal peoples throughout the world who go to their shamans, or spiritual healers, when illness strikes. And many of those who count on spiritual healing get better.

*Karen's Added Dimension.* A few years ago, one of our patients suddenly began showing remarkable improvement in just a few months' time. Karen was a young woman who had been chronically ill for years. We had not made any significant changes in her medication or health regimen, so I wondered what had made the difference.

The only change I could find was in her behavior. She had formerly been withdrawn and depressed about her health. Now she could be seen in the waiting room pulling other patients out of *their* funks by laughing with them, listening to their problems, giving them advice and encouragement.

When I saw Karen in my office I told her that the results of her blood and urine tests showed a sudden improvement. She didn't seem surprised. I then asked her if she had changed her medication. She shook her head and smiled. Rather confused, I asked her if she knew, then, what accounted for her rapid improvement. With some embarrassment Karen said simply, "I guess I've rediscovered love."

She explained that she had attended church with a friend of hers and the sermon had been about the healing power of love. She was impressed with what she heard and she surely needed healing, so she just started to give help and understanding to her family, friends, and whoever else seemed to need it.

As a kind of "side effect," as she phrased it, she started to feel better. "And it seems to make other people feel better, too. My family and I are much closer now," she told me. I told her that I had noticed my other patients seemed to be benefiting from it as well.

I proceeded with Karen's examination and as I was going through her chart I noticed that on her initial questionnaire she had written "agnostic" as her religion. I could not help but ask her if she had "changed her mind" about that.

"No," Karen replied. "I'm still an agnostic. But now I feel that even if there isn't a God we should all treat each other as if there were." Then she added, "Anyway, all I know is, it works. It makes me feel better; it makes other people feel better. And that's all I care about."

What had happened to Karen—and to her immune response? To this day, Karen is a different person, like someone with an added dimension. And her health has reflected that. She has resumed an active life-style, something once prohibited by her illness, and is making new friends. She comes in only for periodic checkups now.

I thought about what she had said for some time, looking for some label to attach to her, something to replace "agnostic." But finally I understood: Karen had become spiritual. She said that she had "rediscovered love." She had obviously discovered, or rediscovered, the spiritual side of her nature, which she expressed through love.

If you are an agnostic like Karen or an atheist, do you still believe in the importance of understanding, generosity, empathy—in short, love—as a vital force for transforming your life and your health? And if you believe in God, are you aware of the power of His love, and the importance of expressing it to others? As Boerne wrote in 1824, "Love is a form of flattery which pleases all . . . even God."

All religions seem to agree on one thing: There exists something larger than ourselves, something that affirms we are not alone, we do not have to suffer alone. There is a purpose in life. Once you have found a higher authority to believe in you can harness and nurture that belief and see changes in your life—and others' lives.

One thing we have learned from Karen and other patients is that "healing begets healing." As you reach out to people you will find they need someone to listen to their problems, to care about them, just as much as you do. Too many of them just don't know how to ask for love or even for a willing ear. And listening to other people's problems puts our own into perspective. Giving unconditional love makes us feel better about ourselves. We are more likely to receive love in return.

We are not suggesting that you go out and buy a hundred valentines and stamps. It is not easy to make such an effort overnight. But you can start by reading this self-checklist to see any areas in which you may need to rediscover or liberate the spiritual part of yourself.

- Is my relationship with each member of my family as close as it could be?
- Is there any unresolved animosity between me and any member of my family?
- (If you have a spouse, boyfriend, or girlfriend) Have I done everything to make our relationship as strong and loving as possible? Do I listen to his/her problems, share laughter, say what I think makes him/her special? Does either of us fight over trivial things just to show "who's boss"?
- Have I encouraged any of my friends to feel that they can call me whenever they need me? When I feel "down" is there any friend I can call just to talk things over?
- (If you work) Is there a good feeling between me and the people I work with?
- When I meet a stranger who needs assistance, how do I respond? Am I the kind of person who holds doors open for others, doesn't mind giving directions, smiles back at

someone who smiles at me, isn't afraid to engage in friendly conversation on the bus, in line at the supermarket, in the doctor's waiting room?

- Do I feel lonely much of the time?
- Do I feel misunderstood?
- Do I like myself? If I don't completely like myself, do I still love myself?
- Am I able to forgive imperfections in others? One wise man once said, "The day I'm perfect is the day I can expect perfection in others."

S. R. Hirsh wrote in 1836: "Respect your own body as the receptacle, messenger, and instrument of the spirit." If you are not happy with some of your answers to the questions, are you ready to do something about it? Do you *believe* you can make a change for the better?

## Placebos and Faith

In a 1957 issue of the *Journal of Projective Techniques,* Dr. Bruno Klopfer described an often-cited true story about a man who demonstrated the spectrum of the power of belief. Mr. Wright was in a hospital dying of cancer and was not expected to live more than two weeks. When he heard of a new cancer-fighting drug, he "begged so hard" to receive it that his physician complied.

His doctor had left him bedridden and gasping for air; a few days later he found him walking around the ward, chatting happily. His tumors were half their original size.

The injections were continued and within ten days Mr. Wright was discharged from the hospital. Practically all signs of his disease had vanished.

All was well with Mr. Wright until about two months later when conflicting reports began to emerge about the drug. He began to lose hope and rapidly relapsed into his original state. His physician then decided to tell Mr. Wright that he had an improved formula for the drug, following which Mr. Wright's optimism reached a new high.

After receiving the new injections, really consisting of water, Mr. Wright again recovered his health; tumor masses melted, chest fluid vanished.

Unfortunately, Mr. Wright heard further reports about the drug's uselessness and was readmitted to the hospital, where he died within two days.

Should Mr. Wright have believed in a useless medication? If someone is given a sugar pill, a placebo, and thinks he took a powerful drug and feels better, is that just a useless trick of the mind?

Questions like these surround the term *placebo effect*—a much-maligned phenomenon. The placebo effect really refers to a thought or set of assumptions that, in turn, triggers emotional impact and biochemical change.

Actually, the placebo effect is what we have been talking about: faith. The faith is placed in the medicine. And while the placebo effect is a mistaken cognition, it is nevertheless effective. The remission, the getting better, is real.

The placebo effect is, therefore, as valid as any effective drug or surgery if it accomplishes the same thing. The placebo effect *is* medicine, administered by belief rather than by a pharmacist. We just are not used to thinking of ourselves as having within us the power to heal. It takes a while to understand that positive belief is a form of healing, too.

We mention the placebo effect because, at its best, it is an excellent illustration of how our faith—belief plus expectation—affects our health. It also testifies to the mind-body connection.

So, was Mr. Wright right to die? Given the fact that he did not know he was curing himself, any other outcome seems unlikely. But today a physician or psychologist, understanding the principles of neuro-endocrine immunology, could have put aside the useless drug and taught Mr. Wright to use his impressive belief system, perhaps to put his cancer into remission. Or, more likely, his belief system could have been used in combination with other effective cancer treatments.

## Three Steps of Faith

How do you start implementing the powerful belief system within you? It seems appropriate to turn to the words, found in Scripture, of a wise and deeply religious man: King Solomon. Here is a three-step formula to enhance your bond of body, mind, and spirit:

### Body

*"A heart at peace gives life to the body" (Proverbs 14:30).*

The first principle for developing a healthy belief system is to be at peace with yourself. Anyone with $PS^2$ cannot afford to harbor unresolved guilt, fear, or any of the other negative internal emotions we discussed in the last chapter.

If you have $PS^2$, it is important to take an inventory to see if there are any unresolved issues you are carrying around that cause continuing aggravation. Then you can learn new, healthier ways to react to what you cannot change. It may help to talk with a friend, rabbi, clergyman, or therapist.

Sometimes when life is at its most uncomfortable, it can also be a vehicle for learning about courage.

This notion brings to mind the exceptional spirit and extraordinary will of Viktor Frankl, M.D., a psychiatrist who survived the loss of almost his entire family at the hands of Nazis. He himself was in a concentration camp, which he talks about in one of his remarkable books, *Man's Search for Meaning*. As most of his life was being snatched away and he was losing all he held dear, he still believed he had the freedom "to choose his attitude, in a given set of circumstances." He rose above his outward fate by finding meaning in his suffering.

### Mind

*"Pleasant words are . . . sweet to the soul and healing to the bones" (Proverbs 16:24).*

The second principle for developing a healthy belief system is to be at peace with others. Use your mind, your will, your emotions to make a conscious effort to reach out to others. Chronic resentment and anger most assuredly make $PS^2$ worse. But pleasant words spoken with a kind attitude are a healing balm—not only to the one who hears them, but also to the one who speaks them.

**Spirit**

*"Remember your Creator . . . [before] the dust returns to the ground it came from, and the spirit returns to God who gave it" (Ecclesiastes 12:1, 7).*

The third principle is to be at peace with God, or whatever higher power you believe in. Even the most scientific and technically oriented among us realize that we get nothing from nothing. The universe did not form from nothing. There was some power at work that is far greater than anything we can understand. Whether or not you believe that "something" to be God, or you view it as another dimension of infinite energy and power, become resonant and in touch with Him or with it. Your body will return to dust one day, but your spirit will live forever. Now is the time to "remember your Creator."

As you put these principles into action, as your belief system is strengthened, then your potential for $PS^2$ reduced and you will find that your body and mind reap rewards of healing from your spirit.

# 5

# Foods to Boost Your Defenses

Few factors improve your health as easily and simply as eating the right foods. They have enormous impact on your neuro-endocrine-immunological system. In fact, I am convinced that the condition of your mind-body connection actually *starts* with nutrition.

Think of your brain as the control center over all your body's biochemistry. To orchestrate effectively, it must have a regular supply of proper nutrients. A nutrient, quite simply, is anything that the body needs for nutrition. Your brain must have the right materials with which to work. Good nutrition assures you of this.

Many patients define poor nutrition as a deficiency of certain necessary vitamins and minerals. This is one important component, but too many vitamin supplements can also be a factor in poor nutrition. The answer? Balance tempered by common sense.

*Patricia's Junk Food Interludes and Irregular Menstrual Periods.* Take Patricia, a young patient of mine. I saw her for the first time when she was sixteen years old and 74 pounds overweight. During the previous four years, Patricia had gained and lost more than 100 pounds, bouncing from one crash diet to another. In between diets, however, she had practically lived on chocolate candy bars, hot dogs, and soft drinks.

During this four-year nutritional dearth, Patricia had endured irregular and painful menstrual periods, excessive fatigue, and constipation. Lab tests showed that her ovaries were not functioning properly.

Her treatment? A low-calorie, nutritionally sound diet along with exercise. Within fifteen months she had lost the excess weight. While she still had some monthly cramping, her menstrual cycle had returned to normal and she has been able to maintain her ideal weight.

Patricia's case exhibits clearly the detrimental effects of poor nutrition. Probably you do not live for months at a time on hot dogs and soft drinks, but chances are you can improve your nutritional intake.

## PS$^2$ and Food

Good nutrition is essential for good health—especially if you have Profound Sensitivity Syndrome. This is because PS$^2$ affects the internal workings of the body—the way your body is able to *use* food.

If you have PS$^2$, your body is reacting adversely to sensitizers, those events that cause a stress response in you. Imagine this as racing your car's engine while in park. Chemicals are being pumped into your body and causing stimulation throughout. Your metabolism increases, along with your heart rate, respiration, and the speed with which your body metabolizes nutrients. You are "soaking up" what's there and needing more.

Thus, you might lose weight without changing your caloric intake. Or, as was the problem with Kathy, if you are under emotional stress you might lose weight while you are actually eating more.

*Kathy's Mild Malnutrition.* Kathy was a 43-year-old woman who had been my patient for many years. She was hypersensitive to many foods and inhalants but had done well in treatment. She had PS$^2$ but few symptoms.

One day she called me and was quite upset about having lost ten pounds during the past month. She said she was eating more than usual because she was concerned about her weight loss, but no matter how much she stuffed into her mouth she was still losing weight. She was particularly frightened that she might have cancer, as one of her relatives died of cancer after a sudden, unexpected weight loss.

A thorough evaluation showed Kathy to be in tip-top health—except for the weight loss. As for stress, she acknowledged that she had some tension in her job, but nothing, she felt, that could be affecting her so strongly.

I put her on a high-caloric supplement to meet her nutritional needs. It slowed down her weight loss but did not keep her from losing more. As oftentimes is the case when I cannot come up with a physical cause for a physical event, I look for input from a mental health practitioner. I referred Kathy to Dr. Lipton hoping he could dig down into her unconscious mind for a "mental" explanation of this problem.

According to Marc he did not have to dig very deeply. Kathy apparently was an intellectualizer, meaning someone who finds reasons for her problems while burying her feelings inside. This is like steam in a pressure cooker. As evidenced by the hissing steam, tremendous pressure is building inside to the point of explosion.

Kathy's job was causing her much more stress than she realized. Her boss was a crude and rude individual; his insults were causing her great inner turmoil. Her sympathetic nervous system was apparently in a high-output stress reaction, pumping cortisol, epinephrine, and norepinephrine into her bloodstream. Because of her extreme sensitivity, those stress hormones caused her metabolism to skyrocket. Thus, even though she had increased food consumption, she was burning up an enormous number of calories, and burning body fat and muscle tissue to supplement her energy requirements.

Along with biofeedback training, Dr. Lipton counseled her to help her stop personalizing her boss's behavior and to develop assertiveness skills to deal with him. Within two weeks she started to regain the weight she had lost.

Kathy's was an instance of mild malnutrition. We know scientifically that severe malnutrition causes immune abnormality, which causes increased infection. While I believe mild malnutrition also causes changes in immune function, there is no hard clinical evidence to prove it. Ninety percent of the testing done for mild malnutrition is research testing, and the majority of it is done in animal models—not human ones.

Still, in studying volumes of patients' records I have found cases showing, I feel, that mild malnutrition affects immunity and creates greater incidence of certain clinical problems. Malnutrition particularly causes the body to be deprived of the protein it needs to function. This is one factor that can lead to immune problems. Actually, a person can lose protein in one of two ways: by being sick or simply by not eating enough of it. (Even though all we need is six ounces a day.)

Because of the way $PS^2$ made Kathy's body respond to stress, she was not consuming enough protein and, therefore, showed signs of protein deprivation. She was burning her own body fat so as not to deplete her own protein supply.

It is worse for your health to lose protein by a disease than by malnutrition because, in the former case, the body often will not switch to the mechanism that burns fat instead of protein. If you were to put someone on a complete slow starvation diet, you could show some immune defects, but the person would not die from a defective immune system. Someone who had intense and prolonged protein deprivation because of a disease, however, could die from loss of immunity and subsequent infection.

A person who loses weight because of disease also loses his or her cell-mediated immunity. This means the cells no longer function properly, particularly the T-cells. Ultimately loss of cell-mediated immunity means increased infection.

There is an interesting connection with allergies here. One of the immunological results of protein deprivation is losing allergic response. The allergic response works to help you knock out infection. Thus, when you lose it, you have a harder time combating infection.

I have seen people with asthma or a lot of allergies who went on crash fad diets, deprived themselves of protein, and subsequently lost their allergic response. At that point they appeared to be healthier because they no longer responded allergically to whatever substance had been bothering them previously. In truth they were sicker but did not know it.

For instance, say someone who normally has a severe reaction to poison ivy goes on a starvation diet or a diet lacking in protein, such as the Stillman Protein Deficient Diet. Before very long he or she would be able to touch poison ivy and have no physical reactions. This is because he or she would have knocked his or her immunity down to the point that it could not respond. Now he or she would be in danger of picking up an infection and being unable to fight it.

Dr. William Beisel at the Johns Hopkins School of Hygiene and Public Health has delved deeply into the effects of nutrients on immunity. In a 1987 issue of the medical journal *Comprehensive Therapy* he wrote, among other findings, that "malnutrition can be caused by a poor (or excessive) intake of one or more essential nutrients. . . ."

Notice that Dr. Beisel said poor *or* excessive intake of nutrients can lead to malnutrition. This means that it is unhealthy to ignore your body's need for, say, vegetables or fruits, and that, for example, it is equally unhealthy to take large quantities of such vitamins as A and D. These fat-soluble vitamins in excessive amounts can get stored in fat tissue and cause problems.

*Jerry's Bad Cholesterol.* The effects of nutrient deprivation were painfully clear in the case of Jerry, a 49-year-old postman whose job had put him under tremendous pressure, especially when people began complaining that their mail was not being delivered on time.

Before this he had not had many physical troubles to speak of. Now he started to suffer a crushing sensation in his chest, pain down his left arm, nausea, sweating, and anxiety. He was rushed to a hospital where the diagnosis was myocardial infarction. He was subsequently referred to me to see if some metabolic problem could be related to his heart condition.

A thorough history, physical examination, and laboratory testing confirmed that he had an increased amount of "bad" cholesterol—low-density lipoprotein—and a decreased amount of "good" cholesterol—high-density lipoprotein—circulating in his system.

The first step for Jerry was a proper diet plus a tailor-made set of exercises. This was done in conjunction with the relaxation techniques we will be teaching in chapters that follow. The result over time was an increase of good cholesterol and a decrease of bad cholesterol. Jerry was able to return to his job with restored good health, lighter of spirit.

It is interesting to note that researchers are suggesting that life-style changes alone—diet, exercise, and relaxation techniques—appear to halt or reverse atherosclerosis, a hardening of the arteries.

In November 1988 the preliminary findings of Dr. Dean Ornish, who is heading a research team to study this phenomenon, were reported.

He randomly divided fifty patients into two groups. One group received traditional treatment including advice on lowering their cholesterol levels and blood pressure, plus advice on quitting smoking. The second experimental group was put on a low-fat vegetarian diet in which fewer than ten percent of the calories came from fat. (The average American consumes three to four times that much.) Along with exercise and relaxation techniques, those who smoked were required to quit.

After a year those who received customary care had more dangerous blockage in their arteries. Those in the experimental group had less blockage.

This confirms the importance of life-style choices (such as we are teaching here) as preventive medicine.

*Joyce: Food as Tranquilizer.* Another patient, Joyce, age 37, came to see me because of her inability to lose weight. At a height of five-feet-five inches, she weighed 260 pounds. She told me, further, that she had increasing susceptibility to respiratory infections and a variety of other maladies. Most of the weight gain had occurred over a seven-year span, a time of intense stress as she tried to juggle her job on the police force along with returning to school for her degree and caring for her home and family.

As we talked, Joyce was practically in tears. "I've tried every diet I could find," she said. "I've starved myself to the point that I only eat when I actually feel faint from hunger. Nothing seems to work.

"And" she added, "I seem to get hungry at the strangest times. I might have had lunch just an hour before and suddenly I become so famished I can't stand it and have to have something to eat. I know what I'm doing to myself, but I can't seem to do anything about it."

The pressure not only caused her to eat more, but, because she had $PS^2$, created a response in her that cried out for increased nutrients for proper body function. Because the foods she consumed did not provide a properly balanced diet, she suffered from both obesity and the weakening of her immune system.

As we talked further it became clear that Joyce was using food as a way to make herself feel better—a way of coping with all of the activities in her life.

Her laboratory test results confimed that she had dangerously high levels of stress hormones and that her immune function was below normal. She also had subclinical deficiencies of most of the water-soluble B vitamins as well as iron and zinc.

Joyce and I worked to develop a diet plan for her that was low enough in calories to bring about weight loss, yet would, at the same time, replenish her vitamin deficiencies. We spent some time going over her diet in order to include some of her favorite foods, as well as those foods that I believe help combat stress. (These are included in the plan in this chapter as well.) I also prescribed a complex multivitamin, Slice of Life (SOL), which is a 130-calorie liquid protein drink that contains at least 100 percent of the recommended daily allowances (RDA) of nutrients. It is taken before eating a meal, as a preload. This results not only in eating less food, but feeling more satiated, allowing weight loss on a nutritionally sound program. I developed the program 25 years ago and have had thousands do well on it.

It was, therefore, no surprise that Joyce kept to her diet and during the next six months lost 70 pounds. Furthermore, her facial expression changed to one of happy confidence. In another ten months she lost 72 more pounds and reached her ideal weight of 118. And she was able to maintain it.

I would estimate that, like Joyce, anywhere from fifty to eighty million Americans may now suffer from undetected vitamin deficiencies, a danger I wrote about several years ago in *The Truth About Weight Control*. Today we are learning new ways to diagnose such health dangers. One blood test, for instance, developed by Dr. Herman Baker, is known as a protozoal assay. Protozoa are microscopic organisms that thrive on specific vitamins, some on one, some on another. A one-ounce blood sample is taken, processed in a lab, then "fed" to various vitamin-loving protozoa. If the organisms thrive on it the vitamin is present in sufficient quantities. If they do not thrive, a deficiency exists. In my estimation, this method of testing is still in the experimental phase.

Here is a review of some important vitamins and minerals believed to enhance immune function. Following this is a compilation of different types of problems that I have seen in patients who lacked certain vitamins or minerals.

## Vitamins and Minerals

### Vitamin C

Vitamin C in a high concentration is available to us in citrus fruits, tomatoes, cabbage, papaya, cantaloupe, strawberries, and potatoes.

It can help the thymus gland produce more T-cells, help maintain interferon levels, and reduce histamine release, thereby helping control allergic reactions.

Lack of vitamin C prevents neutrophils (white blood cells) from being mobile and going after invading bacteria. If someone is starving, therefore, he makes less hydrochloric acid and is unable to kill stomach bacteria. He has an increased likelihood of salmonella, tuberculosis, and cholera. You see this in the very young, the very old, and, of course, the malnourished.

Dr. Beisel, quoted earlier, has told me that he feels people are abusing vitamin C. He believes that increased vitamin C, such as more than one gram a day, can cause kidney stones, intestinal upset, and, most importantly, increases the enzymes in your body that *destroy* vitamin C. He believes that once the supplements are stopped it can take a couple of months for the enzymes to get back into balance.

He postulates further that anyone who takes an increased amount of vitamin C and then stops taking it may show an increased incidence of infection for about a month. That's because he or she now has a vitamin C deficiency.

### Vitamin A

Vitamin A is plentiful in dairy products, eggs, dark green, orange, and yellow vegetables, liver, cantaloupe, and apricots. It is beneficial to the production of T-cells and also helps the kidneys filter debris from the blood.

Decreased vitamin A can cause atrophy of the lymphoid system and bring about decreased immunological function. In animal studies, increased vitamin A increases B-cells. High, toxic levels of vitamin A may cause headaches secondary to increased brain pressure.

**Vitamin E**

Vitamin E is found in whole grains, seafood, wheat germ, nuts, and sunflower seeds. It makes T-cells respond more quickly, helps the body produce antibodies, and also helps rid the body of "free radicals" that can injure the immune system. It also helps maintain the effectiveness of vitamins A and C.

In animal studies, increased vitamin E causes a better response to vaccines that increase antibodies.

**B Complex**

The entire range of B complex, all the water-soluble B vitamins, can be found in meats, liver, dairy products, eggs, brewer's yeast, legumes, brown rice, and nuts.

They affect major aspects of the immune system. For instance, B vitamins stimulate antibody responses, help keep the thymus gland active, and help in the attack on bacteria. They benefit the endocrine system, aiding in the production of hormones and steroids.

A deficiency of $B_6$ (pyridoxine) blocks B- and T-cells and decreases antibody production. A deficiency of $B_{12}$ causes decreased cell replication, meaning they do not multiply as well. It also leads to decreased red blood cells and decreased lymphocyte function. Decreased folic acid (another B vitamin) causes decreased cell replication, decreased neutrophils, decreased red blood cells, and decreased lymphocyte function. All of this means there is less ability to fight infection. There is no good data on what they do in excess.

**Potassium**

Potassium is a mineral that comes from bananas, dairy products, oranges, legumes, tomatoes, seafood, avocados, meat, raisins, and potatoes. It helps keep the immune system well-balanced.

**Iodine**

Iodine is in seafood, iodized salt, and kelp. It helps the body manufacture antibodies and the thyroid gland to manufacture and secrete thyroxine and triiodothyronine, two hormones that optimize the functions of the immune and endocrine systems.

**Iron**

Iron comes from meat, organ meats, legumes, spinach, dried fruits, brewer's yeast, and whole grains. It affects the lymph nodes, energizes T-cells and killer lymphocytes, and is needed to produce the biochemical reaction used by macrophages to kill bacteria.

It has been shown that patients who have a protein deficiency and an increase in iron also have increased susceptibility to infection.

A decrease in iron causes anemia. It often decreases the lymphocytic count (and that means the lymphocytes cannot readily gobble up the bacteria).

**Zinc**

Zinc comes from meats, legumes, liver, eggs, nuts, and whole grains. A balanced amount aids immune helper cells and suppressor cells.

Decreased zinc leads to decreased cell-mediated immunity, and, therefore, numerous problems, including increased infection. There is a rare hereditary defect called acrodermatitis in which children cannot absorb zinc. Unless treated, they will usually live to only one or two years of age.

Sometimes patients who are getting intravenous fluids for

long periods, such as for burns, can develop decreased and delayed wound healing and increased infections because they are not getting enough zinc in their systems.

## Physical Signs of Nutrient Deficiency

This chart, derived from a study of my patients' records, shows the types of physical problems associated with vitamin and mineral deficiencies:

### Protein-Calorie Deficiency

| ORGAN | PHYSICAL SIGNS |
|---|---|
| Hair | Becomes fine, dry, brittle, stiff, straight; is easily and painlessly pluckable; outer one-third of eyebrow may be sparse in hypothyroidism |
| Skin | Edema (pitting); "flaky paint" or "crazy pavement" dermatosis |
| Face | Brown, patchy pigmentation of cheeks |
| Teeth | Malposition, a line across upper incisors, becomes filled with yellow-brown pigment; tooth decay (caries); tooth may break off |
| Muscles | Muscle wasting, weakness, fatigue, inactivity, loss of fat |
| Liver | Enlarged liver (fatty infiltration) |
| Gastrointestinal | Diarrhea |
| Central nervous system | Apathy, irritability; psychomotor changes |

### Iron Deficiency

| ORGAN | PHYSICAL SIGNS |
|---|---|
| Nails | Ridging, brittle, easily broken, flattened, spoon-shaped, thin, lusterless |
| Eyes | Inside lower eyelids are pale |
| Skin | Pallor |
| Vulva | Inflammation of the inside of the vagina and the outside (vulva), and candidiasis |
| Tongue | Sore and abnormally red |

## Vitamin A Deficiency

| ORGAN | PHYSICAL SIGNS |
|---|---|
| Eyes | Poor twilight vision; loss of shiny, bright, moist appearance; loss of light reflex |
| Gums | Inflamed and bleeding |
| Skin | Dry; rough "gooseflesh," "sharkskin," "sandpaper skin" |

## Vitamin $B_2$ (Riboflavin) Deficiency

| ORGAN | PHYSICAL SIGNS |
|---|---|
| Eyes | Difficulty with vision |
| Mouth | Cracks and sores; difficulty swallowing |
| Nose | Excessive oil production; cracks and sores around nose, eyes, and ears |
| Lips | Inflammation of the mucous membranes of the lips and the loss of clear differentiation between skin and mucous membranes of the lips |
| Tongue | Magenta in color |

## Vitamin $B_{12}$ Deficiency

| ORGAN | PHYSICAL SIGNS |
|---|---|
| Eyes | Inflammation of the optic nerve causing difficulty in vision |
| Skin | Pale, jaundiced |
| Central nervous system | Numbness and tingling in fingers and toes, loss of balance |
| Gastrointestinal | Loss of appetite, flatulence, diarrhea |

## Vitamin $B_6$ (Pyridoxine) Deficiency

| ORGAN | PHYSICAL SIGNS |
|---|---|
| Nose | Itchy flaking |
| Eyes | Inflammation of eyelids |
| Tongue | Sore, smooth |
| Central nervous system | Dizziness, convulsions, forgetfulness, mental deterioration |

## Vitamin $B_3$ (Niacin) and Vitamin A Combination Deficiency

| ORGAN | PHYSICAL SIGNS |
|---|---|
| Gums | Inflamed and bleeding |
| Tongue | Scarlet, raw; fissures |
| Skin | Redness; increased pigmentation (even in blacks); thickened, inelastic, fissured, especially in skin exposed to sun; scaly, dry |
| Central nervous system | Psychotic behavior (dementia) |
| Gastrointestinal | Diarrhea |

## Vitamin C Deficiency

| ORGAN | PHYSICAL SIGNS |
|---|---|
| Gums | Bleeding |
| Skin | Dry and rough; poor healing |
| Muscles | Deterioration |

## Folic Acid Deficiency

| ORGAN | PHYSICAL SIGNS |
|---|---|
| Mouth | Canker sores |
| Tongue | Painful, sore, smooth |
| Skin | Pallor |

## Fluoride Deficiency

| ORGAN | PHYSICAL SIGNS |
|---|---|
| Teeth | Decay |

## Phosphorus Deficiency

| ORGAN | PHYSICAL SIGNS |
|---|---|
| Teeth | Decay |

## Iodine Deficiency

| ORGAN | PHYSICAL SIGNS |
|---|---|
| Neck | Neck mass (goiter) |

### Vitamin K Deficiency

| ORGAN | PHYSICAL SIGNS |
|---|---|
| Skin | Hemorrhages |

### Calcium Deficiency

| ORGAN | PHYSICAL SIGNS |
|---|---|
| Bones | Osteoporosis (in association with low protein intake and fluoride deficiency) |

### Vitamin D Deficiency

| ORGAN | PHYSICAL SIGNS |
|---|---|
| Muscles | Poor muscle tone, spasms |
| Bones | Osteoporosis; rickets in children; bone softening in adults |

### Vitamin $B_1$ (Thiamine) Deficiency

| ORGAN | PHYSICAL SIGNS |
|---|---|
| Muscles | Leg cramps, weakness |
| Central nervous system | Mental confusion |
| Cardiovascular system | Enlargement of the heart; congestive heart failure |

### Magnesium Deficiency

| ORGAN | PHYSICAL SIGNS |
|---|---|
| Central nervous system | Tremor, convulsions, behavioral disturbances |

## Rules of Good Eating to Boost Your Immunity

Along with nutritional needs, each of us has personal preferences for the foods we consume. As Herman Melville put it, "Feed all things with food convenient for them. . . . The food of the soul is light and space; feed it then on light and space. But the food of the body is champagne and oysters; feed it then on champagne and oysters."

To help you provide what your body needs as you eat the

foods you enjoy, I recommend following these few basic good rules, which are incorporated into the diet plan that follows:

1. Eat a variety of foods to attain the best nutritional balance possible. Include fruits, vegetables, breads and cereals, dairy products, as well as meat, fish, and poultry products in your diet. That way you will get all the vitamins, minerals, and nutrients you need from food.
2. If you have been sick recently or are sick now, you can take vitamin tablets because illness causes increased metabolism of vitamins and minerals. Your doctor can tell you what you need and what you do not need.
3. Maintain your ideal weight. We will be discussing weight control in a later chapter.
4. Avoid too much total fat, saturated fat, and cholesterol. Higher levels of blood cholesterol are associated with greater risk of heart disease and atherosclerosis (hardening of the arteries from fatty deposits). You can lower your levels of fat and cholesterol by selecting leaner cuts of meat, draining off meat drippings, limiting the amount of margarine or butter, using lowfat and skim milk, limiting fried foods, watching the amount of salad dressing you eat, and staying away from rich desserts. Cook with safflower, corn, or soybean oils.
5. Eat foods with adequate amounts of starch and fiber. These are found in fruits, vegetables (including potatoes, sweet potatoes, yams, corn, and peas), and whole grain cereal products (including brown rice, oatmeal, and whole wheat cereals and breads).
6. Avoid too much sugar. Watch out for soft drinks, candy, desserts, jams, jellies, and syrups.
7. Avoid excess sodium and salt. Start by taking the salt shaker off the table. Avoid obviously salty foods like pretzels, ham, and bacon. Remember that commercially prepared foods may be high in salt content. When you shop, be sure to read the labels. We generally forget that items such as catsup, barbecue sauce, pickles, meat tenderizer, canned soups, and monosodium glutamate are high in salt or sodium.

## The Stress Correction Plan to Boost Your Defenses

Based on years of clinical observation I am convinced there are some foods that tend to reduce the detrimental effects of those stressful sensitizers on your body. These foods can help make up for the draining effect. Otherwise, the depleted stores of nutrients will allow the effects of stress to worsen.

The best plan is one worked out for you in consultation with your doctor. The following diet plan will act as a guide as you formulate your own plan.

It works by furnishing the proper proportions of protein, carbohydrates, and fats, as well as the vitamins and minerals needed by the body to function at an optimal level of efficiency.

This basic plan provides 1,800 calories a day, a maintenance level for women. Men can use the plan for slow weight loss or to maintain their weight by increasing quantities specified by approximately one-third. Women can reduce their weight by reducing quantities specified by one-third.

Items that actually contribute to stress should be avoided as much as possible. These include salt, animal fats, and junk foods. Also lower your caffeine consumption.

- Salt retains water in the body, leading to weight gain. Animal fats tend to cause tension and irritability because they are hard to digest. Saturated fats, such as those in butter, cheese, and fatty meats, are real culprits. They should be replaced with unsaturated fats that the body can break down more easily, such as safflower, corn, and soybean oils.
- Junk foods, like candy, are foods that are high in calories because of simple sugars and are also low or deficient in vitamins, minerals, or important nutrients. These foods along with high caffeine trigger the release of an excessive amount of insulin, causing blood sugar to fall and thereby creating a desire for still more sugar.
- The intake of foods rich in potassium and vitamins B and C should be increased.

- In addition, drink two quarts of fluids, including two glasses each of skim milk (unless you are allergic to milk) and water. This will increase the renal excretion of stress-producing impurities from your body.
- Ingestion of bulk foods, such as fresh fruits, vegetables, and whole grains, supplies fiber, which helps assure regular bowel movements. Dietary fiber is simply the part of a plant that is not broken down by chemical action during the process of digestion. Because fiber holds water, the resulting stools are softer and pass through more easily.

In sum, the Stress Correction Plan to Boost Your Defenses will benefit a number of the body's systems. I encourage you to discuss this with your doctor to tailor it to your specific preferences.

## The Stress Correction Plan to Boost Your Defenses

(1,800 Calories Per Day)

*DAY #1*

*Breakfast*

1 cup skim milk[†]
¾ cup oat flakes
1 corn muffin with unsweetened strawberry conserve
1 soft-boiled egg
½ grapefruit

*Lunch*

1 cup raw spinach salad with fresh mushrooms, Zero Dressing[*]
1 Salmon Salad Sandwich[*]
½ banana
Orange-flavored club soda

---

[†] People allergic to milk should substitute soy milk for skim milk.
[*] Recipe included at the end of this plan.

*Dinner*

1 cup skim milk†
½ cup asparagus
3 oz. Sautéed Liver in Sherry with ½ cup onions*
1 "Home-Fried" Potato*
1 small whole wheat roll with 1 Tbsp diet margarine
1 cup fresh raspberries or strawberries

*Night Snack*

12 whole wheat crackers
¾ cup fresh sliced pineapple

*DAY #2*

*Breakfast*

4 oz. nonfat yogurt with 1¼ cups fresh strawberries
½ cup skim milk†
½ cup cooked oatmeal
½ pumpernickel bagel with unsweetened raspberry conserve and 1 Tbsp cream cheese
1 poached egg

*Lunch*

1 cup lentil soup
1 Turkey Salad in a Pita Pocket*
1 fresh peach
Sugar-free lemonade

*Dinner*

1 cup Tossed Salad* with Zero Dressing*
1 cup cooked turnip greens
3 oz. broiled swordfish in dry white wine, lemon juice, and ½ Tbsp diet margarine, melted
1 cup whole wheat noodles with ½ Tbsp diet margarine and sprinkle of parsley
½ cup orange juice

*Night Snack*

1 cup skim milk†
6 graham crackers
½ cup fresh fruit

<u>*DAY #3*</u>

*Breakfast*

1 cup skim milk†
¾ cup wheat flakes
1 whole wheat English muffin with 1 Tbsp peanut butter and unsweetened blueberry conserve
1 fresh orange

*Lunch*

2 cups cantaloupe, cubed, tossed with ¾ cup lowfat cottage cheese
4 whole wheat breadsticks
1 cup tomato juice
2 Tbsp cashews

*Dinner*

1 cup Marinated Vegetable Salad*
½ cup green peas
3 oz. baked pork chop with 1 Tbsp diet margarine
½ mango
Sugar-free iced tea with lemon

*Night Snack*

1 cup skim milk†
1½ oz. whole wheat pretzels

<u>*DAY #4*</u>

*Breakfast*

1 Banana Shake—frozen or fresh*
2 whole grain waffles with diet pancake syrup
1 scrambled egg
½ cup cooked oatmeal

*Lunch*

1 cup Cole Slaw*
1 Tuna Taco*
1 fresh nectarine
Sugar-free lemonade

*Dinner*

1 cup pea soup
1 cup cooked spinach with lemon
3 oz. Chicken Piccata*
⅔ cup mashed sweet potatoes with orange liqueur
¾ cup fresh grapefruit sections
Lemon-flavored club soda

*Night Snack*

1 cup skim milk†
1 kiwi, sliced
2 small bran muffins

*DAY #5*

*Breakfast*

4 oz. plain nonfat yogurt with 3 Tbsp wheat germ and ¾ cup mandarin oranges
½ cup skim milk†
¾ cup cornflakes
1 slice toasted pumpernickel or rye bread with unsweetened peach conserve and 1 Tbsp diet margarine

*Lunch*

Twin Seafood Salad Sandwiches*
Raw zucchini sticks with ½ cup cherry tomatoes
2 small tangerines
Sugar-free fruit punch

*Dinner*

1 cup spinach salad with fresh mushrooms and Zero Dressing*
4 oz. Turkey Meatballs* heated in
½ cup tomato sauce in place of spaghetti sauce
and poured over 1 cup cooked spaghetti

½ cup cooked broccoli
1 slice whole wheat Italian bread with 1 Tbsp diet margarine
1 cup fresh melon balls
Sugar-free iced tea with lemon

*Night Snack*

½ whole wheat bagel with 1 Tbsp cream cheese
1 cup skim milk†
2 Tbsp raisins

## *RECIPES*

**Zero Dressing**
Blend:
½ cup tomato juice
2 Tbsp lemon juice or vinegar
1 Tbsp finely chopped onion
1 Tbsp chopped green pepper
⅛ tsp black pepper
¼ tsp salt
½ tsp dill weed
⅛ tsp fresh garlic clove, chopped

**Salmon Salad Sandwich**
2 slices rye bread
¾ cup canned, drained salmon
Mix:
2 Tbsp reduced-calorie mayonnaise
dash lemon juice
chopped celery
chopped cucumber
dash onion powder
lettuce

**Sautéed Liver in Sherry**
Spray frying pan with vegetable oil spray. Sauté ½ cup onions, add 1½ Tbsp sherry, and simmer 5 minutes. Add 3 oz. liver, simmer until tender and browned.

### "Home-Fried" Potato

Spray small casserole dish with vegetable oil spray. Preheat oven to 375° F. Cut one baking potato into 8 chunks. Put chunks into pan and spray with vegetable oil spray. Do not cover. Bake for 1½ hours or until brown and crunchy. Season as desired.

### Banana Shake

Blend:

- 1 cup skim milk†
- ½ frozen banana
- dash vanilla extract
- crushed ice

### Cole Slaw

Mix:

- 2 cups raw shredded cabbage
- chopped carrots
- chopped green pepper
- minced onion
- chopped celery
- 2 Tbsp reduced-calorie mayonnaise
- dash vinegar, dash salt, dash celery seeds, sprinkle of low-calorie sweetener

### Tuna Taco

Fill 1 taco shell with the following:

- ½ cup tuna fish, drained
- 1 Tbsp taco sauce
- 2 Tbsp shredded cheddar cheese
- shredded lettuce

### Chicken Piccata

Blend:

- 1 Tbsp melted diet margarine
- 2 Tbsp lemon juice
- 1 clove garlic, minced

Spray with vegetable oil spray. Pour over 3-oz. chicken cutlet in a small casserole pan. Cover, bake at 375° 1 hour. Spoon sauce over chicken while baking.

### Turkey Salad in Pita Pocket

½ whole wheat pita

Mix:

2 oz. cooked turkey cubes
1 Tbsp reduced-calorie mayonnaise
Dash paprika, onion powder, garlic powder

Fill pita with turkey salad. Top with diced cucumber and diced hot peppers or shredded carrots.

### Tossed Salad

Toss together:

Raw endive, escarole, Chinese cabbage, chopped celery

Sprinkle with 1 Tbsp sunflower seeds and 1 cup lowfat croutons.

Croutons:

Day-old bread, cubed. Season with garlic powder and onion powder. Bake at 350° F. 10 minutes until browned.

Top with Zero Dressing.

### Marinated Vegetable Salad

Combine:

Raw cucumber sticks, raw zucchini slices, raw mushrooms, chopped celery, radishes, and raw spinach.

Combine:

¼ cup wine vinegar, 2 Tbsp vegetable oil, dash of dill seeds.

Marinate vegetables in dressing, refrigerate.

### Twin Seafood Salad Sandwiches

2 small whole wheat buns
3 oz. cooked shrimp, tuna, salmon, halibut, chopped

This can be baked at 350° F. 10 minutes until easily flaked

1 Tbsp reduced-calorie mayonnaise
dash lemon juice
chopped celery, chopped cucumber, chopped radishes
dash onion powder, dash garlic powder
lettuce

Mix all salad ingredients, place on whole wheat buns, and top with lettuce.

**Turkey Meatballs**

Mix together and form into small meatballs:

- 1 lb. ground turkey
- ¾ cup flavored bread crumbs
- 1 cup spaghetti sauce with mushrooms
- 1 tsp salt
- ⅛ tsp pepper
- 1 tsp onion powder
- 1 onion, chopped
- 1 small green pepper, chopped

Pour 3 additional cups spaghetti sauce with mushrooms into saucepan. Heat until simmering. Place meatballs in sauce. Simmer on low heat for 45 minutes. Serve over spaghetti.

Makes 4 servings.

# 6

# Gain without Pain

You have probably heard the expression "No pain, no gain." It generally relates to exercise, suggesting that if you really want to improve your body, you have to suffer a little in the process.

I find two errors in that concept. First, it suggests that health and physical fitness are synonymous. Actually, fitness relates to good muscle tone, strength, endurance, and suppleness. Health involves a lack of disease and the body's ability to fight off infection. Each has specific needs related to exercise.

Second, pushing yourself to continue in an exercise program in the presence of pain is asking for trouble—muscle strain, for instance.

This does not mean that we can go the other route and avoid exercising: Your body generates energy by use. The right amount of exercise helps control the body's production of insulin; reduces the effects of sensitizers; improves heart function; relieves depression; helps you sleep better, eat less, have more energy; and increases your life expectancy. And for those with $PS^2$, exercise has a direct relationship to your immune system. This is the area I would like to focus on in this chapter. I want also to share a specially designed exercise program that will give you the right amount of physical activity, for fitness *and* health.

The point, as with nutrition, is to understand balance and control. Extremes are rarely effective. Let me show you what I mean.

*John's Recurrent Infections.* John, age 26, appeared not to be exceeding the normal limits of an exercise program, yet we found out later this was not the case. In fact, it was through John and his apparently healthy exercise program that I first learned how too much exercise can harm the immune system.

On the evening he first came to see me, John was wearing a jogging outfit. It was soaked with perspiration and his conversation was punctuated with sneezes. He was quick to apologize—both for his sneezing and his appearance.

"Early evenings are the only time I have to run," he explained. "I run about ten miles every day. Sorry I didn't have time to change."

John's cold was not the reason he had come to see me. He had had a number of colds during the previous two years, several serious infections (one had put him into a hospital for three weeks), a generally run-down feeling, and trouble sleeping.

Yet, to all appearances, John led a healthy life. His weight was right for his height, he had quit smoking and drinking four years earlier, his diet was nutritionally sound, and he certainly got plenty of exercise.

A battery of lab tests revealed that all was normal except for John's hormone levels: He was loaded with stress hormones. It seemed the mystery had been solved. All we had to do was identify the source of his stress and teach him to deal with it.

I spent an hour with John before he convinced me his life was relatively stress-free. This was something I had never seen before: elevated levels of stress hormones with no obvious reason for them. I asked John to try a special allergy-identification diet for a couple of weeks. And because of his cold I persuaded him to abandon his exercise program until the infection passed.

When John arrived for his next appointment his cold was gone and he told me he felt better than he had in months. Just as I was about to ascertain whether or not his problems were caused by a food allergy, he admitted that the diet had been too bland for him and he had ignored it.

He had, however, refrained from his exercise program and now wanted to resume his daily runs. At the time I knew of no reason why he should not.

It was not until about a month later that the mystery was solved. Actually, John solved it. He called me filled with excitement over a clipping he had found in a magazine. It reported on research done in 1981 by two Soviet scientists. N. I. Ivanova and V. V. Talko had conducted tests on subjects who had just performed exhaustive exercise, such as running ten miles. They identified a significant drop in the formation of T-lymphocytes and an increase in the platelet-forming cells in the blood. Those and other changes pointed to an imbalance in the immune system due to the strenuous exercise.

Soon I was able to find reports of confirmations. In a similar test Dr. Lee Berk at Loma Linda University in California also found suppressed T-cell activity in relation to strenuous exercise and was able to narrow the effects further. He found that exhaustive exercise increases the number of suppressor cells and reduces the number of helper cells.

From the University of Cape Town in South Africa came the report that, like John, long-distance runners were suffering chronic respiratory infections.

Dr. Thomas Tomasi at Roswell Park Memorial Institute in Buffalo, New York, detected decreases in antibodies in the saliva of cross-country skiers and bicyclists. Dr. Tomasi also found that the decreased natural killer cells (T-cells that kill bad bacteria and viruses) in the bicyclists remained lower for 24 hours after the exercise.

There is still much to be learned about the effects of exercise on immune function. From what has been researched, however, it appears that the body perceives hard exercise as a stress reaction—just as it does a bad day at work or a fight with a spouse—and responds with normal stress hormones.

If this happens infrequently the body recuperates from

stress-hormone exposure rather quickly and without ill effects. If this goes on regularly as with those who exercise too hard too frequently, the body does not recover. Instead it starts to suffer some of the same immune depression characteristics of individuals who are in chronic states of stress. If Profound Sensitivity Syndrome is present, the effects are long-lasting.

Thus, in John's enthusiasm for a healthy life-style he actually suppressed his own immune function. Frequent infections can be expected in someone whose immune capacity is being turned down during each evening's exhaustive exercise session. And his fatigue was probably the result of efforts by his weakened immune system to overcome the many infections.

John and I worked together to bring his "unhealthy healthy" life-style into balance and find his ideal level of activity. We succeeded. The recurring colds tapered off and the infections disappeared.

Why have millions of Americans gone overboard exercising? Partly because the need for balance in an exercise program has not been stressed as heavily as the benefits that can be achieved. And partly because we discovered what is known as "runner's high." This is a pleasant physical state caused by the release of chemicals that originate in the brain and intestines. These chemicals, called beta endorphins, act as the body's natural opiates, fighting pain or excessive physical stress. When the stress ends, the endorphins have nothing to combat and, instead, give the body a mild, pleasant elevation. The key is to strike an appropriate balance between the potential negative consequences and the positive chemical benefits.

## Heart Rate and Exercise

Everyone has an ideal level of activity, which changes with each new level of fitness achieved. Your current level is found easily by monitoring your heart rate while exercising.

Your heart rate—the number of contractions of your heart muscle that occurs each minute—increases with physical activity. The harder you work, the harder and faster your heart must work. By raising your heartbeats to a number within a certain range for twenty to thirty minutes you will be working aerobically to stimulate consistently the pulmonary and cardiovascular systems.

The range should be high enough to be beneficial, but not higher than your maximum heart rate. This maximum heart rate is not the highest number of beats the heart is capable of, but the highest number that is safe and medically advisable.

There is a good deal of disagreement as to where this safety starts and stops. I believe that many fitness programs recommend heart rates that are too high and, therefore, detrimental to overall health.

I did not come to this conclusion without evidence. In my fascination with the workings of the endocrine system, I have researched and studied extensively its relation to the heart and the immune system. I found, for instance, that during stressful situations the adrenal gland oversecretes three hormones—cortisone, corticosterone, and aldosterone—that in excess amounts affect the heart adversely. When I was training at Johns Hopkins Hospital, my being given the Schwentker Award for my work on the interrelationships between the endocrine system and heart functions led to my work for two years with Dr. Nathan Shock at the National Institute of Health's National Heart Institute.

Thus, with the knowledge we have now, that the body considers exhaustive exercise as a type of sensitizer, I feel compelled to recommend a lower number of beats per minute for maximum heart rate than most physical fitness trainers advise. Many aerobic programs, while perhaps giving the heart a good workout, are too stressful for the body.

*Frank's Heart Palpitations.* Frank, age 43, came to me because he had developed a number of recurrent sore throats and bronchial infections and feared that something was wrong with his heart.

An examination revealed that Frank did have palpitations and fluid retention. A slight arrhythmia showed up on the electrocardiogram.

A detailed history uncovered that a year earlier Frank had been twenty pounds overweight, out of shape, and feeling older than he was. A friend recommended he go to a local gym where a professional trainer would develop a program to help him reestablish his vitality.

Unfortunately, the trainer advocated an approach to exercise that he called "maximum effort." This was defined as going all out until you could not go any longer. Frank's program was to work through a number of exercise machines and then go "full-out" on a stationary bicycle.

After entering the program, Frank lost weight and was increasing the amount of time he could endure on the exercise machines. Although he looked trimmer, which provided reinforcement for the program, he started developing viral infections and began to feel something was wrong with his heart. Instead of connecting this with his exercise program he pushed himself even harder to "become healthier."

When I learned this from Frank it became obvious what had happened to him. First, he was exercising at maximum cardiac output, and second, he was terminating the exercise abruptly, not cooling down gradually. This produced decreased cardiac output, fluid retention, decreased oxygenation, palpitations, arrhythmia, decreased immune function, and increased infections.

After thirty days of a more appropriate exercise regimen his arrhythmia, palpitations, and viral infections subsided. He had been ruining his heart and immune system by overdoing it. The theory "no pain, no gain" simply is not true. The correct approach is *gain without pain*.

To calculate a safer, yet fully effective range of heartbeats per minute use this formula*:

* This formula is applicable to healthy men and women up to age seventy.

*Upper limit of target heart rate:* Take the number 220, subtract your age from it, and multiply the number you get by 0.70.

*Lower limit of target heart rate:* Take the number 220, subtract your age from it, and multiply the number you get by 0.60.

Thus if you are 40 years old: 220 − 40 = 180 × 0.70 = 126; 220 − 40 = 180 × 0.60 = 108. While exercising, your heart should be beating in the range of 108 to 126 beats per minute. If it is above 126, slow down; if below 108, speed up.

The easiest way to take your pulse is to place the index and middle fingertips of your left hand on the right underside of the wrist bone approximately one-and-a-half inches below the base of the thumb. Count the beats starting with zero, for ten seconds and multiply the total by six.

It is somewhat difficult to keep track of your pulse while you are playing tennis or swimming. In that case a good rule of thumb is to see whether or not you can carry on a conversation, breathing normally without gasping for air. If you are alone you can gauge your level by breathing in through your nose and out through your mouth. You have achieved the right level when you are able to do this comfortably.

## First Things First

I have included here an exercise program that is safe, will benefit your health, and will increase your fitness level. Before starting this or any exercise program, however, ask yourself these questions and review the rules that follow:

### Checklist

1. Do I have dizzy spells or feel faint as often as once a month? ____Yes ____No
2. Have I ever been diagnosed as having cardiovascular problems, problems with my heart or blood pressure? ____Yes ____No

3. Do I occasionally get a pain or feeling of tightness in my chest or shortness of breath when I have not been exercising? ____Yes ____No
4. Has my doctor ever told me I have arthritis? Do my joints become painful on occasion? ____Yes ____No
5. Have I suffered a back injury from which I have not yet fully recovered? ____Yes ____No

If you answered yes to any one of these questions or if you have any doubts about your health, *please consult your doctor before starting any exercise program.*

## Some Important Rules

- Select a physical activity you enjoy. When exercise stops being fun, people stop exercising.
- Other than moderate walking, which is fine to do every day, I recommend that you exercise every other day. It is generally accepted that it takes approximately 48 hours for muscles to recover and regenerate from the effects of exercise. This will also minimize immune suppression.
- Check your heart rate periodically during the activity.
- If you have not engaged in a physical activity for the last three months or more, you should consider yourself sedentary, even if you exercised regularly previously. *If you are in this category, start slowly.*

  Begin by walking briskly (120 paces per minute) for fifteen minutes a day, three days a week for two weeks. Increase your walks to thirty minutes a day, three days a week for another four weeks. Then you should be able to walk thirty minutes a day, five days a week or one hour a day, three days a week. This level of fitness will burn about 1,000 calories a week and win you all of the health benefits that exercise can bring—with no reduction in immune activity.
- Watch out for pain. The key to determining whether or not an exercise is deleterious can be judged by noting when discomfort or pain begins.

  That is, if you start to do sit-ups and on the first or second one feel a good deal of pain, you can conclude immediately that you are not appropriately positioned and are doing yourself harm.

If, however, you start to feel pain after the twentieth sit-up, then the pain is probably coming from normal muscle fatigue. This kind of discomfort can be labeled as harmless. In other words, if the pain and discomfort are there from the beginning of the exercise, stop it immediately. If they do not set in until you are well into the exercise, then use your best judgment about stopping. As I discussed previously, it is not, as some experts argue, necessary to experience such pain to benefit from the exercise. If you have any questions about your body's reaction to exercise, talk with your doctor.

## A Healthy Fitness Workout

Here is a moderate aerobic workout developed for our readers by Evalee Harrison, a Physical Fitness Specialist in Berkeley, California, and Executive Director of the Health and Movement Institute. Do these exercises at a pace that keeps your heart rate in the range you calculated earlier. Do not, however, start off at a gallop. Overdoing it at the beginning is one reason many never reach the end.

By performing each "action" sequence ten times, you may be able to complete the program in as few as ten minutes. Increase that number as you become more limber. You will want to maintain your raised heart rate for twenty minutes and can achieve this either by performing each action sequence more times, or by repeating the entire program.

### To Start

Stand straight, but not stiffly, with your knees relaxed, your legs apart, toes pointing forward, and feet placed slightly wider apart than your hips. Your arms should be hanging loosely at your sides. Try to keep your stomach pulled in and your buttock muscles tight.

Take a full, deep breath, inhaling through your nose and

exhaling slowly through your mouth with your lips parted slightly. Remember to breathe with your diaphragm.

Begin with ten action sequences of every exercise.

**Yes and No**

Drop your head forward, lowering your chin to your chest. Hold. Return to center.

Turn your head slowly to the right until your chin is over your shoulder. Hold. Return to center. Hold. Turn your head to the left. Hold. Return to center.

I call this sequence the "yes and no exercise." When you are turning your head to the right and left it appears as if you are shaking your head slowly indicating "no." Tilting it forward appears as if you are nodding, indicating "yes."

Repeat this (and every action sequence) ten times.

**Shoulder Shrug**

Raise both shoulders toward your ears slowly. Hold. Lower them in an exaggerated shrug. Roll both shoulders forward. Hold. Press them backward. Hold.

**Frame Up**

Grip your arms at the elbows and lift them slowly over your head until you have made a frame for your face. Your elbows should be either beside or behind your ears. Stretch your waist upward, away from your hips, as though you were trying to make yourself taller. Hold. Lower your arms slowly until they are flat against your body.

**Body Bend**

Again, grip your elbows and lift your arms overhead. Bend your upper body to the right. Hold. Return to center. Repeat to the left. Return to center.

Now turn your chest to the right side with a gentle twist of your upper body. Hold. Return to center. Repeat to the left. Return to center.

Note: If you feel any discomfort in your back, try pivoting on the sole of the foot opposite to the side to which you twist. If discomfort persists see your doctor.

**Touch the Ceiling**

Lift both your arms overhead and flex your hands at the wrists so your palms are flat toward the ceiling. Stretch one arm, then the other, as if you were trying to press the ceiling with your palms. Tilt your head back slightly and focus your eyes on each hand as you do the lifts.

**Full Circle**

With your arms still overhead, clasp your hands, lacing your fingers. Lower your arms to the right, then down and across your thighs and up toward the left until they are back overhead. You will be making a large circle with your arms. Now make a circle in the opposite direction. Your elbows should be gently rounded throughout each circle, your torso erect.

**Press and Swing**

With both feet on the floor, toes pointing forward, bend your knees and press your hips forward. Swing your arms forward at the same time. Hold. Now straighten your knees and raise yourself up onto the balls of your feet, swinging your arms out to the sides. Hold.

**Swimming**

Lean your upper body forward from the hips, keeping your knees slightly bent. Reach forward with one arm, then the other, pulling them back and forth in a swimming motion ten times.

Turn your body to the right and repeat. Turn to the left and repeat.

**Foot Action**

Put all your weight onto your right foot and kick your left foot forward with your heel flexed. Now shift your weight to the left foot and kick your right foot, heel flexed. Continue to alternate your weight as you shift back and forth from side to side. Repeat ten times.

Now repeat the exercise, but this time point your toes. Try to make your movements steady, rhythmic, and moderately paced.

## Overcoming Dizziness

I want to include here a nonstrenuous exercise that I teach the growing numbers of patients I am seeing for dizziness. To correct the problem I use a simple exercise I learned at the Johns Hopkins medical institutions. Deana is one example. Her dizziness was caused by an abnormal reflex between her eyes and her brain. No medication was necessary—just simple exercise.

*Deana's Cure for Dizziness.* Deana, age 37, developed her trouble with vertigo suddenly; she had been in good health until that time. Then she found herself becoming dizzy whenever she moved her head.

For instance, if she was driving and turning her head, the street signs would appear out of focus; if she stopped the car she could read them perfectly well. Or while grocery shopping and wheeling her cart down the aisles, product labels would seem to leap out at her; if she stood still she could read them. And while sitting still watching television, if she became excited by the program and her heart began to race, the picture appeared to jump out at her. (This was because her racing heartbeat caused a slight motion in her body. That movement caused her dizziness and made the moving picture appear to blur.)

I diagnosed her problem as an inner ear disorder, the cause of most cases of recurring dizziness. If you are one of its victims, your doctor can tell simply by looking at the way your eyes move when you move your head.

The following exercise is an effective treatment. It consists of moving into and out of the offending head position. Sit on the edge of your bed. Lie down quickly, turning your head to the left. Feel the vertigo, rest quietly until it goes away, and then sit back up. If you become dizzy again, wait until the dizziness goes away. Then, lie down, turning your head to the right, wait, and sit back up. Do this about fifteen times, three times a day.

It's very simple, and invariably—as well as you can say invariably in medicine—in two or three days the symptoms subside. This syndrome often gets better on its own as well. It may come back on occasion, but again, is quickly cleared up with this exercise. If, however, the dizziness persists after one week you should seek medical attention.

People who have a hard time getting started with any kind of exercises are often depressed, which increases procrastination. Exercise, however, is a natural antidepressant that can pull you out of your rut. Your behavior has the power to change your mood. So start slowly, but do start. As Lazerov said earlier in this century, "Bad habits are easier to abandon today than tomorrow."

# 7

# Time Out for Relaxation

When you think of relaxation, what picture comes to mind? Lying on warm sand under swaying palm trees? Stoking the fire in a snow-covered cabin in the woods? Curling up in your favorite chair with a cup of tea and a good book?

Depending on the image you summon, you may be under the misapprehension that relaxation is an impossible dream, a luxury of time or money you cannot afford. In truth, you cannot afford *not* to relax.

Relaxation is critically important to your overall well-being. It restores your mind, enabling it to focus better on life's problems. It restores your body by giving your biochemistry time to reset and balance itself. It benefits, further, your heart and immune system.

How do you go about relaxing? First, by not thinking you have to plan a vacation in order to succeed. In fact, many vacations are anything but restful. While you do need to get away from it all periodically, we want to teach you several simple ways to relax your mind and body wherever you are, in whatever situation you find yourself.

Here are ten questions I often ask my patients in order to help them understand their inborn ability to relax. Answer true or false to get an idea of where *you* stand.

## Relaxation Test

| True | False | |
|---|---|---|
| ____ | ____ | 1. You worry occasionally about getting your next pay raise. |
| ____ | ____ | 2. You become somewhat embarrassed if a stranger visits your home and it hasn't been dusted or cleaned during the past week. |
| ____ | ____ | 3. You rarely read books, preferring newspapers or magazines. |
| ____ | ____ | 4. You get great satisfaction from winning at competitive sports, or from increasing the distance you walk or run during exercise. |
| ____ | ____ | 5. When you are sitting, you often tap your fingers or move your toes. |
| ____ | ____ | 6. You get at least two colds every winter and suffer from a variety of small aches and pains that seem to have no medical basis. |
| ____ | ____ | 7. You become restless if you are forced to sit for more than a few minutes without some distraction. |
| ____ | ____ | 8. You rarely do things without a reason. |
| ____ | ____ | 9. You often feel uptight, tense, even fearful, and you don't really know why. |
| ____ | ____ | 10. You have occasional dizzy spells or become out of breath for no apparent reason. |

If you answered *true* to three or more of these statements, you should probably take a long look at your capacity to relax effectively. Your body may not be getting the rest it needs to recuperate and function optimally; your mind may not be getting the refreshment it needs to take on new challenges. You could be in danger of letting yourself succumb to needless illness and fatigue.

*JoAnn's Herpes.* JoAnn, an eighteen-year-old college student, was perfectly healthy until about a month after making love with her boyfriend for the first time. He had not been feeling good and said he felt tired all the time. JoAnn developed similar tiredness, malaise, headaches, chills, high fever, and sore throat. She also had swelling of her eyelids and around the orbit of her eyes.

After a thorough examination, I found that she had been infected by the Epstein-Barr virus, one of the herpes viruses. Her liver had also been affected by the virus. The diagnosis was made primarily by patient history, blood-smear examination, and serological tests to look for various antibodies. (I did the CEBV-specific seria diagnostic tests, which are now available in several laboratories across the country. We will talk more about this virus in chapter 10.)

Bed rest was the first step for JoAnn until her liver returned to normal and the acute phases of fever and fatigue passed. I also treated her with appropriate vitamin and mineral supplements.

JoAnn scored poorly on my relaxation test; her score was 8. She was skeptical at first, but agreed to change from chest breathing to diaphragmatic breathing and did the Total Body Relaxation technique—both of which we will be teaching you in this chapter—for twenty minutes a day for two weeks. She was able to return to school with a reduced load and attributed her success and her new positive outlook on life to the relaxation techniques.

JoAnn has remained symptom-free for the past two years and has resumed her full load of courses. She is engaged to her boyfriend and is making wedding plans.

Dr. Herbert Benson, who first coined the term *relaxation response,* has made a thorough study of its effect on the mind-body link. Among his findings he states that relaxation appears actually to decrease sympathetic nervous system activity. This involves physiological changes such as improved oxygen intake, lowering of heart and respiratory rates, less clogging of arteries, brain-wave activity associated with lower stress, and stabilization of muscle blood flow, which relates to adequate blood supply.

Other medical professionals have reported amazing results in their patients who practiced relaxation techniques, from dramatically improving a severe and chronic asthmatic pattern, to lowering cholesterol levels, controlling anxiety and depression, and improving T-cell activity.

Dr. Lipton and I had similarly fascinating results from relaxation techniques taught to a patient who came to me concerned about his symptoms of sexual dysfunction.

*Walter's Diabetes and Decreased Sexual Function.* A physical examination told me that Walter had Type I diabetes mellitus. This was complicated by mild neuropathy that desensitized some nerves in his genitals and constricted the arteries. The result was restriction of the blood flow needed for a healthy erection.

Further, he had enormous levels of stress hormones: elevated glucagon from the pancreas, increased catecholamine output from the adrenal medulla, and elevated cortisol from the adrenal cortex. All are capable of raising blood sugar levels and of suppressing immune function.

I explained to Walter that his body's inability to handle sensitizers was touching off a biochemical reaction that was exacerbating his diabetes and his sexual difficulties; in short, Profound Sensitivity Syndrome was at work. This was being further aggravated by chronic hyperventilation, meaning he was breathing too rapidly and using the wrong muscles, causing respiratory alkalosis (the opposite of acidity) and a lack of oxygen.

Walter's unstable insulin levels were directly related to the emotional reactions he felt as a result of rather consistent distortions in thinking. To him, everything that happened was a prelude to disaster. On the first day I met him, for instance, he was upset and talking about the muffler falling off his car on the way to our appointment. He was sure now, he said, that his transmission and engine were going next, and he didn't know how he could buy a new car as he was having financial problems. Furthermore, he was afraid that without reliable transportation he might lose his job.

I taught him to self-inject the insulin he would need every day, outlined nutritional and exercise programs, and put him in touch with Dr. Lipton, who began by helping Walter learn the relaxation techniques outlined in this and subsequent chapters. Soon Walter was able to stabilize his levels of stress chemicals.

About three months after my first meeting with Walter, I witnessed an unexpected turn of events. During the early weeks of his treatment, Walter's insulin needs had stabilized predictably. Then his need for insulin began to drop, and continued dropping. Finally, seven months after the initial diagnosis, he no longer needed to inject any insulin. His body's insulin production was sufficient to meet his needs!

I had never seen anything like it in a patient as severely diabetic as Walter. A few years later I read a report by Dr. Joan Borysenko, founding director of The Mind/Body Clinic at New England Deaconess Hospital. Using relaxation techniques, Dr. Borysenko helped diabetics lower their blood sugar levels. Though she was quick to point out that her study numbers were small and the results preliminary, I felt her findings supported the results with Walter.

I suspect $PS^2$ had so badly crippled Walter's immune system that it had turned on him, worsening the diabetes and sexual dysfunction. Learning how to unwind was the key to controlling his physical health.

The exercises that follow are the same ones that helped Walter—and many others—find relief. I have had some patients, high-achieving Type A personalities, who hesitate to learn relaxation exercises because they are afraid it will interfere with their body's capacity to react quickly to the struggles of life. They fear becoming less effective if less "hyper."

It is true that the body needs to produce some stress chemicals in order to respond to the pressures and adversities of day-to-day living. Relaxation exercises do not decrease these chemicals; they simply help the body respond to them in a healthier way. People who practice relaxation have the appropriate level of hormones in their blood in times of stress. The negative effects of those hormones, however, are reduced significantly.

Since not every relaxation exercise works for every person, Dr. Lipton and I have examined the most effective programs in controlled breathing and relaxation, modified them to meet our criteria, and taught hundreds of patients to use them effectively. Let's start with a simple but crucially important first step.

## The Breath of Life

Learning to breathe properly is one of the easiest means we have to combat $PS^2$ and, believe it or not, one of the most important steps you can take toward good health. It reduces stress and anxiety, increases your energy level and sense of well-being, and over time can even increase your immune response. It costs nothing and comes with a lifetime guarantee.

Breathing primarily brings oxygen to the body and removes carbon dioxide. Normal breathing makes use of the diaphragm, a dome-shaped muscle that, when expanded, creates a negative pressure in the chest cavity. This negative pressure results in sucking air from outside the body into and over the lungs. Using the diaphragm exposes our lungs to fresh air and removes the air after it has been exposed to the lungs.

We tend, however, to breathe with our chests, that is, thoracically, using our intercostal rib muscles instead of our diaphragms. This is particularly so for $PS^2$ patients and, as we will see later, is how damage is done.

As a child you breathed properly, and even today, when you are sleeping or completely relaxed, you will revert to diaphragmatic breathing. In our culture, however, we are taught to stand with our chests out and stomachs in. We also wear tight clothes that constrict the diaphragm.

*Judy's Chronic Hyperventilation.* Judy, a petite young woman, 28 years old, came to me about her severe allergies. She was a universal reactor, that is, allergic to everything from soup to nuts. She was also clearly suffering from $PS^2$, with cold hands, high levels of stress hormones, and visible anxiety.

After starting her on a program to assess and treat her allergic problems I asked her to see Dr. Lipton for biofeedback training. Later Marc told me the following story.

He trained Judy in thermal biofeedback, but she was having a lot of difficulty learning to raise her hand temperature. He also noticed that she was suffering from chronic hyperventilation. That is, when Judy was breathing her chest (not her diaphragm) would go in and out rapidly and shallowly.

Dr. Lipton attempted to train her to breathe diaphragmatically first by verbal instruction techniques and, when that failed, by hooking her up to a computerized breathing biofeedback apparatus. This did not work either. She just could not seem to get her diaphragm to go in and out instead of her chest. She was breathing in such a fashion that her carbon dioxide/oxygen exchange was producing an elevated blood pH (less acidic blood) and was clearly aggravating her overall state of poor health.

Finally, after weeks of trying to help her, Marc said that he must have been looking particularly frustrated (and in his line of work it takes a lot to get him frustrated!) when he told her that for some reason she was the first patient he had been unable to help learn to breathe correctly.

Judy responded somewhat sheepishly with, "Dr. Lipton, could a girdle interfere with my breathing?"

Taken aback by this question from a woman who weighed 107 pounds, Marc says he responded in a manner somewhat lacking his usual decorum. "Judy! You? Wear a *girdle?*"

She finally admitted that she felt her strongest asset was her hourglass figure and she wanted to accent it as much as possible.

The answer, of course, to Judy's question was that a girdle not only interferes with, but can completely prevent diaphragmatic breathing. Judy adjourned to the ladies' room, removed her girdle, and started immediately to breathe with her diaphragm and to warm her hands to the appropriate level. Within a week and a half her health had improved dramatically.

Once the habit of thoracic breathing is established, it tends to perpetuate itself; and the only way to retrain ourselves to breathe correctly is to become aware of our breathing and perform exercises such as the ones described here.

As simple as it seems, I cannot emphasize enough how important this is. Inadequate breathing can damage your health.

## The Biochemistry of Breathing

While teaching patients this simple exercise, I often find them incredulous that their incorrect breathing can have a major impact on blood chemistry and disease states. But, as with Walter, I have found that a vast majority of patients suffering from $PS^2$ suffer from chronic hyperventilation. That is, they breathe rapidly and shallowly with their chest muscles, rather than with their "stomach" muscles.

Dr. Lipton and I suppose this occurs because many of our $PS^2$ patients are in states of ongoing stress. Their stress seems to have two causes. First are the life factors and experiences they face. Second is the fact that physical illness itself produces ongoing stress on their bodies, which tends to produce this chronic, unhealthy breathing pattern.

It would seem, then, that when we are stressed we breathe in this incorrect way; and as we continue to breathe this way we tend to weaken our body's capacity to fight off disease.

We do not know everything about the biochemistry of this

weakening, but we do know a little. Using our thorax muscles instead of our diaphragms utilizes only about 66 percent of lung capacity. The thorax muscles do not create enough negative pressure in the chest cavity to bring in sufficient air. As a result, we have inadequate exchange of oxygen and carbon dioxide.

The ratio of this exchange is critical. When we hyperventilate and use only two-thirds of our lungs we decrease the amount of carbon dioxide and oxygen that go into the blood. This disrupts the balance in the blood known as the pH level, which refers to how acidic or alkaline the blood is. Carbon dioxide combines with water in the blood to form carbonic acid. Less carbon dioxide means less carbonic acid, and the blood becomes too alkaline. This increase in alkalinity is considered to have serious biochemical effects on our overall health and organ function. Plus, the decrease in oxygen to the blood affects the metabolism of all of our body's cells, including making it more difficult to lose weight.

Again, we don't know as yet all the mechanisms resulting in greater susceptibility to disease and immune suppression. But, based on what I have observed in my patients, and the substantial physical changes in blood pH, I believe the impact is severe. I cannot emphasize strongly enough that by learning to reestablish diaphragmatic breathing and stopping hyperventilation, you will have a major positive impact on your blood chemistry and physical health. This is no small matter.

*Charlotte's Up-and-Down Weight Battle.* From the onset of puberty Charlotte had had weight problems. During the next 35 years she had lost and gained more than 1,000 pounds—a victim of the yo-yo syndrome. Each time she lost weight she regained the original amount plus an extra ten to fifteen pounds. Her fat was confined primarily to her breasts, abdomen, hips, and thighs. Now post-menopausal she complained further about being unduly tired, having brittle nails, dry skin, and increased numbers of black-and-blue marks.

I made the diagnosis of adipose genital dystrophy. This condition is characterized by obesity in the four areas Charlotte exhibited. Because the accumulation of fat around her abdomen made it too difficult for abdominal breathing, she used only her chest. Blood tests confirmed that she was hyperventilating.

The accumulation of abdominal fat was caused, in part, by her deficiency in female sex hormones. She had a low blood $CO_2$ level and a low blood-oxygen level. The latter made it difficult for her to burn up her calories properly.

When she was treated with proper female hormones and trained to breathe from her diaphragm, she felt much better. Within eighteen months she achieved and began to maintain her ideal weight and has been free of her former symptoms.

### How to Breathe Correctly

You can practice this technique as many times as you like during the day. We recommend you spend at least five minutes, three times a day, every day. Ideal times are before you get out of bed in the morning, before you fall asleep at night, and around midday.

In order to differentiate between abdominal and chest breathing, begin by lying comfortably on your back with a small pillow under your head. Your feet should be slightly apart. Place one hand on top of the other and let them rest on your stomach. Close your eyes and concentrate on the next few breaths. Notice how your stomach moves. No movement or a flattening of the stomach indicates chest breathing.

Now breathe abdominally. Place one hand on the center of your upper chest and the other on your abdomen just above the navel. Be sure to inhale through your nose (unless blocked nasal passages prevent you from doing so), and exhale through your mouth.

Concentrate on your breathing. You should not feel any motion in the hand that is on your chest. The hand on your abdomen should be rising as you breathe in and falling as you breathe out. Later, when you no longer have to be concerned about your chest moving while you breathe, you may prefer to rest both hands on your abdomen or place them at your side.

After a few breaths you should notice that you are becoming more relaxed. Your respiration should be smooth, gentle, and even, with no pauses between inhaling and exhaling. It is not necessary to try to force your breath. In fact, you should be able to breathe deeply now without effort.

As you inhale count slowly to four (about four seconds) and without stopping or holding your breath, exhale to the same count. If in the beginning you find it difficult to use a four-second count you may shorten it, but try to increase it to four as soon as you can do so comfortably.

Each time you exhale you may be aware of a relaxed feeling as the tension flows out with your breath. Continue with this pattern for at least five minutes.

Once you achieve even abdominal breathing, try to slow down the rate at which you exhale. You will be changing your breathing rhythm so that for every one count that you inhale, you will exhale for two. Most people find that counts of 2–4, 3–6, or even 4–8 work well.

Once you have mastered abdominal breathing while in a reclining position, practice it while sitting and, later, standing. One of the easiest ways to switch from chest to abdominal breathing while you are standing is to take a deep breath and exhale it as completely as you can through your mouth. This will cause your stomach to flatten. As you inhale through your nose you should feel your stomach expand—an indication that you have shifted into a pattern of abdominal breathing. Do not attempt to force or take deep breaths with this first inhalation. Just relax and continue your even, gentle breathing. You will find that once you have become proficient at shifting into an abdominal breathing mode you will be able to use the technique anytime, anywhere.

Keep in mind that you are not trying to fill and empty your lungs completely with every breath. You do not need to force your body to take in air. It will take in as much as it needs. Trying too hard could lead to dizziness or hyperventilation. If this occurs, stop the exercise and return to your normal breathing pattern.

## Body Relaxation

By relaxation we refer to the easing of tension. This includes both muscle tension in the body and emotional tension from outside pressures. In this section we will teach you six exercises to master relaxation.

Let's start with a total body technique often called progressive muscle relaxation, because you move from one body muscle group to the next until you have relaxed all of them.

### Total Body Relaxation

Start by lying on your back with your legs apart comfortably. Stretch your arms out along your sides, about six inches from your body. Turn your palms upward.

Take five abdominal breaths. After each breath picture yourself sinking more and more into the floor or mattress as you let go of the muscle tension holding you up. If you prefer, think of yourself as floating weightlessly with the release of tension. After the last breath you should feel as if your muscles have relaxed their grip on you.

For each muscle group listed below, first inhale and tighten the muscles as much as possible. Hold for a count of three. Then exhale and relax the muscles, feeling the tension leave. Take a second breath and relax the muscles further as you picture that now-relaxed part of your body either sinking into the floor or mattress or floating weightlessly. Continue with

- Your left foot and calf. Feel the tension leave.
- Your right foot and calf. Make the muscles as tense and hard as you can before letting go.
- Your left thigh.

- Your right thigh.
- Your buttocks.
- Your lower back. Picture your back flattening out against the bed or floor.
- Your stomach. Push it out as far as you can.
- Your chest. Reach as high as you can.
- Your left arm and shoulder.
- Your right arm and shoulder.
- Your fists. Clench each tightly in turn.
- Your neck. Try to pull your head as far away from your neck as possible.
- Your facial muscles. Yawn with your mouth as wide open as possible.

When you yawn your brain is putting out a *Do Not Disturb* sign. If your yawning is observed by others around you, often they, too, will yawn as you help them relax for that moment.

**The Relaxalot Technique**

Here's a relaxation technique that is extremely effective and can be used anywhere at almost any time. It takes only a few seconds and combines techniques including breathing and visualization in one simple approach.

You can sit, stand, or lie down. You may want to close your eyes.

For this exercise, simply take a deep breath and imagine that you are inhaling into your lungs all the tension, stress, and anxiety from every corner of your body. Do not think of yourself as inhaling air from the outside, but picture yourself "inhaling" internally. Then get rid of all of that tension in one quick exhalation. Keep your mouth half-open as you visualize all that internal tension leaving your body.

You can picture the tension from your whole body entering your lungs at once, or you can focus on various parts of your body with each inhalation. For example, you can concentrate on sucking up into your lungs the tension in your feet, calves, and legs. Then exhale and let go of that tension. On your next inhalation, focus on all of the tension in your pelvis, stomach, and chest. Then continue until you cover all parts of your body. Inhale and exhale about ten times for this process.

Your ability to visualize this in a focused, clear way is the key to the success of this technique. The results are amazingly positive.

### Take Ten

Seconds, that is. Here is another easy, powerful relaxation technique you can employ anytime, anywhere. It will slow down your heart rate and reduce the amount of stress chemicals being secreted into your bloodstream. It will rid you of acute anxiety and even improve your overall performance. It is a modification of a breathing meditation technique that has been used for centuries.

Close your eyes, inhale normally and naturally, and when you exhale count to yourself, *Number one*. Inhale again and on your second exhalation, count to yourself, *Number two*, and so on until you get to number ten.

After number ten, before you open your eyes, take a deep breath and let it out through your mouth slowly for about seven seconds. Then open your eyes.

### Stretching While Seated

This is a way to increase your relaxation by stretching like a cat. We recommend this as an alternate exercise if you find it too painful to do the exercises that require muscle tensing.

Do this exercise three times a day sitting in a chair and repeat each sequence five times.

1. Open your mouth wide. Hold. Return to original position.
2. Bend your head toward your chest. Hold. Return.
3. Move your head just slightly backward. Hold. Return.

4. Bend your head toward your left shoulder. Hold. Return.
5. Bend your head toward your right shoulder. Hold. Return.
6. Pull your shoulders down toward your feet. Hold. Return.
7. Stretch both arms over your head. Hold. Return.
8. Stretch both arms forward at shoulder level. Spread your fingers and stretch. Hold 5 counts. (Do not hold your breath.) Return arms to lap.
9. Inhale and curve your back backward. Hold. As you exhale curve your back forward.
10. Stretch your legs wide apart. Hold. Return.
11. Stretch both legs forward, thighs resting on chair. Hold extended legs 5 counts. Lower feet to the floor.
12. Stretch both legs forward. Stretch your feet by flexing your heels, then pointing your toes. Lower feet to floor.
13. Stretch your entire body from head to toes. Hold. Return.

## Imaging

This is probably the most common mental relaxation technique. You may already be somewhat familiar with imaging, or visualizing. The number and types of images you can use is limited only by your imagination. If you run short, you can borrow someone else's or get an idea from posters, magazines, or films.

The more the image captures your imagination, the more you will relax. Imaging is like playing a movie through your head; you might keep the camera still, focused on one scene, or you might move it around through many scenes.

The more you practice imaging, as with any skill, the better you become at it. Common sense dictates that, as with physical relaxation, you should remain quiet and undisturbed for about fifteen to twenty minutes. The more sensory detail and true-to-life vividness you can put into your images—that is, the more you can see, hear, feel, taste, and touch—the more relaxing they will be. You may find calm, peaceful, still images the most relaxing and diverting. Or you may prefer action-packed, quickly changing scenes. Here is one suggested calm mental image to serve as an example of how to use all your senses in choosing your relaxing place.

Lights lowered where you are sitting or reclining, eyes closed, begin.

### A Day at the Beach

Ho hum. Nothing to do, nowhere to go. No responsibilities. Time is frozen for a day, so you have no worries or commitments. This beach is specially reserved for you; no one else is allowed unless you say so.

You're lying on your back, wearing shorts or swimsuit, with your head comfortably propped on a pile of fluffy towels. The sky is a cloudless blue. Under your visor you see a sailboat, or someone windsurfing out on the water. The sail is white and billows out. Nothing else is on the horizon.

You push your pillow of towels aside and roll over on your blanket. You feel as free and happy as a child. The sun is very warm on your back and the backs of your legs, but a soft breeze fans you. First you feel the hot sun and then you feel the cool breeze. The sun, then the breeze, warm and cool, back and forth.

Your thoughts sail out over the water like birds, till they hover where the sea blends with the sky. You let your mind rest there awhile—far, far away from the problems of daily life. They are far behind. Time is not moving for a day.

You can hear the rhythm of the waves making a whooshing sound, then silence. Whoosh, silence, over and over. The cool, soft breeze whispers over you when the waves sweep in. The warmth of the sun takes its place as the waves roll quietly back. You can barely smell the sweet scent of the suntan oil on your skin—tropical flowers. It's like a background to the faintly salty smell of the clean sand around you.

You have a tangerine wrapped in the bundle of towels beside

you. You could munch the bite-sized pieces of fruit, one by one. That would be nice. But there's no rush. The tangerine will be there when you want it. Until then you'll think about sand castles and pearls, coral reefs, swaying palm trees, seahorses, and whatever else floats through your mind.

Then you'll slowly return to your everyday reality, feeling relaxed and refreshed.

**Meditation**

To meditate means simply to engage in contemplation or reflection. For our purposes, it is the intentional focusing of your attention away from the tension and trauma of the outside world.

As we recommend for the other exercises, give yourself fifteen to twenty minutes for each session. Try to practice meditation twice a day and at the same times each day. Choose those times when you will not be disturbed.

- Get comfortable in a sitting position; have a clock nearby.
- Close your eyes.
- Begin slow, abdominal breathing.
- Become aware of your breathing. Notice your breath coming in through your nose. Notice your stomach expanding.
- Notice your breath going out through your mouth. Notice your stomach relaxing.
- Think of nothing else but your breathing.
- Continue to think of your breathing as you inhale and exhale. Nothing else.
- Thoughts will wander through your mind. Let them pass through like a parade. Do not concentrate on any thought.
- As you think only of your breathing and let other thoughts pass through, you will become more and more relaxed.
- Have someone softly call you after fifteen or twenty

minutes or gently open your eyes, look around slowly, eventually looking at your watch or a nearby clock.

You may want to focus on a particular word or thought instead of your breathing. Just be sure to keep your breathing deep and regular. If you use a word, the word is best kept simple—not more than one syllable. And stretch out the sound of the word. For instance, when unwanted thoughts come into your mind say to yourself *calm*, only say it as *caaaalm*.

One word about these techniques you have learned. The basic secret of strengthening your mind-body link is practice. All the methods we recommend, when perfected, build up a conditioning effect on the brain's capacity to influence the body's physiology and biochemistry. The more you experience this, the stronger and more effective the mind's control becomes.

Why not plan for the next thirty days to practice one or more of these exercises? All of them will help you maintain or improve your own mind-body link.

Remember, these mind-body regulating approaches protect you from the damaging effects of chronically high levels of stress hormones, such as epinephrine (adrenaline), norepinephrine, glucagon, cortisol, and others. Remember, too, that like most everything else in life, "Nothing in, nothing out."

In other words if you don't do it, it won't work. And if you *do* do it, you will find that relaxation is not the impossible dream you may once have thought it to be.

# 8

# How to Strengthen the Connection Between Your Mind and Your Body

*Sandra's Raynaud's Syndrome.* Sandra came into my office on a hot, muggy day in August, but was rubbing her hands together as if to warm them. "Is the air conditioner working overtime in here?" she asked. "My hands are freezing."

"It might be a little on the cool side," I said. "Would you be more comfortable if I opened a window?" She nodded enthusiastically. In a few moments the summer air had filled my office.

"I don't understand it," she said. "My hands are so numb I can barely feel them."

I looked at her hands and saw that her skin was mottled blue. As we talked about the particular physical problems for which she had come to see me, I questioned her about her hands as well.

Sandra told me she had suffered with coldness in her hands since she was a teenager. Now, at 26, she was troubled because of increasing episodes of numbness, tingling, and severe pain in her fingers. Sometimes the coldness lasted only a few minutes; other times it went on for days. It always got worse, she said, when she was cold or faced emotional pressures. Lately the attacks had been coming on almost daily.

Although I was not certain of the cause of Sandra's poor circulation, I had a pretty good idea and confirmed my suspicions with a simple office test. I had her put her hands into a bucket of ice and observed the blanching of the fingers. There seemed to be little doubt that Sandra had Raynaud's Syndrome.

As Sandra described other complaints—frequent respiratory infections, difficulty sleeping, chronic fatigue—I felt sure that she was a victim of Profound Sensitivity Syndrome as well. Laboratory tests for $PS^2$ disclosed high levels of norepinephrine and cortisol.

Curiously, probably because it is made worse by emotional distress, Raynaud's Syndrome is a condition I have identified in many patients who suffer from $PS^2$. It occurs when the small arterioles—tiny blood vessels with muscle coats around them—of the hands and feet go into spasm, reducing or even cutting off the flow of blood. While the early stages are merely uncomfortable, the advanced stages can be disabling.

Sandra agreed to try my Stress Correction Plan and program of moderate exercise. I also prescribed a medication that helped decrease the severity and frequency of the spasms. I recommended she try to protect her hands and feet from cold and avoid emotional conflict and pressure. Because nicotine constricts the arterioles even more, I advised her to quit smoking. I taught her the basics of my stop-smoking program, which I will share with you in chapter 9. (If you or someone you know wants to quit, this will help.)

When I explained why I thought she could benefit from particular relaxation techniques Dr. Lipton could teach her—specifically, thermal biofeedback and hypnosis—she agreed to meet with him as well.

Thermal biofeedback seemed particularly appropriate for Sandra because this technique is based, as we will see, on turning up an internal thermostat that warms the hands in order to relax the body.

When Sandra returned for her follow-up examination eight weeks later, there was little doubt she had benefited from our combined treatments. Her symptoms were much less severe and tests showed that her body biochemistry had stabilized. By sticking to the program, she continued to find relief.

Biofeedback and hypnosis are relaxation techniques that help your brain reprogram certain detrimental activities in your body's systems. When you master these skills, you can harness the therapeutic power of your mental processes to improve your physical and emotional health—and combat $PS^2$. Let's start with biofeedback.

## Thermal Biofeedback

The human body is an amazingly complex message center. The brain, nervous system, endocrine system, and immune system interact with one another constantly. Most of the chemical and electrical messages they send back and forth travel outside our conscious awareness and, until recently, also lay outside our control.

Now with the increasing understanding of biofeedback, we are able to translate some of these messages into an information format that we can see, feel, and understand. Once this information is made available to the brain on a conscious level, we learn to direct healthy responses in areas that hitherto we have been unable even to sense.

The technique we will be teaching you is called thermal biofeedback, or peripheral temperature control. Remember, $PS^2$ is the inability to stop the body's response to sensitizers. The simple technique of thermal biofeedback will help your body learn to overcome that inability.

The goal is to use your brain to warm your hands. Why focus on your hands? Because when you are stressed your sympathetic nervous system, the one that controls excitement, becomes stimulated. This, in turn, produces many complex biochemical reactions.

One of these, caused by the stress chemical norepinephrine, is the constriction of the muscles within the walls of the body's arterioles, making those tiny blood vessels smaller. As a result, the blood flow through them is reduced and does not reach the cells in the surrounding tissues. This is particularly noticeable in the peripheral circulatory system with the hands and feet. Thus, when you become anxious your hands may become cold and "clammy." The amount of blood to the hands, which is needed to warm them, has been restricted.

Thermal biofeedback overrides those reactions by reducing norepinephrine and other stress chemicals in your bloodstream. When you warm your hands through biofeedback you are actually permitting those arteriole muscles to relax and increase the blood going through them. Warming your hands by using your brain is the same as reducing the stress reaction of your sympathetic nervous system. The warmer you can get your hands, the lower will be your level of anxiety.

And the lower your level of anxiety, the less tension you will have in other systems controlled by this part of the nervous system as well. You will reduce blood pressure, slow down your heart rate, relax electrical activity in your muscles as measured by electromyography (EMG), and reduce the secretion of harmful chemicals into the bloodstream.

The benefits of thermal biofeedback go even beyond the sympathetic nervous system; they can affect your entire body. If you are already healthy, they can help maintain your immune defenses. If you have Profound Sensitivity Syndrome, they can bring the endocrine system back into balance, cutting off the flood of hormones that disrupts immune function. Internal relaxation is a remarkably effective therapy.

*Helen's Thymoma.* Helen, age 36, started to develop recurrent infections when she was about 22. They were followed by chronic diarrhea, mouth sores, arthritis, wheezing, and, most recently, signs of diabetes. Her physician made the diagnosis of acquired immunodeficiency (not to be confused with AIDS) and referred her to me for consultation.

I found that she had a slightly impaired antibody response to injected antigens, as well as a low lymphocyte count and a Giardia parasite infection. X rays showed further that she had a mass in her chest (the anterior mediastinum). The compression from the mass caused her to wheeze. I confirmed her doctor's diagnosis of immunodeficiency—with thymoma, a tumor of the thymus gland—and returned her to his care with several recommendations.

Before she left, Dr. Lipton taught her how to relax through biofeedback and autohypnosis. To my amazement, of all the treatments—including removal of the thymoma—Helen feels that the relaxation techniques and her new positive attitude have made her feel the best.

*Maxine's Cytomegalic Virus Infection.* This was also true of Maxine, age 33. Her symptoms were sudden fever and pain in the upper part of her abdomen just under her right rib cage. She also had chronic tiredness. Examination and testing revealed that she had cytomegalic virus infection (CMV). Although this is frequently a congenital disease, she had acquired it through contact with the virus. CMV, one of the "slow-acting viruses" or "salivary gland viruses," is a member of the herpes family and may be acquired at any age by contact with infected saliva, urine, semen, cervical secretions, blood, or milk. It can range in severity from being a "silent" infection to causing fever, hepatitis (liver inflammation), or brain damage.

Once the diagnosis was known and treatment begun, Maxine learned to help herself with some of the symptoms through biofeedback and hypnosis. She has a recurrence of low-grade fever or tiredness occasionally, but is now better able to cope with it.

While biofeedback is a relatively new addition to the clinical arsenal, medical science has well documented its usefulness, when combined with traditional medical therapies, in treating a wide variety of emotional and physiological problems. The combination of medical treatment and biofeedback appears to be more practical for some conditions than either of the two alone.

Take irritable bowel syndrome (IBS) as an example. IBS is a movement disorder that involves the small intestine and large bowel, causing abdominal pain and severe constipation or diarrhea. As many as fourteen percent of all Americans, perhaps thirty million people, suffer chronically from this condition.

The exact mechanisms that create IBS are not well understood, but we do know that it involves overstimulation of this part of the gastrointestinal system and has a high correlation with emotional upset. It is not surprising, then, that I find many patients with IBS who also have suppressed immune function and the physiological problems that such suppression involves.

Generally, I treat irritable bowel syndrome with slight modifications in diet and a regimen of mild exercises. Some people with IBS are also found to be suffering from food allergies. Because of IBS's direct relationship to stress, treatment involving relaxation and thermal biofeedback is also useful.

Drs. Debra F. Neff at the Medical University of South Carolina and Edward B. Blanchard at the State University of New York at Albany studied six men and thirteen women with IBS. Ten of the patients received biofeedback training. Nine acted as a control group. After just ten weeks, six of the ten receiving biofeedback training reported that their symptoms had decreased by fifty percent or more.

The study of the mind-body connection and physical health got an enormous boost in the spring of 1988 when Dr. Daniel Hernandez at the University of Southern California proved that some stomach ulcers originate in the brain, not in the stomach.

Medical science has known for many years that the reaction to stress affects the formation of stomach ulcers, but until Dr. Hernandez's study, we did not know the physiological mechanisms involved.

He discovered that during emotional distress or physical trauma, the brain stem, which connects the spinal cord and brain and is responsible for autonomic (automatic) functions, emits thyrotropin-releasing hormone (TRH). This biochemical stimulates the flow of gastric acids that can cause stomach ulcers.

According to Dr. Hernandez: "It appears that the coping response to stress is initiated centrally in the brain and that chemical messages are sent out to the peripheral organs of the endocrine system, causing the release of stress-related hormones. These hormones, in turn, act on specific receptors in the stomach that [normally] protect the gastric mucosa from the damaging effects of stress. So the brain is pivotal in initiating a cascade of events."

Thus, if through thermal biofeedback we can get our brains to reduce the effects of those tension-inducers, or sensitizers, on our sympathetic nervous systems, we will also be reducing the emission of TRH, which will, in turn, reduce the stimulation of ulcer-causing gastric acids.

Raynaud's Syndrome, IBS, stomach ulcers, high blood pressure, heart rhythm disturbances, headaches, facial pain, asthma, allergies, arthritis, diabetes, insomnia . . . these and other health problems are greatly reduced by thermal biofeedback. Here is the technique.

## Thermal Biofeedback Exercise

Begin by purchasing a small thermometer from a five-and-ten-cent or hardware store. It will be easier for you to read than the thermometers used to measure body temperature. You should remove any brackets or holders attached to it.

To measure the temperature of your hands, place the bulb of the thermometer on the pad of your index finger, the part opposite the nail, and secure it—snugly, but not too tightly—with a piece of Scotch tape. If the tape is too tight you will cut off circulation to that part of your finger and inhibit accurate measurement of blood flow.

The thermometer is your source of biofeedback, providing

you with visual reinforcement, proof that you are actually raising the temperature of your hands. Remember, hand warmth and deep relaxation are intimately linked; reducing sympathetic nervous system arousal lowers your level of anxiety and permits the arterioles in your hands to allow more blood to flow. As you warm your hands, you relax your mind and body more and more. It is that simple.

Thermal biofeedback cannot be overdone, only underdone. In order to get maximal benefits biochemically, set aside about twenty minutes for each session. Depending upon your particular needs, you can do this once a day or three or four times a day. For example, if arthritis pain is particularly bad, practicing several times a day is advisable. If migraines or other headaches are persisting, several twenty-minute sessions daily can be very helpful. Here we go.

Turn the phone down or unplug it if possible and try to prevent any interruptions. Restrictive clothing such as belts, tight waistbands, collars, shoes, and the like should be loosened or removed. You may either lie down or sit in a comfortable chair. Once you have attached the thermometer to your finger, place your arm and hand in a position that allows you to read it simply by opening your eyes. You will be composing your own script in your mind. All you have to remember to help guide your thoughts are two words: *heat* and *muscles.*

Before closing your eyes, glance at the temperature reading on the thermometer. Make a mental note of it. Now close your eyes. Take a deep breath and let it out very, very slowly through your mouth. Do this again. Good.

First, *heat*. Think of a scene that, with the use of your active imagination, allows you to experience a sensation of warmth in your hands. Some people think of their hands in warm gloves or in buckets of warm water. Others imagine their hands being warmed over a crackling campfire, in warm sand at the beach, under an electric blanket, or holding rocks warmed by the sun. Use whatever scene or scenes allow you to experience a warm, pleasant, secure sensation of heat to your hands. Every now and then say to yourself the words *warm, heavy hands*. These words will begin to condition your brain. You will soon be able to elicit the desired response on cue. Actually employ your active imagination to "feel" heat in your hands.

Now switch in your mind to the second word that guides your thoughts, *muscles*. Say to yourself: "Relax the muscles in my eyelids, my face, my jaw, relax the muscles in my neck. Let all the tension leave the muscles in my back, my chest, my shoulders, and my arms. Let all my muscles unwind slowly as if they were tight rubber bands. Relax all the muscles in my hands, my abdomen, my pelvis, legs, feet and feel the deep, deep, deep relaxation all the way down to my toes." Now switch back to *heat*. *Warm, heavy hands*. Focus on a sensation of pleasant, secure warmth to your hands. Just defrost completely. Just let yourself go completely. Become limp as a noodle floating around in chicken noodle or minestrone soup. *Warm, heavy hands*.

Every few minutes open your eyes and peek to see if the temperature on the thermometer is going higher. At the beginning you may actually see it going lower. If so just relax and continue to practice. Remember, this is not a competition. This is not something that you force to happen the way you would slide a dish from one place to another. This is something that you permit to happen by letting yourself go completely, by becoming limp as a noodle. What you will learn is that sometimes in life the best way to achieve control is just by letting go completely. This is called passive control.

So for approximately twenty minutes you are switching back and forth between the two words that guide your mental script—*heat* and *muscles*—and every few minutes or so looking at the thermometer to see if you are warming your hands. Even though you may not, at first, notice any changes in how you feel, many bodily functions are now undergoing subtle changes. As long as you are relaxed, as long as you are visualizing . . . comfortably and casually . . . warmth and heaviness in your hands, relaxing all the muscles in your entire body . . . the process is working. *Warm, heavy hands.*

Allow thoughts to enter and leave your mind casually. Some thoughts and ideas will blend and mix with your images. Drift back to images of warm, heavy hands when you become aware of having lost them for the moment, but do so smoothly and in an unconcerned fashion. Relax all the muscles in your body.

Before opening your eyes, repeat a few phrases to yourself that describe how you feel, how calm you are, how good you feel. . . . Become aware consciously of your sense of control. *My hands are warm. My muscles are relaxed. I am at peace with myself.* Choose a phrase or two that has personal meaning. Tune into the physical sensations, thoughts, emotions, and images that accompany your relaxed state.

Take a few long, slow breaths as you did at the beginning of the session. Stretch leisurely as if awakening from a restful sleep. Smile. Glance at the thermometer. You are learning to control the temperature of your hands as well as your state of mind.

A few comments. Many people prefer to keep their eyes open rather than to close them so that they can look at the thermometer and get more constant feedback as to what they are doing with their hand temperature. You may wish to do this at the beginning but you will find that learning thermal biofeedback is like learning to ride a bicycle; once you get it, you've got it, and you won't forget it. After several weeks of practice you will be able to do it without the thermometer, the same way you get rid of training wheels when you learn to keep your balance on a bike. Then you will need to use the thermometer only once in a while just to make sure you're still keeping your "thermal" balance.

There are a few pitfalls to try to avoid. Thermal biofeedback is not usually something you can learn in one session. You may have to spend a week practicing before you see a rise in hand temperature. It's important to remember this so you do not generate unrealistic expectations and get upset when you don't meet them. Many $PS^2$ sufferers tend to be very self-critical and hard on themselves. The biggest pitfall in learning biofeedback is to become frustrated or competitive with yourself. If you do you will see your temperature go down instead of up. Just relax and keep practicing; you will finally get it.

Everyone always asks, "I've seen biofeedback tapes; should I buy one or make one?" Although some practitioners recommend such tapes, we definitely do not. You customize and control your own script in your own mind. A tape recorder externalizes rather than internalizes a sense of control. Besides, your brain is portable, you can take it wherever you go, and it never runs out of batteries.

Thermal biofeedback has two general purposes. First, practicing it twenty minutes a day will help protect the body from the consequences of stress and help ameliorate the various conditions described here.

Second, the more you practice warming your hands, the more your brain becomes conditioned to the idea and the less time it takes to elicit the physiological benefits. Eventually, simply saying to yourself, "Warm, heavy hands," and relaxing, can increase peripheral temperature.

This technique can be used, therefore, as an instant tranquilizer no matter where you are. If you are about to make a presentation to the boss and feel nervous and stressed, all you have to do is say, "Warm, heavy hands." Simply allowing yourself to perform thermal biofeedback for thirty to sixty seconds will achieve a substantial, deep, calming effect.

The success rate of thermal biofeedback depends on making it a part of your life on an ongoing basis. This is also true of the next relaxation technique we would like to teach you: self-hypnosis. Self-hypnosis, like thermal biofeedback, can redirect brain function for rapid emotional and behavioral change.

## Self-Hypnosis

Self-hypnosis is one treatment in which the person doing it is completely responsible for its success. Even when a therapist is assisting, it is the patient alone who achieves the hypnotic state, which we call Enhanced State of Consciousness—the patient alone with an individually tailored "treatment plan" that effects relief. We use ESC synonymously with self-hypnosis.

During self-hypnosis the brain can trigger and direct a number of the body's systems. It can control functions of the central nervous system, such as heart rate, body temperature, blood flow, and pain. It can trigger the limbic-hypothalamic system and the endocrine (glandular) system. It also appears to be capable of stimulating various neuropeptides, believed to be the basic tools of the body's immune system.

In short, the proper use of hypnosis can have a major impact for good on every aspect of your physical and emotional health. Dr. Lipton has taught the principles of hypnosis to patients with a wide variety of needs and has helped them improve their emotional as well as physical health. Cases vary from the young woman who suffered frequent and painful episodes of herpes simplex II, which I also treated medically, to that of the Sunday school teacher who hoped hypnotic training would help her overcome her fear of public speaking. In the former case, the young woman learned to control her pain—as well as her feelings of anger and helplessness at being host to such a malicious virus. In the latter case, the teacher reported happily that her fears had subsided.

Successful hypnotherapy involves three phases: *training,* during which you learn to use your active imagination; *application,* during which you form a treatment plan to achieve your goal; and finally, *induction,* in which you enter ESC and put your treatment plan into effect. You do not need a therapist with you in order to perform self-hypnosis. You can simply follow these guidelines.

As I describe each phase I will relate it to the experiences of three patients, each of whom came to us with troubling complaints that had not been alleviated by other means.

But before we get into actual training, let me first dispel a few pervading myths about hypnosis. Many people have nothing but optimism about the concept; others feel some hesitation, or worse. Perhaps this exposition will help overcome any doubts you may have.

**Myth:** A person loses control under hypnosis.

**Fact:** Contrary to this common belief, no one loses control during hypnosis. If you are focusing on, say, upsetting information from the past, you might become upset. But you will never lose control of yourself and do something detrimental to your well-being.

**Myth:** You must be naïve and gullible to be hypnotized.

**Fact:** Entirely false. The best hypnotic subjects are intelligent, focused people. This myth has probably found credence because of the use of the term *suggestible* in relation to hypnosis. *Suggestible* means simply that a person is able to take the hypnotic suggestions of the hypnotist or his own mind and apply them.

**Myth:** Hypnosis is something the hypnotist "does" to you.

**Fact:** All hypnosis, whether induced by a professional therapist or by you, is *self*-hypnosis. That is, *you* are placing yourself in the Enhanced State of Consciousness. When another person hypnotizes you, he is really only helping you hypnotize yourself.

**Myth:** Hypnosis is self-induced sleep.

**Fact:** Hypnosis is not sleep. Except in the deepest levels of somnambulism, you are aware of what is going on around you. And even in such deep states your conscious mind continues to stand guard and will arouse you if necessary.

**Myth:** You must trust your hypnotist, because once hypnotized you surrender your own judgment and follow the judgment of the hypnotist.

**Fact:** In spite of what movies would have you believe, you do not lose your capacity to make moral and ethical judgments during hypnosis. You cannot be made to do anything under hypnosis—endangering your own safety, for instance, or violating your moral convictions—that you would not do in a fully conscious state.

**Myth:** The hypnotist must have a stronger personality than his or her subject.

**Fact:** Again, all hypnosis is self-hypnosis. The strength of the hypnotist's personality is irrelevant. What is important is the rapport you have with the hypnotist and the extent to which you understand and believe in hypnosis.

**Myth:** A significant danger of hypnosis is that many people have failed to awaken from the trance state.

**Fact:** The only reported cases of failure to awaken immediately from the trancelike hypnotic state have occurred among those few subjects who reached extremely deep and pleasurable levels of hypnosis and chose not to awaken. But even those levels become natural sleep from which the subject soon awakens unharmed. This "problem" is overcome when the therapist tells the subject that hypnosis will never again be possible unless he or she awakens immediately.

**Myth:** Hypnosis is an abnormal state. It runs counter to our basic psychological functioning and well-being.

**Fact:** Hypnosis is a naturally occurring state in humankind. The best example of a natural hypnotic state is what many of us have experienced on occasion—driving for miles without remembering how we did it, because we were so engrossed in our thoughts. This demonstrates how our conscious and unconscious minds can operate simultaneously.

**Myth:** Hypnosis may often lead to serious emotional problems.

**Fact:** There is no basis for this myth. To the contrary,

achieving ESC on a regular basis reduces tension and stress and produces a sense of well-being and increased ability to deal with the problems and challenges of life.

Let's look at three $PS^2$ patients who were helped with different problems and follow their progress as we study the three phases of hypnosis training.

*Marie's Back Pain, Ellen's Weight Problem, and George's Impotence.* At age 46, Marie suffered from chronic lower back pain. Orthopedic surgeons and chiropractors had given her two options: learn to live with the pain or undergo surgery with a fifty percent chance of success.

Ellen, age 35, was overweight. If only she could stop snacking throughout the day, she felt she would be able to get the extra pounds off.

George, age 41, was troubled by impotence. He had taken his problem to therapists, a clinical social worker, a pastoral counselor, and a sexual dysfunction laboratory. Reared by parents who placed strong emphasis on "clean thoughts," George had struggled with feelings of guilt about his sexual relations with his wife throughout his twenty-year marriage.

Each of these individuals faced different types of problems: Marie wanted relief from pain; Ellen wanted to modify her behavior; George hoped to change his emotions.

I worked on the physiological aspects of their difficulties: I had Marie lie on a flat surface day and night for a period of two weeks and gave her a muscle relaxant. I put Ellen on "Slice of Life," that special food supplement I developed that provides the right amounts of vitamins, minerals, nutrients, and the right proportion of fat, carbohydrates, protein, and fiber. This allowed for a release of her body's own cholecystokinin—a hormone that allows you to eat less but be satiated. And I gave George injections of testosterone. Because he had a slightly underactive thyroid, I also placed him on replacement thyroid hormone.

Dr. Lipton approached the psychological aspect of their

problems by tailoring the three phases of self-hypnosis to their individual needs.

As with Marie, Ellen, and George, you can use the following instruction in self-hypnosis to meet your particular needs as well.

**Phase One: Training**

The first step in hypnosensory training begins with learning to stimulate your active imagination. Dr. Lipton calls this "sensory vivification"—making your senses come alive in your mind. Everyone can learn sensory vivification. In addition, you can practice it anytime you can close your eyes for a few minutes—at home, in your office, even on the subway.

The goal is to relive the sense of actually being in the location you decide to picture, such as a restaurant. You will use taste, touch, smell, hearing, speech, emotions, and even the sensation of movement. You are creating not just a picture, but an experience.

Let's start with the sensation of *taste*. You are now in a favorite restaurant. Close your eyes and picture yourself sitting in the chair; you are actually there. Look down at the tablecloth and silverware, the carpeting, the next table. You can see and hear the waiters and other diners. Here comes the waiter with your meal, perhaps an elaborate seafood platter.

Pick up your fork and take the first bite. Focus on the taste. Is it rich with spices? Cooked to perfection? Chew this bite carefully and swallow it. Then take another.

If you have difficulty tasting the food, try something like lemon on your fish. You might even take a tiny bite of the lemon itself. Can you feel your lips pucker? Experiment with different flavors until you can taste the food.

Remember to sip whatever you decided to drink with this meal. Is the wine dry? Does it complement the entrée? Is the water cold and refreshing?

Now focus on the sensation of *smell*. Breathe in the aroma of your food. Sniff the acrid smoke of the cigar the man at the next table has been puffing on so inconsiderately for the last ten minutes. Smell its pungent odor.

Now switch to the sense of *touch*. You have looked at the tablecloth, now feel it. Run your fingers over it. How heavy is it? Is it coarse or smooth? What kind of upholstery covers your chair or booth? Touch your water glass and feel the beads of moisture on the outside and the ring it is leaving on the tablecloth. Feel the breadbasket and the warmth of your coffee cup.

Now listen to the *sounds* around you. Listen to the busboy clearing a nearby table. Can you hear sounds from the kitchen? What are people at nearby tables talking about?

Think about your *speech*. Hear yourself talking to the waiter, asking what he has for dessert. Hear yourself talking as you normally do.

Now pay attention to *movement*. Pour cream into your refill of coffee. Feel the pitcher in your fingers. Feel the movement in your arm as you lift your coffee cup and put it down. Turn your head. Adjust your chair.

Now concentrate on your *feelings*. Are you warm and mellow? Comfortably full? Carefree and lightheaded? You are having a good time; how does it feel?

Now that you have experienced this meal one sense at a time, go back into the restaurant and have a full sensory vivification experience eating the food, tasting, smelling, hearing, feeling, seeing. You are in the restaurant. Experience it.

Try different scenes; some will be more vivid than others. You might visualize getting up in the morning and going through your normal activities until you are ready to walk out the door. You might relive an emotionally moving occasion such as your wedding or the birth of a child. You might try a time of your life in which you experienced a sense of "fearful exhilaration" such as looking down from the top of the Sears Tower in Chicago or the World Trade Center in New York and being thrilled by the view.

After about a week of practicing three or four times a day, you should be ready to move on to the next phase. You will know you have reached this stage when you start to experience things so vividly that you have to remind yourself where you really are.

At this point you have learned an effective way to use your mind to experience great enjoyment. But this enjoyment by itself will not bring about your goal, whether relief of physical symptoms like headaches, a change in behavior like chewing your fingernails, or a change in emotions like overcoming fear of heights. For that we must move on to phase two.

**Phase Two: Application**

Sensory vivification has given you the ability to focus and to "experience" your thoughts. Now, developing a treatment plan will give you a pathway along which your thoughts will travel during hypnotherapy. The four steps in this phase can be adapted to whatever problem you are trying to overcome. They constitute your treatment plan.

While proceeding with this phase, write down your thoughts, what you are actually telling yourself. You will use this later, in the third phase of self-hypnosis.

*Step one.* Using sensory vivification, recreate those senses surrounding the situation you wish to change.

For instance, Marie concentrated on the pain in her lower back and the sense of frustration it gave her. Ellen pictured herself grabbing a candy bar. George recreated a recent scene with his wife in which he felt frustration and failure at being unable to maintain an erection.

*Step two.* Continue to imagine the worst; then change your thoughts and imagine yourself behaving in the way you would like.

For Marie this meant picturing helpful chemicals being

released from her body into her bloodstream, being carried to the affected area, and washing away the pain. (The image of "helpful chemicals" is good for anyone with the problem of pain. You can give the chemicals any appearance you like—any color, shape, or form that appeals to you—and imagine they are washing away the pain, or perhaps disintegrating it.)

Ellen imagined herself resisting the impulse to snack. In her mind she would start into the store for junk food, then turn and walk out; she would grab the loaf of bread to make toast, then put it back. (If you are afraid of heights, you might imagine yourself climbing a ladder; if you are trying to overcome fear of the water, you might picture yourself jumping into a pool, swimming to the other side, and emerging safely.)

George's treatment plan was aimed at overcoming his anxious thoughts related to sex. After creating in his mind as much emotional discomfort as he could and thinking about it as long as he could, George then pictured himself being successful in maintaining an erection.

*Step three.* Experience the relief or joy associated with the removal of the problem.

Marie experienced freedom from pain. She "felt" it go and reveled in the attendant happiness. (If you are taking this approach and feel that the symptom can be removed quickly, then picture it so. If you feel it will take several days or weeks to remove the symptom, then picture it bit by bit, step by step, slowly being removed from your body.)

Ellen felt the enjoyment of controlling her eating behavior, rather than having her desire for food possess her.

George allowed himself to feel happy and in control. He accepted his feelings of intense sexual excitement as positive ones and tried to intensify them.

*Step four.* Congratulate yourself on your success. In your imagination pat yourself on the back and feel good about what you have accomplished.

Before going on to the next phase of hypnosensory training, reread the four steps of your treatment plan that you have been writing down. Study them so that you know exactly what you are going to do when you are in the Enhanced State of Consciousness.

Also, be assured that you will not lose consciousness when you enter a hypnotic state. Your conscious mind will still be aware of what is going on and what you are doing. Your unconscious mind will, at the same time, direct the emotional, behavioral, or biochemical change you desire.

This technique is perfectly safe. During the course of twenty years of working with various forms of self-induced trance states, Dr. Lipton has not once seen negative effects in any of the patients he has trained. Positive results, on the other hand, abound.

### Phase Three: Induction

Before inducing a state of self-hypnosis, if you have trained yourself in thermal biofeedback as outlined in the last chapter, start by warming your hands. It makes your inducement much easier and more rapid. If you have not used thermal biofeedback, that's all right, too.

What appears to be happening in an Enhanced State of Consciousness is that we establish a psycho-physiological climate in which the conscious mind can communicate with and make an impact upon the unconscious mind. The unconscious mind, in turn, can effect the emotional and biochemical changes we desire.

Remember, you will not become unconscious or unaware of what you are doing; quite to the contrary, you will be in enhanced control of your body and your mind.

Now keep in mind that the more *real* your images and feelings, the deeper and better this will be for you. What defines a hypnotic state is the capacity to focus your attention, bypass your critical thinking, use your active imagination, and convert the suggestions you will be giving yourself into *the real thing*.

For example, in this state think of yourself on a roller coaster. If you experience the car slowly climbing the first hill, if you hear the strain of the chain pulling the line of cars loaded with people higher and higher, then if you see, feel, and hear the car tearing down the hill—feeling your muscles tighten, hearing people screaming, feeling yourself pressed against the side of the car as you zoom around the first turn . . . then you know you are in a hypnotic state.

Memorize your treatment plan developed in phase two. This is what you will be experiencing. Review it until you can recall it easily.

If at any time during the hypnotic state you are interrupted, simply stop your forward journey, count quickly from one to twenty, and awaken fully. When the interruption is over you can reinduce the state quickly and proceed with your session.

Set aside about twenty minutes during which you will be free from interruptions. Lower the lights, find a comfortable chair, lean back, and relax. Allow thoughts about work, children, friends, and problems to fade away.

Let's begin. Close your eyes. Suggest to yourself that all the energy is leaving the muscles in your eyelids to the point where there is no energy left in them at all. They are heavy. They feel heavy. They feel solidly closed.

Now raise your right hand and turn it palm upward. Visualize in your mind's eye a very large and heavy book, perhaps a dictionary, placed on your palm. Feel the tremendous weight. Because of the angle of your outstretched arm and hand this book feels immensely heavy, and it is quickly tiring all the muscle fibers in your arm, bicep, and forearm. The book feels as if it weighs twenty pounds, and it is getting impossible to keep your hand elevated. The dictionary is pressing your arm and hand down, down, down. You're not fighting this feeling but allowing it to happen, using your active imagination. When your hand touches your lap or chair, the book disappears and you are just letting yourself go completely.

Remind yourself that the universe of your mind has no limits. The deeper and deeper you go the better you feel, and all you have to do to go deeper and deeper is just to let yourself go completely.

Now, start to count very, very, very slowly backward from 20 . . . 19 . . . relaxing all the muscles in your face . . . 18 . . . letting all the tension leave the muscles in your neck . . . 17 . . . relaxing your shoulders and arms . . . 16 . . . letting the tension leave your hands . . . 15 . . . just letting yourself go deeper and deeper. Try to develop a sensation of movement or velocity, set at your own speed, going deeper and deeper, remembering that the deeper you go the better you feel.

Now, 14 . . . 13 . . . 12 . . . 11 . . . relaxing the muscles in your chest and abdomen . . . 10 . . . 9 . . . letting the tension go in your pelvis . . . 8 . . . 7 . . . 6 . . . deeper and deeper and deeper . . . 5 . . . 4 . . . relaxing all the muscles in your legs . . . 3 . . . 2 . . . feel the relaxation in your feet . . . and toes . . . 1.

Now, at 1, using your active imagination and all of your senses, reexperience a very happy but physically exciting scene from your life such as a roller coaster ride, a fast horse race, going down a high water slide, or some similar experience. Hear it, feel it . . . hold on . . . and when you experience this event *as if you are there* then you know you have succeeded at inducing, by self-hypnosis, an Enhanced State of Consciousness. If you are not successful don't be discouraged. Self-induced hypnosis is like learning to become a good long-distance runner. It takes a lot of practice. Over and over and over.

When you do finally achieve the *you-are-there* experience, continue for the next five minutes to experience the scenes that you developed in your treatment plan—the pain, the healing, the relief—just as you did before. Allow your experiences to become as vivid and real as possible. After approximately five minutes with your treatment plan, clear your mind and develop a comfortable, pleasant feeling.

Allow yourself to enjoy the pleasure you feel. When you are ready to return to a fully conscious state, simply tell yourself you are going to count from one to twenty and when you get to twenty, you will open your eyes. You will feel refreshed, relaxed, and secure. Experience the return as if coming from a distant journey. When you reach twenty you will open your eyes and be fully awake and alert.

You'll notice that the more you practice inducing a state of self-hypnosis, the deeper and the more intense the *you-are-there* experience will become, and the more rapidly you will be able to achieve it. After several weeks of practice, instead of twenty minutes, you will be able to induce yourself in a minute or two. Many people who become proficient induce themselves many times during the day to get repeated exposure to and benefits from their treatment plan.

This is how our patients fared with their training in self-hypnosis.

Marie's back pain receded almost immediately in response to twice-daily practice. Within two weeks she found that one session each day yielded significant relief.

Ellen's snacking stopped. She realized that she felt in control of her life—something she had not felt for a long time. Because of her new attitude she had the self-discipline to begin a regular exercise program and lose the pounds she wanted to shed. She performs her hypnosensory training two to three times a week as "maintenance," and has kept the weight off.

George reported that after a month of practice he and his wife had intercourse successfully on half of their attempts. After three months they were successful nearly all of the time.

You should reach your goal as well if you can practice twice daily for several weeks, particularly if you are trying to alleviate a condition, habit, fear, or behavior.

The two plans outlined here, thermal biofeedback and self-hypnosis, in conjunction with the medical treatment of your doctor and your own desire to observe a sound health program of nutrition and exercise, will help you reprogram your mind-body connection.

And as you do, you will find that Profound Sensitivity Syndrome cannot prevail. You can do a great deal to control your health. You can become the decision-maker, with the new ability to act as you wish.

# 9

# Control Your Smoking

When we say someone can control his or her smoking we mean he or she can *stop* smoking completely, and stay stopped. Sound impossible? Perhaps this chapter will change your mind. I am happy to say that I have seen many converts to this way of thinking. During the past four years, for instance, Dr. Lipton and I have treated hundreds of patients for smoking cessation—and our data shows an 85 percent success rate.

We have outlined here a program that, if followed, will be as effective as the one we use in our stop-smoking clinic. Here is help for you or someone you love who smokes and wants to quit.

## Smoking and $PS^2$

Everything affects people with $PS^2$ more profoundly than those who do not have $PS^2$, and smoking is no exception. Dr. Lipton and I have observed some interesting clinical findings about the characteristics and reactions of $PS^2$ smokers.

First, although some people with $PS^2$ are heavy smokers, the majority smoke between one-half and one and one-half packs a day. Further, there appears to be a higher percentage of $PS^2$ smokers who smoke only between one-half and one pack a day than in the non-$PS^2$ population. We feel that because the effects of smoking on $PS^2$ people are so much more profound, they tend to limit themselves.

Second, unfortunately, $PS^2$ smokers react physically as if they were smoking much more. It is not unusual for a $PS^2$ smoker to be in my office with a heavy hacking cough and say that he or she smokes only from five to ten cigarettes a day. Based on the extent his or her health has been impared, I would expect a response of two to three packs a day.

Although we have not had an opportunity to analyze the data statistically at the writing of this book, it appears that $PS^2$ sufferers who smoke between five and ten cigarettes a day have obstructive lung disease equivalent to non-$PS^2$ smokers who smoke two or three times that number of cigarettes. Although smoking is disastrous to everyone, if you suffer from $PS^2$ stop right now!

*Jane's Asthma.* Jane, a 41-year-old mother of two children, came to me because of her severe asthma. She had seen a pulmonary specialist who placed her on Theo-Dur (a medication for asthma), which made her heart pound and caused her to have difficulty sleeping.

She indicated that she smoked two to four low-nicotine-and-tar cigarettes a day, and that she was advised by her doctor to stop smoking. Because of the low number of cigarettes she smoked daily, she did not feel that smoking caused her asthma.

I gave Jane a pulmonary function test and found she was suffering from severe obstructive lung disease. Based upon her history, her physical examination, her anxiety and depression, her allergic reactions, and a host of other $PS^2$ symptoms, I insisted she stop smoking immediately—telling her that her two to four cigarettes were equivalent to one to two packs for someone else. At first she looked at me as if I were bonkers, but after further explanation she agreed to stop for two weeks.

When I saw her two weeks later she told me it was like a miracle. Her asthma had disappeared almost completely. On top of that she had stopped her medication and felt like a new person. For Jane, smoking even three or four cigarettes a day was disastrous.

## The Effects of Nicotine

Nicotine is a physically addictive drug, which means if you smoke your body comes to depend on it. When you smoke a cigarette the nicotine enters your bloodstream and your body begins to metabolize it or burn it up. Thirty to sixty minutes later the level of nicotine in your blood begins to drop and when it falls below that level to which your body is accustomed, physical withdrawal begins. These symptoms include agitation, gastrointestinal distress, sweating, increased heart rate, and a general sense of discomfort, anxiety, and irritation.

These unpleasant sensations that feel like drug withdrawal are what cause you to reach for the next cigarette. As you inhale the smoke and absorb the nicotine into your bloodstream again, you eliminate the unpleasant feelings, but encourage the vicious cycle to continue. Many people suffer severe withdrawal when they attempt to quit cold turkey. This can make giving up cigarettes difficult, to say the least.

Still, if the physical symptoms of nicotine withdrawal were all you had to contend with, you might be able to overcome the addiction more easily. The first three or four days would create the greatest discomfort as most of the nicotine left your body. The elimination process would continue for several weeks.

Unfortunately, along with suffering *physical* withdrawal you also experience *psychological* withdrawal, and the symptoms of this latter kind of withdrawal can be almost as wrenching as those of the former.

The entire pattern of smoking cigarettes—opening the pack, lighting up, inhaling, blowing out the smoke, flicking the ashes, and the like—is relaxing and reinforcing. You have become accustomed to smoking, and it serves as a means of reducing tension and anxiety. You have made it an important part of your life. This psychological dependency, the way you rely on cigarettes in your day-to-day life, is a powerful force.

That is why our two-prong, Dr. Mind/Dr. Body program is so effective. In fact, we believe it is the most effective smoking-cessation program in the world today. Through diet and behavioral modification techniques we can help you overcome both the physical and psychological withdrawals experienced during smoking cessation. Most important, we can help you reach your goal of leading a healthy, smoke-free life.

## Background of a Relationship

As a physician I had, since the beginning of my practice, been horrified by what cigarettes were doing to the health of my patients. I was also impressed by how, in spite of my clear warnings about their physical conditions, they continued to smoke.

I could not believe it—and felt helpless to do anything about it. They were coming to me to help their breathing, their heart conditions, ulcers, high blood pressure, but I knew that as long as they continued to smoke, their physical health would continue to deteriorate, regardless of what I did to treat them.

I tried every approach, from scare tactics ("Jean, you'll drop dead if you don't stop!") to supportive concern ("You know, Harry, you really should stop smoking. It's so important for your health. I know you can do it."). Nothing worked. I referred them to various smoking-cessation programs that helped only a few.

A further incentive to find an answer to the smoking problem developed after I became Secretary of Health and Mental Hygiene for the state of Maryland. I was amazed at the impact cigarette smoking has on every aspect of our health as citizens, not to mention the incredible cost in terms of dollars, decreased productivity, and loss of life. So I started a search to find what new techniques were available to help people stop smoking.

I heard about a physician in Paris who had a promising new approach, so, in April 1979, I traveled to Paris and met Dr. Michel Bicheron, a specialist in the treatment of arthritis. Quite by accident Dr. Bicheron had discovered that a mixture of vitamins, minerals, and sodium bicarbonate in a procaine base, when injected into the affected joints of his patients, had an unexpected side effect: It curbed their desire to smoke.

His curiosity whetted, Dr. Bicheron learned that one of his colleagues, an acupuncturist, had achieved some success by inserting needles into four acupuncture points. Dr. Bicheron wondered about combining the treatments, and, putting his theory into practice, injected his mixture into the four acupuncture points on the nose and ears. The patients tested reported that their desire to smoke was lessened considerably.

I incorporated Dr. Bicheron's technique into my practice, eliminating the shots in the ears and nose, and over the next eight years made significant improvements. Today I administer medications that substantially reduce the physical craving for cigarettes. I adapted the content of these nutrients into the diet plan that follows later in this chapter so that it offers benefits similar to those available to the patients who take part in my smoking-cessation program.

I believe up to that point it was the most effective stop-smoking program in existence. It got an added boost when a colleague of mine became interested in the psychological aspects of addiction.

*A Colleague's Father's Cancer.* It had started because his father was a heavy smoker—three packs a day. The summer before he was to go to college, my future colleague, who planned to be a brain surgeon, won a National Science Foundation grant to spend three months at a cancer research institute. Before long he decided to study psychology instead. Why? Because he worked with patient after patient who lay in bed half-dead from lung cancer, cancer of the stomach, or other cancers, smoking their cigarettes! It seemed unbelievable.

He went home, confronted his father about smoking, and was dismayed to get this response: "I'd rather live a shorter life than a miserable one" (miserable without cigarettes, that is).

What did he do? As any intelligent and rational student

would, he started to smoke! In no time at all he was up to two packs a day and over the next fifteen years, now as a psychologist, increased to three packs.

This created some professional embarrassment. Whenever a patient became annoyed at him for confronting him or her with an issue, he or she might say, "Look who's talking. What are you smoking for?" To a psychotherapist this was a real handicap. He was further influenced by the fact that he could not walk up three flights of stairs without wanting to lie down and rest.

So in 1981 he stopped smoking. How? Cold turkey. He told all of his patients that he was going to quit smoking. Once he had done this he knew he had no choice but to stop. In his line of work he would have lost all of his credibility—and many of his patients.

It was agony. He considered changing his profession so he could continue smoking but because, as he says, he had no other marketable talent he had to stop smoking, which he did. And this colleague (I am sure you have guessed by now that it is Dr. Lipton) began to address the psychological addiction of smoking, with which he was so familiar. This was the backup my stop-smoking program needed, because I found that some of my patients were returning to smoking in spite of the fact that they had no physical addiction or craving for nicotine.

Sadly, Dr. Lipton's father died in his arms at the age of 64 from cancer of the stomach and pancreas. Perhaps if he had really understood the potential for loss of life and the grief his loved ones would suffer he would have been able to quit many years earlier.

Yet, perhaps not. As human beings we function on two levels, intellectual and emotional. Unfortunately, these two levels are not always well integrated. They oftentimes seem to exist independently. What we know does not influence what we feel, and our feelings tend to call the shots.

I tell you these stories in the hope that it may help you face up to a serious question: Do you want to live a longer, healthier life, sharing it with those who love you, or do you want to think, "It won't happen to me"?

I am sure you are acquainted with the life-threatening effects of smoking. It is a major contributor to everything from emphysema to heart disease. But did you know that once you stop smoking your body will start to heal itself from the damaging effects? Once you have become a nonsmoker the cell-damaging effects of nicotine and other irritants collectively known as "tars" will be eliminated. Your body will begin a healing process that is measurable almost immediately.

For instance, according to pulmonary-function tests, a former smoker's breathing capacity shows improvement in ninety percent of cases after only *one month.* And imagine how much healthier, how much more vigorous you will be after you have quit the habit.

*Deidre's Osteoporosis.* Deidre, 47, was a heavy smoker—three packs a day for 32 years. Up until menopause she had no trouble maintaining her ideal weight and had led a life full of vigor. At that time, however, she began to experience hot flashes, extreme fatigue, headaches, spells of irritability, and steady weight gain. Six months prior to my examination of her she developed pain in her lower back and above her knees.

Lab tests showed that her body was not producing enough female hormones. Bone-density studies showed that she also had decreased calcification, or osteoporosis. This is a common occurrence, easily remedied by giving the patient the proper female hormones and calcium supplements—and getting them to stop smoking. Smoking causes calcium to be leached from the bones and worsens osteoporosis. (In instances in which the patient has a family history of breast tumors, female-hormone treatment is not recommended.)

Deidre began to follow my stop-smoking diet, an appropriate exercise plan, and went through my one-day stop-smoking program in Baltimore. Within six months she had returned to her ideal weight of 118 pounds. Her other symptoms vanished, and the pain from her arthritis and osteoporosis disappeared with the lessening of the weight on her back and knee joints. She regained her former vigor, her headaches vanished, and her disposition became sunny again. It has been necessary for her to continue her hormone medication, calcium supplementation, and exercise.

The reversal of Deidre's osteoporosis symptoms, resulting from a scarcity of female hormones and from smoking, was aided by her smoking cessation. Once smoking is stopped, the bone loss begins to stabilize. Deidre has not smoked a single cigarette in more than four years.

The following are questions about the effects of smoking that we are asked most often by our patients. Please read this information about tobacco abuse, withdrawal, diet, and other important topics and use it as a reference. Read sections out loud to help reinforce the information presented. The greater your understanding about how and why you smoke, the more likely you will be able to give it up for good!

## Answers to Your Questions About Smoking

Q. *What is nicotine?*

A. Found in tobacco, nicotine is a true addictive drug. It has profound and far-reaching effects on the body. When inhaled, tobacco smoke and nicotine are absorbed into the bloodstream instantaneously and alter respiratory, gastrointestinal, cardiovascular, and nervous system functions.

Q. *How does nicotine affect the brain?*

A. Part of nicotine's addictive effect is related to its ability to cause endorphins, the body's natural pain killers that produce a sense of well-being, to be released in the brain.

Without nicotine the habitual smoker's endorphin level drops, causing anxiety, discomfort, and a generally "off" mood.

Smoking another cigarette raises the endorphin level in your brain, an artificial "high" that eliminates those symptoms temporarily. The self-help program we recommend is designed to reduce sharply the uncomfortable effects of cigarette withdrawal.

Q. *Why can't I concentrate well without cigarettes?*

A. Nicotine also affects the nervous system by causing your body to produce adrenaline, a powerful hormone that, in excess, affects many vital organs adversely. In the brain, adrenaline's stimulant action boosts concentration and memory temporarily, although memory is not enhanced above that of a nonsmoker's.

The smoker's brain has been conditioned to high levels of nicotine, adrenaline, endorphins, and other stimulants. During the time between cigarettes, the smoker may suffer mild deficits in memory and concentration as these chemicals wear off. Smoking another cigarette alleviates these withdrawal symptoms and the cycle of addiction continues.

Q. *How does smoking affect my heart?*

A. Cigarette smoking is a major risk factor in the development of many heart and circulatory system ailments:

- In the heart, adrenaline and nicotine raise your pulse rate making your heart work harder than it should.
- Noradrenaline and nicotine both act to constrict and damage blood vessels throughout the body. Hardening of the arteries (atherosclerosis) develops as cholesterol builds up inside these damaged arteries, blocking blood flow to vital organs. In the brain, a stroke can result. In the heart, chest pain (angina pectoris) or heart attack

(myocardial infarction) may occur. Severe leg cramps (intermittent claudication) can develop as the leg muscles cry out for more blood. Hands and feet often become cold.

- High blood pressure develops as a result of narrowed arteries (more work for your poor heart). As a result, heart failure, stroke, kidney failure, and heart attack are more likely to occur.
- The carbon monoxide in cigarette smoke (also found in automobile exhaust) seriously lowers the level of oxygen in your blood, another insult to your heart, brain, and aching legs.

*But,* even if you already have chest pain from narrowed coronary arteries, or if you have suffered a heart attack, by ceasing to use cigarettes you will reduce significantly the risk of having a first (or second) heart attack. *This advantage starts as soon as you stop smoking and continues to increase each day you do not smoke.*

Q. *Is it true that smoking can cause or aggravate ulcers?*

A. Yes. Smoking has an impact on the development of, and recovery from, ulcers of the stomach and the first portion of the small intestine (duodenum). Studies have established that an individual who has an ulcer and who smokes will experience delayed healing of the ulcer, as compared to an individual who does not smoke.

Similarly, ulcers are more likely to occur in smokers as compared to nonsmokers. It seems that nicotine stimulates the abnormal flow of stomach acids and digestive enzymes, thereby making ulcer development more likely.

Q. *What are some of the effects of smoking on nonsmokers?*

A. Cigarette smoking is dangerous to the health of those around you. Unintentional exposure to cigarette smoke—

known as passive smoking—results when a nonsmoker is subjected to a smoker's exhaled air as well as to "side-stream smoke" that pours off the tip of a burning cigarette.

- The children of smokers have more respiratory illness and miss more school than do children of nonsmokers.
- Persons with heart and lung diseases have increased symptoms of illness (chest pain, shortness of breath) when exposed to passive smoke.
- Passive smokers' allergies are worsened as a result of exposure to smoke.
- Women who smoke during pregnancy deliver lower weight babies than do nonsmokers. The unborn baby becomes a passive smoker and is forced to "smoke" each time the mother does.

Q. *Is there really such a thing as "smoker's wrinkles"?*

A. An experienced observer can pick out the smokers in a crowd by looking at their faces. Smoking can be linked to the development of facial wrinkles and crow's feet, partly because of reduced levels of oxygen in the skin. Once these wrinkles occur, cessation of smoking will not make them disappear. Stopping will prevent their further development.

Q. *If I know cigarette smoking is so bad, why do I still smoke?*

A. Smoking is identified as a source of pleasure. The endorphins released in the brain while smoking bring about a sense of well-being. This is especially pleasurable when endorphin release helps modify the unpleasant effects of stressful situations.

The main drive to continue smoking, however, is physical addiction to nicotine and the avoidance of nicotine withdrawal.

Q. *Why can't I just switch to a low-tar, low-nicotine brand?*

A. Studies have shown that people smoke the number of cigarettes necessary to maintain a given level of nicotine in their bloodstreams. The fallacy behind low-tar, low-nicotine brands is that they do not decrease tobacco use. One simply smokes more cigarettes, inhales more deeply, and holds the inhalations longer in order to maintain the same blood nicotine levels obtained from smoking "regular" cigarettes.

Q. *Why do I smoke more when I'm tense or when I drink coffee and alcohol?*

A. Tension of any kind causes an increased loss of nicotine into the urine. Tension also has an acidifying effect on urine, and nicotine is removed from the body faster under these conditions. More cigarettes are consumed, therefore, to replenish the nicotine and alleviate withdrawal symptoms.

Alcohol is another potent urine acidifier. This chemical, through the same urine-acidifying mechanism, stimulates the urge to smoke just as stress does.

If you drink decaffeinated coffee, use a brand in which the caffeine has been removed by a water process. Otherwise the chemicals used in the decaffeinating process cause endorphin levels to drop. The result? An urge to smoke!

Q. *Can altering my diet help me stop smoking?*

A. Absolutely. Through the dietary changes outlined in this chapter, the urine can be made less acidic, slowing nicotine loss and reducing the urge to consume tobacco under stress. Withdrawal from nicotine can be made easier as a result.

Q. *What part does behavioral conditioning play in the psychological addiction to nicotine?*

A. Behavioral conditioning can be thought of as "habit." This conditioning is another important reason why people continue to smoke, in addition to nicotine's addictive properties. Once a smoker becomes accustomed to lighting up twenty, forty, or more times a day, it seems impossible to get through the day without cigarettes.

People tend to smoke in certain situations. It can almost become a ritual: after a meal, while talking on the phone, with coffee and/or alcohol, or when tense or nervous.

Along with the physical addiction to cigarette smoking, behavioral conditioning is responsible for the psychological addiction to tobacco use. If you are accustomed to craving cigarettes under certain conditions, you may continue to crave them even after your physical addiction to nicotine has ceased.

Q. *What can I expect to experience when I actually stop smoking?*

A. Cravings for a cigarette will likely come in waves with the most severe during the first three or four days. During this acute period you must cope with both your physical and your psychological addictions.

The intensity of these cravings will decrease over the days and weeks that follow. This is not to say that all of a sudden a high wave won't come along now and then. But, in general, as time continues, the height and frequency of the waves will gradually become more and more manageable until, finally, they all but disappear.

The secret to becoming a nonsmoker is *time*—resisting temptation for a long enough period to allow the physical and psychological cravings to weaken and weaken and weaken. Never again take that first cigarette.

Q. *How tough will it be?*

A. Kicking any addiction is not easy and you must anticipate discomfort during the first several weeks as big waves of craving come along. But you can be assured that the discomfort you will feel giving up cigarettes will be much less than would be experienced if you did not follow the steps outlined here for you.

There is no technology available to eliminate the cravings you are likely to have. Their intensity will depend on how long you have smoked, the strength and quantity of cigarettes you are used to smoking, how deeply you have inhaled, and whether or not you have $PS^2$.

Some heavy smokers report surprise at how easily they were able to quit while other, lighter smokers report great difficulty. The experience is a highly personal one. I recommend that you anticipate the worst. You may be pleasantly surprised that it is much easier to quit than you had imagined, but do not count on it.

## The Stop-Smoking Program

### Step 1: Calculation

This plan will reduce the level of nicotine in your bloodstream gradually and, in conjunction with the other steps, lessen symptoms of withdrawal when you quit.

The calculation is quite simple. If the average number of cigarettes you smoke each day is fourteen or less, starting tomorrow decrease the number you smoke each day by one until you smoke none.

If the average number of cigarettes you smoke daily is greater than fourteen, divide the number of cigarettes smoked by fourteen. This is the number of cigarettes you should eliminate each day, starting tomorrow. (If it is a fraction, go to the next highest number.)

As an example, suppose you smoke 28 cigarettes a day; $28 \div 14 = 2$.

Consumption, therefore, should be reduced as follows:

| | |
|---|---|
| Day 1 of reduction: | 28 − 2 = 26 cigarettes a day. |
| Day 2 | 26 − 2 = 24 |
| Day 3 | 24 − 2 = 22 |
| Day 4 | 22 − 2 = 20 |
| (etc.) | |
| Day 14 | 2 − 2 = 0 |

Here is a chart to get you started:

Day 1: ____ − ____ = ____ cigarettes a day.
Day 2: ____ − ____ = ____
Day 3: ____ − ____ = ____
Day 4: ____ − ____ = ____
Day 5: ____ − ____ = ____
Day 6: ____ − ____ = ____
Day 7: ____ − ____ = ____
Day 8: ____ − ____ = ____
Day 9: ____ − ____ = ____
Day 10: ____ − ____ = ____
Day 11: ____ − ____ = ____
Day 12: ____ − ____ = ____
Day 13: ____ − ____ = ____
Day 14: ____ − ____ = ____

**Step 2: The Stop-Smoking Diet**

This diet is designed to decrease the effects of nicotine withdrawal so that you can give up smoking with less craving for nicotine and without gaining weight. It is a well-balanced, healthy meal plan that is designed to counter the excess acidity in your body produced by tobacco abuse.

Most studies have shown that when people stop smoking only about one-third gain weight. Another third lose weight, and the remaining third show no change in weight.

One tip about eating: Many people report that sunflower seeds reduce the craving for cigarettes, so purchase a supply of the roasted, unsalted variety to munch on freely. Also get some low-calorie hard candies to suck on during the difficult period of nicotine detoxification. This will help satisfy your needs for oral gratification as a substitute for cigarettes.

Follow this diet for fourteen days *from the time you start to cut back.*

## Dr. Solomon's Stop-Smoking Diet

156 grams carbohydrates
40 grams fat
78 grams protein
1302 calories

### Breakfast

½ cup orange juice or ½ fresh grapefruit
¾ cup high vitamin/mineral cereal
1 cup skim milk*
Water-processed decaffeinated coffee, tea
Saccharin

### Morning Snack

1 fruit choice—see Lists, p. 199

### Lunch

Choose one of the following protein products (may be hot or cold):

¼ cup lowfat cottage cheese
¼ cup water-packed tuna or salmon
2 slices lean roast beef; roast veal
2 slices roast turkey or chicken without skin
1 egg—poached, hard-boiled, soft-boiled
1 slice low-fat cheese food
5 small boiled shrimp

1 cup vegetables, served hot or cold without margarine or butter—see Lists
1 cup salad—see Lists

* If allergic to milk, substitute soy milk and delete any cheese.

Salad dressing should be a good low-calorie product. No more than 1 Tbsp is to be used with each serving.
1 cup of skim milk or 1 cup plain low-fat yogurt
1 Fruit Choice—see Lists. If yogurt is chosen in place of milk, fresh or canned fruit can be added to it for dessert.
Diet soda, water-processed decaf coffee, tea, low-calorie lemonade

**Afternoon Snack**
1 Fruit Choice—see Lists

**Dinner**
Choose one of the following protein products:

3 ounces of lean roast beef; corned beef; ground round steak; tenderloin; rib roast
Veal—leg, loin, shank, cutlets
Poultry—chicken, turkey, Cornish hen, pheasant
Pork (limit to no more than once a week) loin, shoulder arm roast, lean chops, ground ham, center ham slices

Meat products may be baked, broiled, roasted, steamed.
All visible fat should be removed prior to cooking.
Skin should be removed from poultry products prior to cooking.

1 full cup vegetables—see Lists
1 full cup salad—see Lists
2 teaspoons margarine, if desired.

Choose one starch from the following:

½ cup mashed potatoes
1 small baked potato
1 small potato, boiled
¼ cup sweet potato
½ cup green peas
½ cup lima beans
1 slice white, rye, pumpernickel, or whole wheat bread
½ hamburger bun
½ plain or onion bagel
1 small dinner roll
½ cup rice
½ cup noodles

1 Fruit Choice—see Lists
Diet soda, water-processed decaf coffee, tea, low-calorie lemonade

**Evening Snack**
1 cup skim milk or 1 cup plain yogurt
1 fruit choice—see Lists

## LISTS

**Fruit Choices**
½ cup orange juice; ½ cup grapefruit juice
1 fresh peach; pear; apple; orange; apricot; tangerine
¼ fresh cantaloupe or honeydew melon
2 canned (sugar-free) peach halves; pear halves; apricot halves; pineapple slices
½ cup unsweetened applesauce; grapefruit sections; orange sections

**Salad**
Includes any or all of the following:

lettuce, romaine, endive, Chinese cabbage, radish, watercress
fresh greens such as kale, spinach, beet greens
bean sprouts, alfalfa sprouts
green pepper slices
tomato wedges
sliced mushrooms

1 Tbsp low-calorie salad dressing

**Vegetables**

| | | |
|---|---|---|
| asparagus | cauliflower | beans—string or wax |
| beets | celery | yellow squash |
| broccoli | cucumbers | zucchini squash |
| carrots | greens | sauerkraut |
| tomatoes | tomato juice | V-8 juice |
| turnips | okra | rutabaga |

## SAMPLE MENU

**Breakfast**
½ cup orange juice
¾ cup Total, with saccharin, if desired
1 cup skim milk
Water-processed decaffeinated coffee

**Morning Snack**
1 fresh peach

**Lunch**
¼ cup water-packed tuna stuffed into large tomato
1 cup salad with 1 Tbsp salad dressing
1 cup V-8 juice
1 cup skim milk
¼ fresh cantaloupe with lemon wedge
Low-calorie lemonade

**Afternoon Snack**
1 fresh apple

**Dinner**
1 medium chicken breast baked with tomato sauce
½ cup rice
½ cup broccoli with lemon wedge
½ cup carrots with chopped parsley
1 cup salad—1 Tbsp salad dressing
2 tsp margarine (if desired)
½ fresh grapefruit
Water-processed decaf coffee

**Evening Snack**
1 cup skim milk
2 unsweetened peach halves (blend into fruit/milk drink)

**Step 3: Biofeedback**

As discussed earlier, the psychological addiction to cigarettes is a powerful force. Smokers become dependent on the apparently relaxing effects of smoking. It is, unfortunately, a self-perpetuating tension reliever. That is, the absence of cigarettes creates a tension that is relieved when you smoke another cigarette. This association is built up in your mind: tension = cigarette; tension = cigarette.

You can use the biofeedback techniques you learned in chapter 8 to break this conditioning, substituting biofeedback and the tension reduction that results from it as a way to bridge the gap. Thus, you learn a new association: tension = biofeedback = no cigarette; tension = biofeedback = no cigarette.

Practice biofeedback for twenty minutes twice daily during the days of your smoking reduction to lower your overall level of tension. Then, whenever you find your urge for a cigarette to be stronger than you wish to tolerate, all you have to do is practice biofeedback for a few minutes. You will find that your level of tension and the intensity of your craving for a cigarette will diminish. Use this technique as often as you need to resist the temptation to smoke.

You may also want to use self-hypnosis to help curb your desire for a smoke. While you are in the Enhanced State of Consciousness, visualize yourself as a conqueror engaged in winning the battle against cigarette addiction and regaining control over your body and your life.

### Step 4: Exercise

An extremely important part of successful smoking cessation is to increase your level of physical activity. Aerobic exercise can work magic in controlling your cigarette cravings. It releases endorphins, as discussed in chapter 6, giving a naturally soothing effect and making the withdrawal period much more tolerable.

We recommend that you exercise aerobically for twenty to thirty minutes a day during your early stop-smoking days. And, as always when beginning an exercise program, you should be examined by a physician before increasing your level of activity.

### Step 5: Set Yourself Up

One way to help yourself give up cigarettes is to "set yourself up."

Tell everyone whose opinion you value that you have made a *serious commitment* to yourself to stop smoking cigarettes and to remain a nonsmoker. Tell your children, spouse, employer, siblings, parents, or closest friends that you will quit no matter what, if it's the last thing you do. This is the route Dr. Lipton took when he told his patients of his decision to stop smoking, and it was particularly effective for him.

What purpose does this technique serve? Having made such firm commitments to those who are important to you, you will feel stronger about resisting the urge to smoke, rather than disappoint them and embarrass yourself. Plus, they may be able to help you through some difficult times.

If you find out you are unable to make such strong commitments to those closest to you, sit down and try to find out why.

Also, realize that you must conquer any ambivalence about shaking the habit before you can make this commitment to those who mean the most to you. You must be willing to "set yourself up" for potential embarrassment if this technique is to work. It is the thought of being embarrassed that will help you through the times of extreme temptation. Make yourself proud! Make your support system proud!

### Step 6 (Optional): Stopping with a Friend

Many of our patients have reported enhanced success at giving up smoking when they joined with a friend and did it together. We have found that this approach can be extremely successful as long as you understand that one huge pitfall is involved. First we will describe how the system should work and then the pitfall.

Although nicotine withdrawal can be highly individualized, you and your buddy will be experiencing many of the same discomforts. Provide each other with lots of encouragement and follow these suggestions for best results:

1. Agree upon a mutual day you will quit for good. Arrange your charts so you begin tapering off at the same time and quit at the same time. (You will be able to celebrate your smoke-free anniversaries together!)
2. Contract with each other that you will *without fail* talk on the telephone or in person at least once a day for the first thirty days. Be flexible with your agreed upon times, changing them as necessary, but do not fail to speak with one another each and every day.

3. Be supportive, taking turns *really listening* nonjudgmentally to each other's feelings and concerns. This is a healing process and benefits the listener as much as the speaker.

4. Keep in mind that the physical and psychological alterations experienced by a new nonsmoker are unique to the individual. Try to avoid comparing yourselves step-by-step throughout the program. Rather, be available to listen and to care.

Now for the big pitfall of the buddy system, which is why this step of the program is optional.

Stopping smoking with a friend is fantastic—as long as you and your friend stop smoking. The problem comes when your friend does not make it. You now have a convenient excuse to fail as well. After all, you don't want to make him or her feel like a failure.

We have also observed that the one who fails tends unconsciously to *want* the successful partner to fail. Comments oftentimes go like this: "So, Harriet, you're still not smoking, huh? Amazing. I would never have guessed it. I'm happy for you, really I am. I knew you were a much better person than I am and had so much more self-discipline and control. And I don't want you to feel guilty, either. You were a good friend and the few days you didn't call me as we had agreed really wouldn't have made any difference, I'm sure, in my continuing not to smoke."

Get the picture? Unless you realize from the inception that you stop smoking only for yourself and that the only one who is going to take care of your own health is you, then joining a friend to stop smoking may be a bigger liability than an asset.

## Two Pitfalls

There are two major pitfalls along the road to successful smoking cessation. These are particularly disastrous during the crucial first thirty days, when you are formalizing the image of yourself as a nonsmoker. These two dangers are good friends who smoke and alcohol.

Your smoking friends may seem encouraging and supportive of your efforts to kick the habit. True friends certainly want the best for one another, and no one is likely to discourage or condemn you outwardly.

But on an unconscious level your resolve to stop smoking represents a significant threat to them and stirs up many emotions about their own smoking habits. Thus, smokers who are confronted with those attempting to quit will—inadvertently, unconsciously—find themselves undermining their friends' efforts.

This occurs in subtle, but nevertheless destructive, ways. A friend who says, "Good luck. I've tried to quit so many times I've lost count," does not bolster your resolve and commitment. "Why quit? It's never worked for me. How can it work for you?" are not the positive, encouraging words you need to hear. Some friends become even more blatant in their undermining behavior by offering you a cigarette or suggesting that you wait until another time to quit.

Being prepared for this ahead of time will help you deal with it. Practice some responses that would be appropriate in this situation, such as, "I've made a commitment to myself and I believe I can stick to it."

Or "share the blame" for your desire for a healthier life-style with someone else, such as: "My doctor said I should quit, and I trust his judgment" or "My wife finally convinced me I shouldn't smoke with a new baby in the house" (or "around the grandchildren"). It shouldn't be too hard to find a co-conspirator.

Alcohol is responsible for more failures to give up cigarettes than any other single factor. Let us stress it: If you drink alcohol while trying to quit smoking, you will likely fail.

The very nature of alcohol reduces inhibitions, including the commitment you have made not to smoke. It is absolutely imperative that you be aware of the dangers of consuming alcohol—for the first thirty days and thereafter.

Parties are particularly hazardous because of peer pressure. Many people, many friends, will be smoking, thereby creating great temptation to smoke, and alcohol will be present as an additional threat to your resolve. Again, forewarned is forearmed. Be careful with your alcohol consumption—better yet, avoid it!

## Further Tips

During the first thirty days while developing the "new you," choose social activities where smoking is limited or prohibited. Visit museums and libraries. Go to a theater or a movie. Spend time out-of-doors enjoying the fresh air. Socialize with nonsmoking friends as much as possible. Request seating in nonsmoking areas of restaurants, planes, trains, and at work, if possible. Learn to enjoy the pleasures of freedom from tobacco smoke, continually building up the image of yourself as a nonsmoker.

Think about the benefits. You know the long-term benefits, such as those that relate to your physical health. To the person who has just quit, however, these can seem too remote to provide adequate rewards for his or her efforts.

So think about these other benefits. After you get over the initial hump, your energy level will increase and your concentration and thinking will sharpen. Sexual functioning will be enhanced as the arterioles and capillaries—tiny blood vessels—are released from the constricting effects of nicotine. Your mood will lift as you feel like the master of your own destiny. You will have an improved sense of smell and taste. Many reformed smokers report improved vision and hearing as well. Improved blood flow to the skin will result in better tone and decreased wrinkling.

## Back in Control

*You can and will succeed at licking the powerful nicotine addiction ruling your life.*

The power of positive thoughts like this one should never be underestimated. Many smokers fail to realize that their sense of control has been eroded as a result of being enslaved to the cigarette habit. Unfortunately, this feeling of helplessness can spread into the rest of the smoker's life as well.

Those who kick the habit, however, develop a realistic and well-deserved increased sense of control over their lives. There are few things that require more self-discipline than saying no to cigarettes. Each and every time you do, you are enhancing your sense of competence, and this wonderful feeling generalizes itself to your life as a whole.

Your mental attitude is the single greatest determinant of your success. See yourself as a winner. Fix an image in your mind that visualizes yourself as a nonsmoker, a conqueror of addiction to tobacco, a winner who—no matter how intense the craving—will not succumb to temptation.

*I am a nonsmoker. I choose not to smoke cigarettes.*

Believe in yourself. You are a tenacious, immovable, stubborn, committed person. One who resists all temptation to smoke. One who will succeed. A *winner!*

# 10

# Control Your Allergies

When most of us hear the word *allergy* we think of sniffles, sneezes, and wheezes, or, perhaps, hives. We think of pollen and ragweed. We remember hay fever commercials of red-eyed, runny-nosed, miserable people seeking relief in a tablet or a capsule.

We do not usually think of citrus fruits, eggs, milk, wheat, corn, tobacco smoke, perfume, dust, and mold. Yet these are just a few common causes of reactions in people suffering miserably from allergies. An allergy to these—and many other substances—may not make you sneeze. Instead, you might develop a headache, diarrhea, an inability to think straight, depression, ringing in your ears, a weight problem, weakness, fatigue—any number of disturbing symptoms.

Strangely enough, in the case of food allergies, you might actually crave those very foods to which you are allergic. In the case of inhalant allergies, you might like the smell of the substance you are inhaling and yet be allergic to it.

Chemicals in our food, water, and air are increasing the numbers of those with allergic reactions. For instance, in order to make our foods look better and last longer, pesticides, bisulfites, nitrates, ethylene gas, and herbicides are routinely used in growing fruits and vegetables. The shiny look of the red apple in the store should be a warning sign to peel it. And some apples contain Alar, a cancer-causing pesticide. Hormones (steroids) and antibiotics are routinely added to fowl and red meat in order to make them look bigger and better.

Plus, we are subjected to pesticides, industrial wastes, fertilizers, phenol, formaldehyde, and lead exposure in our food and water. And now our indoor air is more hazardous than outdoor air.

Thus, Pat, age 48, passes out if she walks into a fabric store. Gwen, age 43, develops migraine headaches if exposed to pesticides. Michael cannot work in his office because of the presence of fiberglass. Chris, age 27, suffers from sinus congestion, dizziness, and nausea when she comes in contact with gasoline fumes, cleaning sprays, and grocery stores. Jeff, age 14, has joint pain, fatigue, and chest pain when he is around floor wax, gas heat, or vinyl in cars.

It might seem that the fight against allergies is a lost cause since it is often hard to escape from the allergen, the particular substance to which you are allergic. Fortunately, we can control many of the effects of allergies by some simple regimens.

First, I need to remind you that treatment of allergies is a controversial area of medicine that is constantly in flux. Many schools of thought exist. I can only present to you my best insights, which I have used in treating allergy patients for years. My insights grew partly out of my thorough grounding in the basic sciences when I studied for my Ph.D. in physiology, minoring in biochemistry and biophysics; they also grew out of my medical training and experience with patients at the Johns Hopkins Hospital.

These strands of experience have by no means yielded the last word, possibly because the more we learn, the more new thoughts evolve. I can offer only what has worked for many of my patients, most of whom have shown improvement.

Before we look at treatment, let's look at Shirley's case in which a combination of untreated allergies to milk, molds, and formaldehyde caused internal stress and made her Sjögren's Syndrome symptoms go out of control.

*Shirley's Sjögren's Syndrome.* Shirley, 45, was well until four years ago when she went to her gynecologist complaining of dry vagina and pain during sexual intercourse. He prescribed an estrogen cream that helped somewhat. She then saw her family doctor because various joints began hurting. He diagnosed rheumatoid arthritis and referred her to me to see if we could find a reason for the continued vaginal dryness.

We found that Shirley had a number of other symptoms, including the fact that her decreased secretion involved her entire respiratory tract, vagina, and skin. She had rheumatoid nodules, a slightly enlarged spleen, burning and itching eyes, difficulty swallowing, and decreased taste acuity. Her tongue was large, red, and smooth, and she had cracks and fissures at the corners of her mouth.

Shirley said her symptoms worsened when she drank milk, or if she went into a carpet store, or if it rained. She was tested and found to be allergic to milk, molds, and formaldehyde. Further, her laboratory tests showed, among other results, that she had too much globulin in her blood and positive Sjögren's antibodies. This added up to Sjögren's Syndrome, an autoimmune disorder. Once she was treated for her allergens and for her Sjögren's she showed marked improvement. Biofeedback helped her deal with her symptoms.

This is an example of how untreated, hidden allergies can cause internal stress, which sets off $PS^2$, and, in turn, aggravates the signs and symptoms of Sjögren's Syndrome.

Now let's get an idea of what starts the problem in the first place.

## Histamine

Whatever you are allergic to, be it milk or disinfectants, it is the histamine your body releases in response to it that does the damage.

Histamine is a biochemical substance that is released by mast cells (white cells). It is much like turning a key in a lock to open a door. When a substance you are allergic to, the antigen or key, combines with an antibody on the surface of the mast cell, the lock, then histamine is able to escape from inside the mast cell.

If the histamine goes to your bronchial tubes it makes you wheeze. If it goes to the back of your throat or lungs it makes you cough. If it goes to your nose it makes you congested. If it goes to your skin you get hives or a rash. If it goes to your GI tract you get diarrhea or abdominal pain.

In my work with allergy patients I have found another effect of allergies tied specifically to $PS^2$. The final pathway in the track of an allergen in your body is at the cellular level. The result is increased permeability across the cell membranes.

This means that the holes in the membranes of the cell become larger. Substances inside the cell that could not fit through those holes before now slip through them and travel out of the cell into the general circulation. And substances outside the cell that once could not get inside through the cell membrane now can. When this happens you get the symptoms of allergies.

This can affect any organ in your body. Allergic response affecting the brain, for instance, causes increased permeability in the brain cells and actually results in fuzzy thinking.

In my treatment of allergy patients I direct my attention toward the basic problem of correcting the cell permeability. Since nutritional deficiencies and decreased blood flow also increase permeability, the cells are strengthened by addressing these problems. Again, this is best done by the team of "Dr. Mind and Dr. Body" working together.

Dr. Mind does his part by increasing blood flow to the cells through relaxation, biofeedback, autosuggestion, and psychotherapy. Dr. Body does it by nutrition and addressing any biochemical deficiency correctable at the cell membrane level, such as prescribing medication in the case of low thyroid or getting rid of an infection, another cause of increased permeability. I also prescribe immunotherapy to desensitize the patient to the allergen.

Do you see the connection with $PS^2$? The basic defect in $PS^2$

is increased cell permeability—which exacerbates the unusual assemblage of symptoms a $PS^2$ sufferer endures. You will see later that a number of symptoms of allergies are also symptoms of $PS^2$. So we are working with the mind-body connection to correct the excess permeability of cells and reverse the effects of $PS^2$. This, in turn, will improve the response to allergens in your body.

If you have wondered whether or not you suffer from allergies, the following listing of symptoms may help you.

## Allergy Symptoms

Symptoms vary from individual to individual but include the following:

*Skin*
Itching, rash, hives, easy bruising

*Eyes*
Tearing, itching, burning, blurred vision

*Ears*
Ringing (tinnitus), itching

*Nose*
Nosebleeds, dry nose, nasal discharge, sneezing, congestion, itching, pale nasal mucous membranes

*Throat*
Dry throat, scratchy throat, burning tongue, sour taste in the mouth

*Respiratory System*
Coughing, wheezing

*Cardiovascular System*
Chest pain or tightness, rapid pulse, heart palpitations, arrhythmia (irregular heartbeat), phlebitis (inflammation of veins), vasculitis (inflammation of the blood vessels)

*Gastrointestinal System*

Bloating, nausea, vomiting, abdominal pain, diarrhea, bad breath, inflammation of the stomach and the small and large intestine, increased gas

*Musculoskeletal System*

Joint pain, muscle aches, leg cramps, back pain

*Genito-Urinary System*

Urinary frequency, urgency, itching

*Reproductive System*

Impotence, frigidity, sterility, vaginal discharge, menstrual disorders

*Central Nervous System*

Dizziness, headache, fatigue, depression, mood swings, forgetfulness, crying spells, "spacey" feeling, decreased attention span and concentration, hyperactivity, inability to reason, mental confusion, diminished short-term memory, anxiety, weakness, exhaustion, increased sensitivity to heat, cold, pain, light, and sound, irritability, short temper, nightmares, insomnia, tremor, decreased coordination, restlessness, stuttering, and some emotional disturbances

*General*

Heavy sweating, fluctuations in weight with fluid retention, increased sensitivity to drugs and anesthesia, post-surgery complications, and recurrent infections

If you have any or a number of these symptoms you might want to turn detective and try to determine what is making them appear. Here are guidelines to help you understand possible causes of what may well be your allergic symptoms.

## Food Allergies

Do you find yourself craving a particular food and then feeling worse minutes to hours after eating it?

Do the symptoms go away if you eat the food again?

Does this happen with carob, wheat, corn, milk, soybeans, eggs, citrus fruits, or peanuts?

Do you stick to a certain diet and feel bad if you change it?

Many people who are allergic to a certain food become addicted to it—that is, they eat a lot of it on a regular basis. If they stop eating it, they feel disturbing symptoms starting up—symptoms that go away as soon as they eat the food again. This makes it hard for many to lose weight. And for some, the unpleasant symptoms do not go away when they start eating the food again.

### Treatment

If you find this is the case, try eating the offending foods no more than every four days if possible. By rotating the foods you help the body clear the offending culprit and diminish or eliminate the allergic symptom. You might want to avoid the foods altogether.

Keep a food diary and write down any symptoms that occur over a 24-hour period. If a food such as egg is considered a possible culprit, eliminate it from your diet for two weeks. Initially the adverse symptoms may actually intensify but after approximately four days you can expect to feel better if you are right about the suspected food.

It will also help if you to eat sensibly and limit sweets, junk food, and food with added salt. Eat more fresh vegetables and fruits, fish and fowl.

## Inhalant Allergies

Do you develop allergic symptoms if you walk into a dusty room?

Do changes in nature in spring and fall affect you physically?

Is it hard for you to be around furry pets?

Does damp weather bother you? If so, suspect a mold allergy.

Common inhalant allergies include grasses (April to June), weeds (August to October), molds (October to March, but this can be perennial), trees (February to April), dust and dust mites as well as cats and dogs. The types of trees, grasses, and weeds that produce inhalant allergies depend on the specific region of the country.

**Treatment**

The type of treatment you use depends on the duration and severity of symptoms. Most inhalant allergy problems can be controlled by avoidance. For example, do not have a cat or dog in the house if you or a family member develops allergic symptoms with exposure to a pet.

Dust and mold are not so easy to avoid, particularly outdoors. Mold exposure not only gives typical allergic responses such as nasal congestion, nasal and eye itching, and asthma, but can cause headaches, fatigue, depression, and joint pain as well. Think of how many people you know who get joint pain in rainy weather or can predict when it will rain.

Try to keep your home as dust- and mold-free as possible. Bathrooms and kitchens are likely sources of mold, as are damp basements, houseplants, dried flowers, upholstered furniture, and carpeting. You could cover pillows, mattresses, and box springs with sealed slipcovers made of vinyl or synthetic materials. Leaving a small electric light on in closets will reduce humidity—and mildew. Check humidifiers, dehumidifiers, and air-conditioning equipment regularly and vacuum often.

Consult with your physician to see if medication is indicated to control the problem. If none of the above helps, consider consulting an allergist to see if desensitizing immunotherapy is indicated.

## Chemical Allergies

Do you feel funny if you enter carpet, department, grocery, or fabric stores?

Does the odor of soap, detergents, colognes, perfume, nail polish remover, shampoos, or household deodorants bother you?

What about insecticides, sprays, mothballs, ammonia, disinfectants, newsprint, fluorescent lighting, paints, ceramics, your working environment, wood-burning stoves, fireplaces, gas heat, diesel, exhaust, or oil fumes?

What about your reaction to commercially or restaurant-prepared foods versus home-prepared fresh foods?

Do you tolerate cooked or peeled vegetables and fruits better than those "fresh" from the store?

### Treatment

Low-level exposures to chemicals can cause severe, debilitating allergic symptoms in some. They can go unrecognized by others but may have a cumulative effect. Important factors include genetic background, the chemical compound involved, the person's nutritional intake, length of exposure, previous exposures, age, sex and "total allergy load," meaning anything that pushes the individual over the threshold, including all types of allergy and both inside and outside stressors.

Here is a list of products to use and some to avoid if you have any of these allergic sensitivities.

| | **Use** | **Avoid** |
|---|---|---|
| Cooking | Glass, iron, or stainless-steel cookware; cellophane bags for storage | Teflon, aluminum or chemically treated utensils, gas stoves, plastic dishes |
| Clothing | Natural fibers such as cotton, wool, silk, linen | Nylon, polyesters, synthetics |

| | | |
|---|---|---|
| Bedding | Cotton mattress covers, sheets, blankets | Foam rubber, synthetics, polyester |
| Floor covering | Hardwood, stone, linoleum, and ceramic tiles; terrazzo; scatter rugs; nylon, wool, or cotton carpeting | Jute backing; wall-to-wall carpeting |
| Pest control | Pyrethrum is the best available at the present time | |
| Painting | Latex, and mix 500 grams baking soda with 5 liters of paint | |
| Heating | Electric; hot water pipes; good filter system | Gas, oil, glued-in insulation |
| Water | Spring or distilled | Chemically treated |
| Furnishings | Metal, glass, hardwood | Synthetics—plastic, foam rubber |
| Building materials | Marble, stone, ceramic tile | |
| Glass cleaner | Vinegar | |
| Clothes washing | Borax, baking soda (one-half cup) | |

Baking soda is also good as a household cleaner, oven cleaner, brass and copper polisher, room deodorizer, refrigerator freshener, deodorant, toothpaste, or mouthwash.

## Allergies at Work

Allergies not only stir up problems of their own, but they often cause or exacerbate other diseases. The following case studies will give you an idea of the unfortunate diversity of allergies in our lives.

### Premenstrual Syndrome

The psychological symptoms of Premenstrual Syndrome (PMS) are easy for a physician to mistake for some other physical problem or for a purely psychological problem, especially if the patient herself does not realize that her crying spells or angry moods coincide with a certain time of the month.

The symptoms of PMS usually appear for a few days before the onset of every menstrual period and get better when the period arrives. For some women, however, the symptoms begin as long as two weeks before the onset of the period. Moreover, the symptoms are not identical for every woman.

The spectrum of physical symptoms includes accumulation of water in the tissues, causing a general puffiness; cramps, often severe, in the lower abdomen and/or lower back; and tender and swollen breasts. The psychological symptoms run the gamut from extreme anger or aggression to frequent crying, melancholy, depression, and anxiety.

I have found that many women with PMS are suffering from an allergic-like sensitivity to their own progesterone. Progesterone is a female hormone that increases in a woman's body from the time of ovulation to just before the onset of the menstrual period. Testing helps determine if progesterone sensitivity is the real problem behind the monthly symptoms. If it is, I treat the patient with small doses of progesterone to decrease her sensitivity and relieve her symptoms.

If, in addition to my treatment, I think counseling would be helpful, I recommend the patient see a mental health counselor to learn to relax and deal with her problems. You see, even if the symptoms of PMS are alleviated, the psychological problems incurred may be deep-rooted. The longer a woman has suffered with PMS, the more likely it is that her terrible mood swings have had a negative effect on her relationships and her self-esteem. A marriage or other relationship can be mortally wounded by PMS, and the confusion and rejection a woman experiences as a result can damage her image of herself.

*Mary's PMS.* I first saw Mary when she came to me about a rash she had had for two weeks. She was in her mid-thirties and seemed a bit shy and passive. She had a habit of sighing when I questioned her, as if she were resigned to her problems.

After some testing we determined that her rash was an allergic reaction. The problem went away after she avoided the substance we had identified as her allergen. As it turned out the rash was a fortunate occurrence in getting Mary to a doctor, because as I questioned her she revealed some much more troublesome symptoms that seemed to suggest PMS.

When I probed further about her cramps and moodiness she just shrugged and said, "I guess I'm just a moody person—always have been. I think maybe I get more depressed around the time of my period, but I'm not really sure. And the cramps, I guess they're inherited or something. My mother always had bad cramps. She called it 'the curse.' " Then she added so softly I could barely hear her, "That's a perfect name for it."

I asked Mary if she could arrange to see me just before her next period was due. She looked at me with some surprise, but agreed. I do not always require this of a patient in whom I suspect PMS, but in a case where the symptoms are not clear-cut I find it helpful.

About a week and a half later a woman resembling Mary showed up. I say "resembling" because Mary seemed to have gained several pounds of water weight, had a puffy face, and her expression was tense with pain. Her eyes were red—from crying it turned out—and this Mary was bursting with anger.

"Well, here I am," she half-shouted as I entered the examining room. "You said you could take the curse off. I suppose you think some aspirin will take care of it."

It took me a moment to adjust, but the change in her manner made me delighted we had scheduled her appointment for this time in her monthly cycle. I assured her I was not going to prescribe aspirin for her but wanted instead to give her another examination and run some tests.

She argued at first that tests weren't going to do any good, but then agreed. I asked her to put on an examination gown.

When I returned to the exam room I found Mary no longer angry, but tearful. "Do you think there's really something wrong with me? Is it something serious? I don't know if I can handle any more problems." I told her that I suspected PMS and that, if she had it, it was treatable. This stopped her tears until I examined her for tenderness and gently pressed her stomach. Her cramps were certainly severe.

As I talked with Mary I asked what she had meant by "any more problems." She was much more talkative in her present mood. Her anxiety and depression seemed to counteract her former shyness.

Mary told me that her husband had complained of her "mood swings," as he called it, and had finally found her "bitchiness and crying," as she called it, "intolerable." I recalled then that she had been divorced not long before. On top of that she said she sometimes "took it out on her daughter," and felt guilty. And she had been in such pain every month that her employer was beginning to get "fed up" with the number of times she couldn't come to work.

Mary's troubles were similar to what I had heard from many of my patients with PMS. I sympathized with her and advised counseling with Dr. Lipton, to which she seemed receptive.

Not surprisingly, Mary tested positive in her response to progesterone, indicating that she was sensitive to her own hormone. After treating her for this condition we found that her PMS symptoms vanished in a short time.

It was not long before I was greeting a new Mary in my office, neither the shy, resigned Mary of our first interview, nor the aggressive, tearful Mary of our second. Mary said she felt inwardly stronger, more cheerful, and, best of all, even-tempered. She had also thrown out her painkillers since the cramping was hardly noticeable.

Before she left my office she asked me how she looked. I answered honestly, "Terrific."

"Not puffy?"

"Not at all," I responded and asked why she wanted to know.

"Because I'm due for my period any day now," she answered happily, as if it were the best news in the world.

PMS patients may have different presenting symptoms but still can have a common treatable problem in progesterone hypersensitivity.

## Candidiasis

Candidiasis, as it is popularly called, is a truly bewildering condition for the many women and men who suffer from it. One of the most common symptoms for women is a vaginal yeast infection that refuses to go away. Of course, if that were the only problem, candidiasis would not be the often disabling health problem it is. Because men obviously cannot contract a vaginal infection, they are less likely to have this condition properly diagnosed. Men, however, can get a urinary tract infection from candida, or they can have an infection in some other mucous membrane or the skin.

Other symptoms include allergic-like reactions to some foods and chemicals. A person may experience fatigue, depression, anxiety, and puffiness in a woman's case, particularly around the time of menstruation. The candida sufferer may feel disoriented and find it difficult to concentrate.

Candidiasis is named after the yeast *Candida albicans.* It lives in our gastrointestinal tracts as a normal part of our bodies. When it grows beyond its normal level it can make us sick.

It is theorized that one or all of the following factors can contribute to candida overgrowth: taking antibiotics, birth control pills, or steroids (such as prednisone or cortisone); a high-sugar diet; or a suppressed immune system. Antibiotics are drugs capable of destroying the balance of healthy intestinal microorganisms, allowing candida to take over and dominate the gastrointestinal tract. Birth control pills cause hormonal changes in a woman's body that can also encourage candida to flourish. Steroids cause immune suppression that can allow candida to overgrow—as can any other cause of immune suppression. And candida loves sugar and carbohydrates in general and will grow more readily in the presence of a high-sugar diet.

*Tracy's Candidiasis.* Tracy was 39 and struggling against poor health to stay in her full-time job. She was pale, her eyes were bloodshot, and she seemed to be in a fog as I asked questions about her medical history. It was hard for her to remember much about the duration or pattern of her symptoms. This forgetfulness obviously upset her.

"Dr. Solomon, I'm not a stupid woman but I can't even type a simple letter without making a hundred mistakes. I don't understand it."

I asked Tracy if she noticed any times when her inability to concentrate seemed worse.

"Oh, yes. There are certain foods I can't go near anymore. I've had to give up dairy products completely. And bread seems to bother me, too. And cheese. And you can forget about beer."

Tracy was developing the food sensitivities that are a common factor in candidiasis. Her sensitivity to bread, cheese, and beer was a dead giveaway. Candidiasis, as I mentioned, is caused by an overgrowth of the yeast *Candida albicans*. As candida grows beyond normal bounds in your system, it can cause your body to react allergically to the candida itself.

Now, since candida is a yeast, you are likely to react allergically to other yeasts as well, since they run in the same family, so to speak. Bread is full of baker's yeast and beer is full of brewer's yeast. And cheese? Mold is a relative of yeast and some cheese ripens from mold. To illustrate, picture a nice hunk of blue cheese. The blue in blue cheese is mold in all its splendor.

But it was not just food that made Tracy feel sick. There is mold in the air, mold under the kitchen sink, in the basement, in the bathroom, under the carpet, behind the wallpaper. The fact is, once candida overgrowth puts your immune system on hyper-alert you can become hypersensitive to almost anything. The fumes of chemicals can be particularly troublesome. Some candidiasis patients feel like wearing a gas mask when they fill up the tanks of their cars. Others suspect that the chlorine in their drinking water is another enemy. No wonder that so many candidiasis patients feel they are living in a constant state of emergency.

Any physician who treats candidiasis patients will tell you, however, that, like fingerprints, no two are alike. One patient may find that she has many chemical allergies but is not troubled by food. Another may complain that he has multiple food allergies, but reacts little to chemicals. Part of our job is to determine which substances a candidiasis patient is sensitive, or allergic, to and try to reverse that situation.

As of now you know more about candidiasis than Tracy did that first day she came to my office. Now you know what diagnosis I was tentatively making as she presented all these telltale symptoms to me.

I asked her to stay away from the things she thought made her feel worse until we got her symptoms under better control. I explained that the overgrowth of yeast, or candida, could not be eliminated until her candidiasis, if that was what she had, was brought under control along with her immune system. We made an appointment for her to be tested for allergies and, meanwhile, Tracy was to tell me if she noticed any improvement in her symptoms by staying away from moldy, yeasty, and sugary foods.

The results of Tracy's tests showed a marked sensitivity to *Candida albicans* and to many other substances, some of which she never suspected, such as coffee and dust. I told her that with treatment she should feel her symptoms gradually fading—including the disorientation and "foggy" feeling. She was particularly concerned about this last symptom because she feared it might be threatening her job. Her employer had asked her on two occasions if she were drinking on the job or taking drugs.

Tracy did improve over the months. I continued to caution her to avoid any of the "trigger factors," such as taking birth control pills or eating too many sugary foods. And, most important, she was to tell me if she got any new symptoms or the old ones worsened. This could signal that there was an offending substance we did not test, or that the candidiasis had become more aggressive, which could have been caused by something like prolonged antibiotic therapy.

One day I received a phone call from Tracy just as we were closing the office. "Dr. Solomon? I can't speak too loudly because I'm calling you from work." I asked if she were ill.

"No, nothing like that. It's something I had to share with you. My boss just told me I'm being promoted to office manager!" I had not forgotten her former problems at her job and was very happy for her. And I was pleased that she wanted to share the good news with me.

"But that's not all," said Tracy. "The promotion gave me the nerve to show my boss the material on candidiasis you gave me. I wanted her to know what my real problem had been."

"And what was her reaction?" I asked.

"She was really interested because the majority of patients are women. And also because we've got an Employee Assistance Plan here. She's going to give the material to the guy who manages the plan."

This was the first time I had heard of candidiasis being added to the roster of health problems on an Employee Assistance Plan. Tracy was already making changes in the office!

### Allergy and Weight Gain

*Becky's Food Binges.* Becky had so dutifully answered the questionnaire we have new patients fill out that I imagined she had not left out a single detail. When I came to the questions about diet I saw that her handwriting ran off the page. I turned it over and there on the back her list of diets continued. It seemed as if Becky, by the age of 27, had tried every fashionable diet in the past ten years, as well as several that were unfamiliar to me.

Some were on the common-sense side in terms of good nutrition. Others were—well, just plain bizarre. She had also tried fasting. I noted that Becky had written that she worked in a health-food bakery. Becky was single with no children.

I looked up from the questionnaire and smiled at her. She smiled back as best she could while chewing her last mouthful of. . . . What was she eating? I looked at the wrapper on her lap: carob granola bar. She swallowed and wiped her fingers daintily on a tissue, explaining, "It's to keep my blood sugar up." I glanced back at the questionnaire. "Health-food diet" was the last thing she had listed.

I started a list of my own. "Since that's the diet you're on now, Becky," I said, "could you give me an idea of some of the things you eat on a regular basis?"

She recited as I wrote. "Let's see. . . . Carob granola bars, carob cookies—the kind without sugar, of course—all-natural potato chips, fruit and honey rolls, you know, those dried fruit things, puffed wheat cereal with milk, all-natural cornflakes with honey and milk, trail mix—that stuff with dried fruit and nuts and sunflower seeds—all-natural corn chips, ice cream sweetened with corn syrup, and flavored sodas sweetened with fructose." Becky came out of her reverie. "That's all I can think of."

I cleared my throat. "That's more than enough," I assured her.

While all of these foods could indeed be found at many health-food stores, they were, for the most part, a poor substitute for a truly healthy diet. She had not mentioned many things that were more than snack foods. I had to admire Becky's persistence, but, without knowing it, she had been fighting a "no-win" battle against the forty or so pounds she carried over normal weight.

"Becky, have you lost weight on any of these diets?" I asked.

"Well, a few pounds here and there."

"Why do you think that it hasn't been more?"

"Because I can't control my blood sugar. I have hypoglycemia so I have to keep eating to keep my blood sugar up. That's why I came to see you. I thought maybe you could help me with my blood sugar problem and then I could lose weight."

Becky was not completely wrong. Her blood sugar may have been irregular, but I suspected from her medical history that her overeating was part of a much larger problem.

I talked with Becky about food allergies and told her that just going over her list of favorite foods presented a picture of a possible food allergy.

"Carob, wheat and corn, and milk are foods you seem to eat or drink repeatedly. Wheat is usually found in the carob bars and cookies you like, and you eat puffed wheat cereal. You also like corn chips, cornflakes, and foods sweetened with corn syrup. And you eat ice cream and drink milk on a regular basis. Corn, wheat, and milk are very common food allergens."

She nodded, so I continued. "Becky, when someone comes to me with a weight problem and 'binges' on particular foods over and over, it's likely she may be addicted to the foods that she is eating."

I explained further that allergies make themselves felt one way or another. In her case the "way" was by a weight problem and the fact that she thought she might have low blood sugar.

"You mean it's not my blood sugar after all?"

"Oh, food allergies can play havoc with your blood sugar, all right. But my guess is that you are also binging because you get a temporary good feeling from these corn chips and granola bars. Then, when you start feeling not so good, you just eat more of the same foods. For example, why didn't you stay on your 'fruit and vegetable diet' or your 'high-protein diet'?"

"I don't know. Those diets just seemed to make me feel bad. I couldn't stand them for more than a few days. Come to think of it, I always felt better when I went back to my usual foods. And that was . . . carob, corn, wheat, and milk."

Becky said that when she went off those diets she felt "sort of foggy, couldn't think straight." Her ears started ringing and she got headaches.

When we went over the results of her tests, I told her that I had been conservative when I suspected wheat, corn, milk, and carob as her allergens. She was allergic to other foods as well, including oranges, almonds, and eggs. Plus, she had some inhalant allergies to mold and dust.

"Dust! I never knew I had a problem with dust. Every time I clean my apartment I feel great afterward. But," she added slowly, "then I always get depressed the next day."

For the next half hour Becky and I reviewed her allergenic foods and inhalants. I recommended that she try to eat each offending food no more often than every four days, if possible. This "rotation" diet gave her a new diet to work on, one that I felt would be more successful than any she had tried, plus we added nonallergenic foods to better balance it. I then told her of some precautions to take when dusting and to keep her apartment as clean as possible. We reviewed ways of avoiding and preventing mold. Finally, we set up an appointment for Becky to start treatment to reduce her allergies.

Soon, slowly but surely, Becky began to lose weight. After losing her first fifteen pounds she said to me, "I can't believe I can get through a week without going on those food binges. And I don't get sick or feel as if I'm starving when I don't eat ice cream."

"And the dust?" I asked.

"No more of those big highs in my moods, followed by big lows, thank goodness."

It was not too much longer before Becky achieved the slimness she had longed for all her life. It also was not very long before I was introduced to another new figure (so to speak) in Becky's life—her fiancé, Nick. She had met him at her new job. (She had found it hard to stay on her diet while working at the health-food bakery.)

After a friendly chat with Becky and Nick I was returning to my office when I felt a tap on my shoulder. I turned around to find Becky looking up at me. She whispered, "Don't try to treat me for my addiction to Nick, Dr. Solomon. I don't want to be cured."

I agreed to this, happily.

**Allergy and Temperament**

*Jim's Food Allergies and Bad Temper.* Jim had been seeing Dr. Lipton about problems he was having with his girlfriend. Jim, age 31, was a newspaper reporter. He was not charmed with the idea of seeing me, but here he was in my office.

I read Dr. Lipton's note to me. It indicated that he suspected Jim of having an inhalant allergy problem. Since he did not like to discuss his clients' emotional problems he wrote only that there was a great deal of tension between Jim and his girlfriend.

I could not yet put this together with inhalant allergies. I looked hopefully at Jim. He was looking down gloomily at his nails.

"Jim," I ventured, "did Dr. Lipton discuss inhalant allergies with you?"

"Yeah."

"Good," I replied, and wondered what to ask next.

"Jim, this note from Dr. Lipton indicates that you've been having problems with your girlfriend. Does this have anything to do with your discussion of allergies?"

"Well, Dr. Lipton says it might."

I waited. Jim saw that I needed an explanation.

"It just seems so crazy to me. I've been going with Alicia for about five months now. We've just got a few personality conflicts to work out, that's all. I don't see what her perfume has to do with it. Or her dog, for that matter."

This sounded interesting. I questioned him further.

"And why do you think Dr. Lipton is connecting your romantic problems with your girlfriend's perfume or her dog?"

"Because he thinks he sees a pattern. *He* says that I almost always fight with Alicia whenever I see her on a Friday or a Saturday."

I was still trying to pull this together. "But why just on Fridays or Saturdays?"

"Well, you see, Alicia's boss doesn't like perfume on the job so she only wears it for our dates on the weekend. When I see her during the week she's not wearing perfume."

"And her dog?"

"Dr. Lipton *also* noticed that I get real crabby when she brings her dog over."

"But aren't you around the dog at Alicia's place?"

"No," he said. "I never go over there. She's got a real idiot for a roommate. She's always blasting the stereo or TV. You get the picture."

I thought that, at last, I *was* getting the picture.

I looked up from my notes and asked, "Do you think Dr. Lipton is right about this pattern?"

"I think it's all just coincidence. Alicia and I just happen to fight on those occasions."

"Does either of you seem to start the . . . misunderstandings?"

He squirmed a little before answering. "Okay. Well, yeah, Dr. Lipton and I figured out that I usually start the fights. But she sure keeps them going."

He started the arguments. This was a useful clue. I tried another line of questioning.

"Jim, Dr. Lipton apparently thinks your anger is a symptom of an allergic reaction. Why do you have a problem accepting the idea that you may be allergic to Alicia's perfume and her dog?"

"Because I love that perfume she wears. And Bonzo's the best old mutt in the world."

"Jim, I have patients who love chocolate. But it makes them depressed or anxious or it gives them headaches. Believe it or not, it's possible to be allergic to something that you really like. In fact, it's usually the case."

Jim leaned forward. "That's what Dr. Lipton says. I'm sorry, but I find that really hard to believe."

Nevertheless, I asked Jim if we could test him for some common ingredients in perfume as well as for dog hair. He shrugged. "Sure. Anything to stop this stupid idea about allergies. In fact, run a bunch of tests."

As was sure to be the case, Jim was allergic to ingredients in perfume and dog hair—and cat hair, tobacco smoke, newsprint, as well as more than a dozen others.

When I saw him again he looked exasperated. "What am I going to do about Alicia? And Bonzo? And my job? [I had ordered the newsprint tests, recalling Jim's job as a reporter.] And strawberries? And potatoes?"

I suggested he sit down and take a few minutes to discuss this.

"Things are not so bleak," I said. "In fact, you are fortunate we found these allergies. If Dr. Lipton's hunch was right—and I think it was—you may find yourself having fewer disagreements with Alicia from now on. Don't you see? Now we can control this problem."

I explained to Jim that he should urge Alicia to give up her perfume—but not her dog. That would be asking too much. I also realized that he could not be expected to leave a job he enjoyed.

I told him how to rotate his allergenic foods and explained the treatment I would be giving him to further reduce his allergic reactions. And his ongoing treatment with Dr. Lipton would now include biofeedback, visualization, and hypnosis to give him more psychological control over his body's allergic responses.

After several sessions of treatment, Jim was discovering symptoms he never knew existed. "Dr. Solomon," he said one day, "I was always so tired before at the office. I thought it was all the deadlines. Now I think it *was* the paper." I smiled and he continued, "This therapy has really improved my overall mood. Even people at work say I'm a different person—you know, less temperamental."

"And how's Alicia?" I asked.

"Would you believe she was tired of that perfume and was only wearing it because I liked it? We're getting along great now. Even when Bonzo's around. But I wish you could do something about her roommate. I'm definitely allergic to her!"

**Headaches**

*Linda's Sinus Problems.* This was one of the most difficult consultations I have ever had with a new patient. Linda, age fifteen, in her sophomore year of high school, had been referred to me complaining of severe headaches and sinus trouble. Her mother accompanied Linda on her first visit. My problem was that I could barely get Linda to answer my questions. Her attention kept wandering. Linda's mother was not particularly helpful either.

"Dr. Solomon, I *told* Linda that she's just got to snap out of this. All the other doctors have said—"at this point she turned to her daughter for emphasis "—that there is absolutely nothing wrong with Linda." Mrs. King turned back to me. "I told Linda there was no point in going to see any more doctors. But she behaved so disagreeably that I gave in. You know, Dr. Solomon, these headaches of hers are just Linda's way of trying to get attention." She sighed heavily. "I suppose it's just an adolescent phase."

"Linda?" I said gently. I wondered for a moment if she were high on something, she seemed so out-of-focus.

"Hmm?"

I decided to forget about taking notes until later. I moved my chair and sat directly in front of her to try to get her attention.

"Linda, how often do you have these headaches?"

"Oh," she replied vaguely, "I guess most of the time."

"Do you have one now?"

"Only a little one."

"A little one?"

She nodded. "Yeah. If I don't get a headache, then I just feel sort of tired and dopey instead."

"Do you feel that way now?"

Linda took several seconds to reply. "Yes," she said and tried to stifle a yawn.

I turned to her mother. "Mrs. King, were you aware of Linda's extreme drowsiness?" I did not see how it could escape her attention. Mrs. King glanced at Linda and shrugged.

"She says her headaches keep her up at night. I suspect she's listening to music or talking on the phone till all hours."

"Mrs. King, I wonder if you would mind if I consulted with Linda privately?"

She looked offended but agreed to leave. I felt it might be easier to find out Linda's problem without her mother's strong opinions in the air. I sat back down and felt like snapping my fingers to bring Linda to attention. I questioned Linda, slowly and painstakingly, for half an hour.

At the end of the consultation I ushered Mrs. King back in. I had gotten permission from Linda to tell her mother what we had discussed.

"Mrs. King," I began as she sat down, "I think Linda's headaches and sinus trouble are quite real. And I think her excessive drowsiness and inability to concentrate are also real." She raised an eyebrow. I went on, pointing out the fact that Linda's grades had dropped over the past year and a half ("Yes, of course we are concerned about that"), that Linda cried a lot ("Oh, no. I'm sure you're wrong about that"), and that Linda binged on candy and cookies every night after everyone else was asleep ("Linda! You know I don't allow junk food in the house!").

"I only mention these things to you, Mrs. King, because I think they form a pattern."

"A pattern?"

"I've explained my tentative diagnosis to Linda. She is

interested in receiving treatment for what I suspect may be multiple food allergies."

Mrs. King looked at me in disbelief. "Food allergies? Linda's never been allergic to anything. Her father's the one with the hay fever. You must be mistaken."

"I may be mistaken," I answered sharply, "but if I'm not we could bring Linda's obvious misery to an end." I waited for a response. I had spoken in a harsher tone than I like to use, but I needed Mrs. King's cooperation if I was to help Linda.

Apparently my tone made a difference. "Linda?" she said more softly. Linda looked up apprehensively. "If I go along with what Dr. Solomon says, will you agree that this going to doctors all the time must stop?"

I wasn't pleased with her approach, but it was better than nothing.

Linda finally spoke. "Yes, Mother. Just let me try this treatment." Her voice was almost a whisper. "I've really been sick."

Linda's mother and I looked at each other. She pursed her lips and sighed heavily again. "Well, what's the treatment?"

I explained to Mrs. King that treatment would follow only if my theory proved correct. To determine that, I would conduct a complete physical exam as well as test Linda for food allergies and some common inhalant allergies. If the tests revealed that Linda was allergic, I would then recommend avoidance of certain foods, a rotation diet of her allergenic foods, and treatment to reduce the allergic reactions.

I would also recommend treatment with Dr. Lipton to teach her psychological control of her allergic reactions. What I did not mention then was the fact that I hoped to get Mrs. King to go to some of Linda's sessions with Dr. Lipton. I thought he would agree that some family counseling seemed in order. But that would be his decision. First things first. . . .

I had Linda tested for the most common ingredients in the foods she told me she binged on, as well as some inhalants. As

I suspected, she turned out to be allergic to several of the foods. She was not allergic to any of the inhalants.

When I discussed the results with Linda and her mother, Mrs. King commented, "Well, there may be something in what you say, but I'm not at all sure this treatment will help Linda."

I decided to bring up the subject of family counseling to Dr. Lipton that very day and the next time I met with Linda and her mother I was surprised to hear Mrs. King agree to counseling—that is, until she said: "Why, of course I'll be going with Linda. I plan to make sure she is receiving *professional* treatment."

Linda looked at me pleadingly. I smiled at her reassuringly.

The next several times I saw Linda she was without her mother—at Dr. Lipton's suggestion. It was even hard for *me* to believe that this alert, intelligent, communicative adolescent was the silent girl I had first interviewed. I assumed that one part of this was the treatment and the other part was the absence of Linda's mother.

One day Linda sat before me with a smile on her face. "Dr. Solomon, my headaches are gone, my sinuses are cleared up, and—best of all—my mother has stopped telling everyone that I'm just looking for attention." I encouraged her to continue. "Well, the rotation diet was hard at first, but now I don't really crave that junk food anymore."

I told Linda that she seemed to be much more "in focus" with the world, less groggy. She nodded. "I could barely stay awake before, much less think straight. Now my grades are getting better."

"And how are you and your mother getting along?"

"Let's face it. My mother's never going to be easy to get along with. She has to be boss, you know." I nodded. "But now that my grades are better and we've both been seeing Dr. Lipton she can hardly argue with success."

I told Linda how glad I was for her and asked her to bring her mother along next time so we could discuss Linda's progress.

"Oh," she said, "you'll be seeing her soon anyway. I was going to tell you."

"Tell me what?"

"That she has made an appointment to see you. Now she thinks maybe *she* has food allergies."

I looked at Linda in astonishment.

"Personally," she said with a giggle, "I think she's just looking for attention."

We both laughed.

**Anorexia Nervosa**

I mention anorexia nervosa in connection with allergies because of the 27 patients I have treated with this problem, 21 of them were found to have some form of allergy. This is not to say that allergy caused the condition, but it was there, and treating it along with the other ailments resulted in improvements in the patients' conditions.

*Olive's Anorexia.* Olive, for instance, a college student, had always worried about doing well in school. When she went away to school she faced increased subject load, less time for studying, and financial concerns.

Although she was five feet four inches tall and weighed 102 pounds (her ideal weight was 120 pounds), she had a distorted concept of her body image plus an abhorrence of obesity. Because of tension at school along with other emotional factors she began to eat excessively, particularly chocolate and coffee with a lot of cream and sugar. She sometimes followed her large meals with induced vomiting (bulimia). Olive began to lose weight and was referred to me for diagnosis and treatment.

She was found to have anorexia nervosa and was allergic to the foods she craved—chocolate, coffee, sugar, and milk products. She was also deficient in vitamins, minerals, and was anemic.

I began her medical treatment and, because she had an

underlying emotional disturbance, recommended she receive counseling from Dr. Lipton.

Olive did exceptionally well with our combined regimen. One year later she had resumed her normal weight of 120 pounds, was eating normally, and was taking her medicine for allergies.

These are just some of the problems that can be associated with allergies. Particularly if you have $PS^2$ you might consider allergy testing. As with the patients listed here, you, too, could be tracking down a source of discomfort and frustration.

11

# Control Your Eating

As an endocrinologist I have always been interested in the problems of weight control and have developed a number of approaches and techniques over the past 25 years to help my patients lose weight and keep it off. During the past several years Dr. Lipton and I have devised new, improved methods to address the issue of weight control from the combined mind-body approach.

Some people who are obese have increased levels of steroids in their blood that are being produced by their adrenal glands. These increased levels of steroids cause a higher level of sodium retention leading to fluid retention. People with $PS^2$ have even more steroids than non-$PS^2$ obese individuals, so are even more prone to excess fluid retention.

Until this problem is addressed, it is very difficult for someone with $PS^2$ to lose weight. Once it is understood, however, biofeedback and relaxation techniques, including clinical hypnosis, can sometimes reduce steroid levels and therefore reduce fluid retention.

*Melissa's Obesity and Hormone Problem.* Melissa, a 31-year-old mother, was extremely obese. She was five feet five inches tall and weighed 295 pounds. She had gained most of her weight after dropping out of high school because of pregnancy. From the stress of her predicament plus the hormonal changes following the pregnancy she gained more than 150 pounds in four years. She had been on many diets but to no avail. She claimed that she had reduced her caloric intake but just could not lose weight.

Upon examination she impressed me as an extremely nervous person. Blood levels of steroids confirmed that her adrenals were working overtime and she was retaining a tremendous amount of fluid.

First, I placed her on a carefully formulated diet to reduce water retention, suggested an appropriately graduated aerobic exercise schedule, and recommended relaxation and biofeedback techniques. As soon as her tension and steroid levels dropped so did her weight. So far she has lost 75 pounds and counting.

First, a few comments about obesity.

Obesity is defined roughly as the condition in which a person weighs more than twenty percent above ideal weight, and the excess weight is composed mainly of adipose, or fatty tissue. It is estimated that more than thirty million Americans are obese by this definition and, in spite of our society's weight consciousness, the problem appears to be getting worse.

There are, generally speaking, two types of obesity. One is referred to as hypertrophic, in which fat cells have increased in size but not in number. The other is referred to as hyperplastic hypertrophic obesity, in which the fat cells have increased both in size and number. People whose fat cells are increased both in number and size appear to have a much more difficult time with weight control than do people whose fat cells are simply larger.

Studies indicate that animals that are overfed from early life tend to develop fat cells that increase in size and number more often than animals that are overfed only as adults. Many studies also indicate, however, that the number of fat cells can increase in maturity. Although these findings have not been confirmed in humans, it is thought likely that the same mechanism is at work.

Both conditions are responsive to reduced caloric intake. Dr. Lipton and I have succeeded in helping both groups who attend our weight loss clinic to lose weight and keep it off. Our six-part program should help you, too.

Why should you worry about excess weight? Without question the obese person runs an increased risk of various types of heart disease with, perhaps, atherosclerosis topping the list. The elevated triglyceride—a molecule that contains three fatty acids—and cholesterol levels in the bloodstream of the obese individual are thought to be major contributors to atherosclerosis and heart attack. If weight is lost, body fat is reduced as are, correspondingly, the level of triglycerides and cholesterol in the bloodstream. This loss of poundage is a plus for persevering dieters.

## Fat and Life Energy

People gain weight, quite simply, because they eat more than their bodies require.

To be a little more specific, food is composed of three basic nutrients: carbohydrates, fats, and proteins. Enzymes and oxygen metabolize fat in our bodies. The energy produced from this process is converted to a chemical called adenosine triphosphate (ATP), which is composed of three high-energy phosphate groups. Energy is released to the body when one of these groups is split off from ATP, which happens whenever there is a need for energy.

The body has two basic energy requirements: first for necessary bodily functions such as heart contraction, respiration, maintenance and repair of tissues; second, for support of the body's overall activity level.

We are in energy balance when the calories produced by the food we eat are equal to the amount of energy required for the body's essential functions plus any physical activity in which we engage. When the number of calories ingested exceeds this level, we are out of balance and gain weight.

The average adult male while at complete rest requires

between 1,200 and 1,500 calories daily to maintain his body weight; a female, between 1,000 and 1,300 calories.

It is estimated that only six percent of the obese can blame the condition on endocrine or metabolic problems, per se. Such problems relate to malfunction in either the pituitary, hypothalamus, adrenal glands, pancreas, parathyroid, thyroid, ovaries, and/or gonads.

Dr. Lipton and I began to notice that some of the overweight patients we were treating for other conditions, such as allergies, arthritis, and essential hypertension were, for no apparent reason, beginning to lose weight. It soon became clear that whatever neuro-endocrine-immunological link we were affecting in our treatment of these other conditions was also modifying the body's weight control equilibrium.

Now, let me emphasize from the outset that while we have had convincing, consistently good results in helping people lose weight, our discussion is only theoretical hypothesizing at this point. The exact mechanism for this desired outcome, whether or not it be through modification in behavioral conditioning, modification of cell metabolism, or increase in motivation, is still unclear and warrants ongoing investigation.

We will, nevertheless, share with you the discoveries that led us to design this specific program and the mechanisms that we believe are at work.

## The Weight Control Program

The majority of people we have treated for obesity were unsuccessful in their many previous attempts to lose weight. These people came to us to participate in the joint neuro-endocrine-immunological program because of the high level of frustration they had experienced in their efforts to shed unwanted pounds. In more than fifty percent of the cases patients lost weight, and the majority kept it off.

There are two general perspectives on obesity related to the mind-body connection. One school of thought maintains that underlying emotional problems cause the obese to overeat. The other holds that emotional problems are a result of obesity and its attendant neurochemical and psychological effects. Interestingly, these two perspectives parallel the idea that the mind and body are independent areas of study.

It is our contention that both perspectives are true and are interactive—that is, emotional problems and habits and learned responses can result in increased eating. Overeating results in overweight, which, in turn, can create emotional problems, which, in turn, can cause and perpetuate overeating behavior. In effect, we have one circular process rather than two separate ones.

Weight control appears to be related to the same neuro-endocrine-immunological connection as Profound Sensitivity Syndrome, the one by which thoughts and feelings affect physical changes. In fact, as an example of the way thoughts can affect weight control, consider the findings of Dr. Judith Rodin of Yale University. Her study, reported in 1982 by Dr. Maria Simonson, Director of the Johns Hopkins University Health, Weight and Stress Program, proved that a number of obese people do have a *metabolic* response to the sight, smell, and sound of food cooking—specifically, coffee perking and steak sizzling.

We know as well that a great many overweight people use food to reduce emotional tension. For many, remaining fat serves another purpose, though more often than not on an unconscious level. When people are uncomfortable with emotions such as fear or anger, eating often reduces the anxiety that not dealing with these feelings creates. In this sense, eating becomes a tranquilizer.

*Joan Ate to Relax.* Joan, a 29-year-old single nurse, came to me because her feet were so painful she was having trouble keeping her job. If you are thinking that I am not a foot specialist, you are right! But Joan was five feet two inches and weighed 284 pounds. Her feet were painful because her weight was actually flattening them out.

Joan worked as a registered nurse in an intensive care unit at a prestigious hospital. I knew her weight problem was more psychological than physical in etiology when I asked her during my examination why she was eating a candy bar. She responded by saying, "I always eat when I'm nervous and I'm afraid you won't be able to help me."

After a brief discussion it became clear that whenever she became nervous or upset, which was many times a day since Joan was apparently easily intimidated, she ate to calm her nerves, a habit she reported having since she was a child. I asked her to work with Dr. Lipton in order to learn how to cope with her stresses by a method other than eating. With Joan's permission, here are his thoughts about this case:

"When I first saw Joan she was a shy, timid, unassertive young woman who dealt with her world by eating herself to death. Her job was demanding and high-pressured, since many of the physicians she worked with were renowned in their professions. Whenever a doctor said something that upset Joan, she ran into the supply cabinet and stuffed herself with candy bars. Unfortunately, Joan was upset dozens of times each day.

"Not surprisingly Joan's problem had its roots in her childhood. Her father was an overbearing, physically abusive man and her mother, her role model, was passive and dependent. Since her father would beat her if she tried to assert herself, Joan resorted to the only thing in which she could find a sense of protection and anxiety-reduction—eating.

"Actually, eating seems to have an intrinsic anti-anxiety effect upon all of us. A full stomach is very relaxing. When it becomes the only way you have to relax and you reinforce this eating-relaxation association enough, you are off and running on your way to obesity. Such was the case with Joan.

"I trained Joan in biofeedback as a way of reducing her anxiety in a low-calorie fashion, so to speak. I also worked with her for approximately one year employing a cognitive and behavioral approach to help her become more verbally assertive, thus overcoming emotionally her fear that her father was going to slap her if she spoke her mind."

After about three months in treatment, Joan started to lose weight, and after a year she weighed 207 pounds. She chose to stop her treatment with us at that point, saying she felt she had gained control not only over her eating but over her life.

As our thinking evolved, it became evident that reducing the physiological and psychogenic sources of tension as an adjunct to diet and exercise might be the basic tactic against overweight. Here is the rationale of our program, our combined best thinking on how you can lose weight and keep it off. And if it helps, you can remember the words of Bavishon, spoken in the year 1600: "When the body gets full, the mind gets dull."

## Step One: Where Your Hormones Fit In

The first step with our patients is to reestablish normal endocrine/hormonal functioning. This change, naturally, must be addressed by a physician. It is the only step you will not be able to perform on your own.

When a person first comes into my office I obtain a detailed medical history and perform a thorough physical examination, which includes comprehensive evaluation of the overall endocrine and metabolic function. I have observed that although a single hormone measured by itself may not technically be outside the normal range, if I look at patterns of hormonal levels I will often find trends indicative of low or high output status in one or more organ systems.

When your doctor addresses this basic issue, he or she then knows what systems, if any, are not working optimally. By helping you make corrections and/or adjustments, he or she will bring you to a point where you are no longer handicapped in your weight loss efforts before you start.

The thyroid is an important gland in your body's regulation of weight. It secretes hormones into the bloodstream that assist in regulating the various activities of your body's tissues. The thyroid gland is largely governed by the pituitary gland, which is governed, in turn, by the hypothalamus, all part of the endocrine (hormonal) link.

Several things can go wrong with the thyroid gland. It can produce too much hormone, in which case a person will suffer from *hyper*thyroidism; or it can produce too little hormone, which will cause a person to have *hypo*thyroidism. The thyroid can also become inflamed, which is called thyroiditis; or a cyst or tumor may develop on the thyroid. A common thyroid condition is a goiter, which is a swelling of the thyroid gland itself. Considering all these possible conditions, it's easy to see why consideration of the thyroid should not be overlooked if a patient's symptoms suggest it. Thyroid problems often run in families, though the nature of the thyroid condition may differ from one generation to the next.

The symptoms of an overactive thyroid, or hyperthyroidism, can include a rapid pulse, sweaty palms, nervousness, weight loss, diarrhea, and shaky hands. At the other end of the spectrum, an underactive thyroid, or hypothyroidism, can bring on fatigue, mental dullness, constipation, brittle nails, thinning hair, dry skin, irregular menstrual periods, difficulty getting pregnant, an increase in miscarriages, and sensitivity to cold. You may exhibit none or all of the symptoms listed in each case. And your symptoms can be easily confused with other medical conditions or for psychological problems. This is why so many cases of thyroid trouble go undiagnosed.

Even if a thyroid problem is suspected, it still may not be diagnosed. This is because one must test for TSH (thyroid-stimulating hormone) as well as T3 and T4. What do all these T's stand for? T3 and T4 are two of the most important hormones put out by the thyroid gland. If the levels of these hormones in your bloodstream are too high or too low, it could spell thyroid trouble.

Your test results can show normal T3 and T4 levels but you could still have a thyroid condition. This is why the TSH (thyroid-stimulating hormone) level must be measured, as well. A TSH level that is too high, for instance, may decrease the T3 and T4 you have *in reserve* rather than circulating in the bloodstream at the time the test is done. This reserve is used for times of stress (remember stress?). If you don't have enough of these hormones in reserve, your body's ability to cope with, and recover from, stress is impaired.

Elevated levels of TSH also affect the yo-yo syndrome. If you have fairly rapid fluctuations of weight loss and gain between five and ten pounds, you may be experiencing the yo-yo syndrome. Medication, radiation, stress, diet, and genetics can all play a part in causing thyroid trouble.

*Ellen's Hidden Thyroid Problem.* Ellen, 32 years old, married, childless, and working full-time, came to see me at a friend's urging because she felt bad most of the time. She was tall, with a large frame, so she could carry some extra fat without seeming overweight. But she still looked as though she needed to reduce. I asked her about this. "I know I'm too heavy, but I'm practically starving myself already. I eat fruit, I eat salads, I gave up desserts—but I still can't lose more than a couple of pounds."

Ellen said she always felt tired no matter how much she slept. During the examination I noticed that her hands and feet were unusually cold. She also said that she had irregular menstrual periods and had been trying to get pregnant for the last eight or nine years unsuccessfully. "I've seen one doctor after another," she said. "They all said there was nothing wrong with me, but I could tell what they were thinking. They said I should take a vacation or see a counselor. The last doctor told me, 'All these complaints of yours, they're all in your head.' I was so mad I could have screamed. But I didn't have the energy. I just walked out on him and swore off doctors for good."

"But you're here," I said.

"Well, not because I *want* to be. My friend Miriam dragged me in here because she's tired of hearing me grousing about my health." Ellen softened a little and admitted, "Well, I guess she's really worried about me. She and my husband. I think they talked it over."

Ellen's records showed that her physicians had responsibly ordered many of the tests that I would have ordered, given her symptoms. The results were normal. I could understand the frustration they must have felt as one after another test came back indicating no problem. For the most part, it looked as if everything had been checked out, but I still didn't see the clue I was looking for.

Finally I found a badly photostated record from four years back of thyroid tests. "Ellen, did any of those doctors mention anything to you about your thyroid?"

"Yes, one did. But all the tests came back normal."

Just as her records said. I put them aside. "Well, Ellen, I know this will make you feel like you're running in circles, but I don't think your thyroid tests were thorough. I'd like to run some more."

"Well, I. . . ." She shrugged her shoulders. "Oh, okay, I guess one more test won't kill me." She added quickly, "You understand, of course, that I'm just humoring you? Just so my friend and my husband will be satisfied?"

"Ellen, thank you for humoring me," I said and ordered the tests.

The tests came back indicating problems with her thyroid. Putting that together with her medical history and symptoms, I was able to tell Ellen that she had been suffering all those years from hypothyroidism. Ellen stared and listened carefully as I explained about the TSH levels, and the treatment I recommended.

Her response to that treatment was gradual, but encouraging. Her weight normalized along with her thyroid, and she lost the extra pounds. Her energy level was improving, and her menstrual cycle finally became regular.

Then about a year after her first visit, she called me to see if

I could recommend an obstetrician for her. She told me happily that she was pregnant.

### Step Two: The Stress Correction Plan

This plan is described in chapter 5. It works by furnishing the proper proportions of protein, carbohydrates, and fats and includes the vitamins, minerals, and fiber needed by the body to function at an optimal level. Be sure, also, to follow these words from the Talmud: "Drink plenty of water with your meals."

We will discuss motivation, a crucial element of following a diet, in step four.

### Step Three: Reducing Your Tension

Reduced caloric intake is a shock to the body's equilibrium. Change produces tension. The body responds by becoming more energy-efficient. This means that the body derives more energy from less food, making it even more difficult to lose weight.

Using biofeedback during dieting, as taught in chapter 8, helps reduce your stress response. It will also help you achieve a deep sensation of internal relaxation, an instant tranquilizer influencing you to eat less.

The quieting effect of biofeedback also helps break the habit of eating to reduce agitation. As mentioned earlier, many overweight people eat to cope with worry and anxiety. Going on a diet is stressful so their anxiety levels increase. The longstanding pattern has been to reduce anxiety and irritations by eating—but they resist the temptation. So the level of exasperation increases.

Day-to-day activities continue, the irritations mount. The anxiety level builds until finally they flare with a conditioned response: Suddenly they are on an uncontrollable binge, eating everything in sight.

This is why so many patients respond to the question, "What was going on in your mind when you let yourself go like that?" with, "I don't know what came over me. I was eating before I even knew what I was doing."

Using biofeedback reduces food craving, and internal disquiet and the upward spiral of increasing anxiety is broken.

**Step Four: Taking Back the Control**

Dr. Lipton and I find that people who are chronically frustrated in their attempts to lose weight, or to keep it off, develop a number of similar emotional attitudes. These, if left unmodified, serve only to create a negative self-fulfilling prophecy.

Unsuccessful dieters all share a common attitude: They feel they cannot take charge of their lives. Although this attitude is more often than not related to their lives in general, it becomes focused on the issue of weight.

Many people report a weight gain after an incident in their lives in which control was taken from them. This may happen after the loss of a job or the death of a close friend. Helplessness, loss of control of their feelings, becomes generalized to other aspects of their lives. A "what's-the-use?" attitude becomes prevalent, takes over their thinking.

If the conditioned response to tension, anxiety, or despair is to eat, the weight gain only serves to confirm the lack of control and effectiveness.

*The best way to lose weight and keep it off is to reestablish control over your life.*

From our earlier discussions, particularly chapter 3 on distorted thinking, we know that there are many things we ourselves cannot change, such as other people. We can, however, restructure the way we think or feel, what we tell ourselves about these people. In these cases we must learn to master our reactions, not to personalize what happens to us. There are other areas over which we can be boss that we must learn to recognize, so that we can do something positive where we can make a difference.

If there is one area in our lives over which we can have 100 percent change of attitude, it is what we put into our mouths. When we learn to curb our excessive eating, our newfound effectiveness will have a profound impact on all other aspects of our lives.

How would you go about reestablishing a sense of mastery and optimism? Several ideas follow that have been effective. But first let's put weight in the right perspective. Here is a not uncommon dialogue between Dr. Lipton and a patient.

Dr. Lipton: "What would happen if I told you to go home and lose forty pounds in the next four months?"

Patient: "If I could do that I wouldn't be here."

Dr. Lipton: "Well, this is just a pretend theoretical question. Indulge me for a minute. Suppose someone kidnapped your son or daughter or mother or father and told you that if you did not lose forty pounds in the next four months you would never see him or her again?" (Dr. Lipton does not include husbands or wives in this example because all too often the patient says, "I would let them keep" him or her!)

Patient: "Well, of course, under those circumstances I'd lose the weight."

Dr. Lipton: "You'd lose the weight?"

Patient: "Well, sure. But that's different. I wouldn't let them die. I'd lose the weight."

Dr. Lipton: "How?"

Patient: "I don't know. I just wouldn't eat much and I'd lose the weight."

Dr. Lipton: "What if someone kidnapped your son or daughter or mother or father and told you that unless you learned to fly by flapping your hands and arms, you would never see him or her again? What would you do?"

Patient: "I'd call the F.B.I."

Dr. Lipton: "Why is that?"

Patient: "What do you mean why? Because you can't fly by flapping your hands and arms, that's why!"

Dr. Lipton: "So, you couldn't fly without a plane, but you could lose the weight."

Patient: "Yes, of course."

What has this dialogue accomplished? It has taken weight out of the realm of impossibility and put it under the individual's control, but only under the right circumstances. Circumstances, otherwise known as motivation.

*How Norma Overcame Her Anxiety and Finally Lost Weight.* I had been seeing Norma, a 36-year-old history teacher, for several years for treatment of her allergies, obesity, and quite recently, a thyroid imbalance. Then, about a year ago, she began to experience anxiety attacks. As they worsened, she felt increasingly anxious, fearful, helpless, and vulnerable. She continued to overeat to compensate for the anxiety, and her weight soared to 247 pounds (Norma is five feet three inches tall.)

She also began suffering from dizziness, rapid heartbeat, and ringing in the ears. She would often wake up at three or four in the morning and not be able to go back to sleep. Several times because of the anxiety attacks she was late for class. In fact, she had to leave school on several occasions because of the attacks. Since the anxiety attacks continued even after the successful treatment of the thyroid problem, I suggested she contact Dr. Lipton in order to learn about biofeedback.

Norma did not smoke or drink and had given up cola with caffeine a few months earlier. Extensive testing had ruled out any medical abnormality. When she consulted Dr. Lipton she told him that her only interest was to learn the biofeedback techniques that would help her control her responses to future anxiety attacks, control her eating, and return to her teaching.

During our talks I learned that most of Norma's interest and energies were directed toward her job and her family. For almost twelve years she had gotten most of her satisfaction in life from her teaching career. She had received outstanding evaluations and felt as if all of the extra time and effort that she contributed to her school were appreciated by at least some of the students, parents, and administrators.

Norma continued to take graduate and in-service courses during the school year and usually spent her summers either participating in curriculum workshops at home or attending graduate courses.

Even outside of school most of the people that Norma associated with were connected in some way with teaching. She held offices in both local and national associations with positions on their executive boards. When discussing the types of people that she came into contact with on a regular basis, Norma was quick to note that she tended to travel in rather limited circles, choosing to be in groups where she felt her abilities would be appreciated and where there was little or no danger of criticism. She was aware that she had a strong need to please others and to receive approval from them. As a result, she had pretty much limited herself to participating in activities in which she could excel, rarely undertaking new challenges unless she was virtually guaranteed to be successful.

Norma reported that during the last two years she had been getting much less satisfaction from her job than she had in the past. She had been assigned a schedule that required her to teach several courses out of her field, the result being that she found herself spending an inordinate amount of time and energy preparing for these new classes. It seemed as though the harder she worked to motivate her students the less success she had. To add to her frustration, for at least eight years she had been trying to transfer to a school closer to her home. No positions were available in her area, however, because of declining enrollments and budget restrictions. Norma felt that, despite her best efforts, she was having less and less control over the direction that her career was taking.

Her family situation was also proving to be a recent source of great concern. She was single and up to this point had never even seriously dated. Except for some professional associates, Norma had few social contacts outside her immediate family. She lived just a short distance from her parents and a married sister, and she saw them quite frequently. Her grandmother had died less than a week before Norma first saw Dr. Lipton and she was now also very worried about her parents' declining health.

It was obvious that these recent changes in what had been the most important and significant areas of her life were causing Norma to experience feelings of anxiety. Furthermore, her tendency to isolate herself and to withdraw from others was keeping her from establishing the support network she so desperately needed. She was more and more seeking solace in food.

Basically shy and extremely sensitive, Norma found it difficult to initiate contact with new people. She blamed part of her problem on her weight, saying that she knew she often kept people at arm's length until she no longer had to worry about rejection. Norma had been overweight for her entire adult life, but now hit an all-time high of 255 pounds.

It was clear that unless some major changes were made in her life, she would continue to be subject to recurring bouts of anxiety.

The first order of business was to teach her to use biofeedback in order to deal with future anxiety attacks. It was also suggested that she exercise for twenty minutes or so in the morning, either by taking a brisk walk or riding her stationary bike, so as to release beta endorphins into her system. We also put her on a diet to control her weight.

Upon returning to her job that fall, Norma reported that several times in the morning she experienced feelings of anxiety and mild dizziness but that she was able to use techniques learned during the sessions in order to relax. Breathing slowly and relaxing as many muscles as she could, she was able, for the most part, to continue with her lessons as she had planned. She noted that the episodes became less frequent after the first week or two back at school and that they were much less severe and of shorter duration each time they occurred. During the last two months, she reported no feelings of uneasiness at all while at work, and she was able to finish out the school year without missing any more time because of anxiety attacks.

The next thing that Norma needed to do was to have contact with more people and to make new friends. Dr. Lipton first suggested that she attend some group meetings for the overweight and for single adults. Finally the idea of meeting new people motivated her to go to both meetings. Though it was difficult she forced herself to keep going. She wanted to learn how to act in life instead of simply reacting to it and to try to gain a serenity and peace of mind that had been missing in her life. She felt that if nothing else, forcing herself to attend meetings would "build character."

Norma began to see that she had had a tendency to hunt for reasons why she wouldn't fit in with various groups. She had wanted "perfect" situations in which she would feel not only comfortable but as if she really belonged. Gradually, instead of concentrating on the differences between herself and others, she began trying to find areas in which they had something in common.

For more than seven months Norma had not attended church services, choosing to avoid the place where numerous anxiety attacks had occurred in the past. After two and a half months of therapy, she was able to go to her niece's confirmation even though she admitted that it would not have taken much for her to back out of it.

Once she was in the church, she found herself experiencing periods of anxiety and uneasiness. She was able, however, to use biofeedback again in order to deal with the problem. During subsequent visits to church, Norma reported additional episodes of anxiety, but in each case she found the techniques she had learned to be extremely helpful in coping with the situation. She still prefers to sit in the back, at the end of the pew, just in case she should have to leave, but, up to this point, has not found it necessary to do so, and she reports that the anxiety attacks have diminished.

For Norma, not only has biofeedback been useful in dealing with anxiety but hypnotherapy has also proved to be a valuable tool. Her concentration and ability to focus made her a good subject for hypnotherapy. While under hypnosis, she was given suggestions dealing with her feelings of confidence, security, and control, as well as her determination to do what she had made up her mind to do.

At this point, Norma has been in therapy for eighteen months. During this time several significant changes have taken place. Her weight has dropped to 137 pounds and her anxiety attacks have disappeared. She has begun to be more comfortable dealing with other people and has been able to get involved with new groups.

Norma's ability to focus on the problems at hand as well as her willingness, determination, and motivation to make the changes that were needed have enabled her to take the steps necessary to bring about significant improvement in her life and weight.

For the first time in many years Norma did not make plans for professional activities over the summer. Instead she said that her project for the summer was to work on herself. She has joined a health club and now works out four or five days each week. She is also continuing with psychotherapy and hypnotherapy on a regular basis and making excellent progress in shedding more pounds. Plus, she has begun dating a man who shares her interests, and is quite happy with the results of her initial motivation to change.

As human beings we all function on two separate levels where motivation is concerned. One is intellectual, the other emotional. The intellectual is our rational, logical thinking. Our capacity to understand facts, to know what makes sense and what doesn't, works on this level.

Our emotional level, on the other hand, represents our

feelings, our reactions, and our responses. Our emotions do not necessarily have to make any sense or possess any rhyme or reason for them to be very real to us.

An ideal state of mental health exists when our intellectual and emotional reactions are integrated and consistent. This is, however, only a theoretically attainable state, an ideal.

Our capability for irrationality is often offensive to us. If we think that our feelings make no sense or that our emotional reactions are offensive in some way and, therefore, threatening to us, we tend to suppress, repress, deny, or in some fashion keep the emotional truth from ourselves.

In the final analysis, however, our emotions usually rule the roost. It is at these times, when there is a gross inconsistency between what we "know" and how we "feel," that we find ourselves not doing what we say we want to do. Our intellect, though, can help mold our irrational, emotional reactions into a form consistent with what we know to be so.

In order to reshape our emotional reactions, we must know what they really are. This is fifty percent of the work simply because we are so good at kidding ourselves and protecting ourselves from unacceptable feelings. Our primary task, then, is to bring to the surface that which eludes us.

How does this relate to motivation and weight loss? Our motivation, which is determined mostly by our attitudes, is often outside our conscious awareness.

*Henry, Monica, and Jack—Losing Weight.* It seems that the key to what you really "feel" can be found by exploring the opposite of what you say. Here are three examples of motivation for weight loss and the conversations these patients had with Dr. Lipton. He posed this question to each of the three: "Why do you want to lose weight?"

Patient 1: "Because I know that if I don't lose the weight I'm going to die young."

Patient 2: "Because I don't want to be single all my life. I want to get married and have children."

Patient 3: "Because I know that being this fat is not very attractive to my wife, and I love her and will do anything to make her happy."

The following discussion ensued with Patient 1 during a therapy session:

"So, Henry, you want to lose weight so you won't die young?"

"Yes, I know I should lose weight for this reason."

"Was either of your parents as overweight as you are?"

"Oh, yes. My father weighed two-hundred-seventy-five pounds and was only five-foot-nine. He lived until he was eighty-two years old."

"Are you more like your father or your mother?"

"Oh, my father, definitely. Everyone says I'm just like him."

"Tell me, Henry. Deep down you don't really feel that you are going to die young, do you?"

"Well . . . no. I guess not really."

"Do you ever become afraid that in your efforts to lose weight you might be messing with something that you shouldn't be messing with?"

"You know? You're right. My uncle, my father's younger brother, was real fat. He went on a diet and lost fifty-five pounds and died three years later at the age of sixty-eight."

On the conscious level this patient experienced repeated failure because every time he tried to lose weight, he became fearful that he was setting himself up for an early demise. His unconscious motivation was to stay fat. This canceled out his intellectual commitment to lose weight, resulting in zero motivation.

Therapy with Patient 2 went like this:

"So, Monica, you'd like to lose weight so you can have a social life, meet a nice guy, and maybe settle down and have kids?"

"Yes, Dr. Lipton. I've wanted this all my life."

"You are a warm and friendly person and have a very

attractive face. Haven't you ever had the opportunity to date since you gained weight at the age of fifteen?"

"Oh, sure. You know, Dr. Lipton, there are a lot of guys out there who have a thing for fat women. I've been asked out quite a bit, but I've never gone because I'm so fat."

"I'm a little confused . . . maybe you can help me. A lot of guys ask you out because they like you as a person and may also have a thing for fat women, but even though you want to date you refuse to go out with them because you're fat. Is that right?"

"Yes, that's right."

"I see. . . . Could you tell me a little bit about what your life was like growing up, say, when you were a kid before you got fat?"

"Oh, Dr. Lipton, I don't want to get into all of that. My life was very bad. My mother was married four times, twice to alcoholics who did terrible things to her and to me and it's just too upsetting to think about. I just want you to help me lose weight. I've been trying for fifteen years so I can have a normal life. Please help me."

Because of the trauma and pain associated with this woman's childhood, it had become more acceptable and less anxiety-provoking for her to place the blame for the lack of "normalcy" in her life on her weight than on her fear of men and of suffering the same fate that befell her mother.

Therapy with Patient 3 went like this:

"So, Jack, you want to please your wife and lose weight?"

"Oh, yes. She's very unhappy with how fat I am."

"How does she express her dissatisfaction?"

"Well, she just speaks her mind. She doesn't pull any punches. That's one of the reasons I married her. I tend to be pretty shy and I admired her spunk and aggressiveness."

"But what exactly does she say to you about your weight?"

"Well, she's pretty blunt and she has a right to be because, as you can see, I'm pretty damn fat, right?"

"Right, but what exactly does she say to you about your weight?"

"Well . . . 'Jack, you're a fat, disgusting slob and nobody in her right mind except me would even consider staying with you. And having sex with you is a real nightmare.' "

"How do you feel when she says such things to you?"

"Well, I know she's right. How can I argue with that? Just look at me."

"But how does it make you *feel,* Jack? You know, *feel?* Happy, sad, glad, mad? How does it make you feel?"

"Oh, feel. Well, I guess . . . I guess . . . I guess I don't like it."

"Jack, does it make you a little angry?"

"Yeah. Sometimes more than a little angry."

"Do you ever tell your wife how angry it makes you?"

"Tell her? You gotta be kidding! You don't just stand up to my wife, no sir!"

Here Jack's unconscious motivation to lose weight was being canceled out by an unconscious resentment toward his wife. The only way he could express his anger was in a passive-aggressive fashion, a manner in which she was not aware of how he was getting back at her. His unconscious motivation was to resist weight loss and to say symbolically to his wife, "I really want to lose weight, my darling, and am trying so hard, my lovey honey, but for some reason I just can't do it, and will drop dead, dear, before I ever give you the satisfaction of enjoying me thin, you miserable shrew!"

How were these people helped? The first step was to make them aware of their unconscious feelings so they could begin to exert control. The second step was to help them use their newfound understanding to deal with their feelings in a more functional, that is, less destructive fashion.

Patient 3, Jack, lost 42 pounds in seven months after Dr. Lipton had helped him become aware of his unconscious anger toward his wife and gain the confidence to express it in a different way that was neither as self-destructive as staying sixty pounds overweight, nor injurious to his wife.

Jack had decided to develop a chronic short-term memory problem due to an allergic response to his wife's three cats. Instead of eating to express his anger, he kept forgetting whatever his wife asked him to do.

You may be wondering why Dr. Lipton suggested an alternative rather than helping this patient deal with his fear of anger and difficulty in being assertive. The reason was that Jack did not really want to become more assertive. He said that he had always been that way and rather liked himself the way he was, and that he loved his wife and had no intention of ever leaving her no matter how much he hated her. All he wanted from Dr. Lipton was to help him lose weight. So he did!

Dr. Lipton helped Patient 2, Monica, see that she was using her weight problem to cover up the painful issues of her childhood and their continuing influence on her life as an adult.

When she became aware of what she had been doing, she cried hysterically, saying, "I don't care. I would rather be fat all my life than dig up those painful memories again."

Dr. Lipton told her that she didn't have to look at any of those issues but that she didn't have to stay fat either. Now that she knew the fat issue was a cover-up, there was no more need for it. That is, she could lose the weight and still decide not to date and not to become involved with men. He emphasized that she was in control and did not need the weight as an excuse.

Her response was, "I never thought of that." She proceeded to lose 38 pounds in six months.

Patient 1, Henry, had spent years trying to lose weight and had interpreted his continual failure as a character flaw; his lack of control over his weight had generalized to other aspects of his life. He had started to feel like a failure and became depressed over his perceived lack of effectiveness.

After several sessions, Henry finally accepted the fact that he really did not want to lose weight because he was afraid of dying young like his thin uncle rather than living to a ripe old age like his fat father.

He had denied his real feelings because they offended his rational/intellectual orientation. So he compromised. He would lose ten pounds to demonstrate to himself that he did have control over his body and his life, but he would stop at that point out of respect for his deep-seated feelings, thus choosing to remain overweight.

This patient experienced tremendous relief in not having to continue to do what he really did not want to do (lose weight) and feeling like a failure on top of it all.

Perhaps you, too, have a weight problem that is causing you to feel that you cannot control your life. Remember that you cannot "just" lose weight. Attempting to lose weight without effecting other changes in your life rarely works. The desire to lose weight has to be embedded within a much larger commitment to improve the overall quality of your life—to enjoy life more, to become healthier, to become more active, to live!

Unless losing poundage has a symbolic meaning beyond simply becoming thinner, failure will ensue. Why? Because no matter what anyone tells you to the contrary, losing weight is not easy. To resist the temptation of eating the forbidden, to exercise continuing restraint and self-discipline is tough.

What distinguishes the successful from the unsuccessful is motivation, motivation arising from a commitment to enhance the quality of life.

Weight loss is no more than a modus operandi, a vehicle for enhancing your health and enjoyment.

**Step Five: Hypnosis**

After patients in my office are endocrinologically evaluated and any imbalances are addressed, after the diet is introduced and psychotherapeutic strategies are employed, some patients learn self-hypnosis. This is designed to modify the body's capability to rid itself of fat. Unlike some hypnosis for weight loss, our approach does not focus on giving patients posthypnotic suggestions not to eat fattening foods. Instead, we train them to put themselves into an Enhanced State of Consciousness (ESC) to redirect the body's biochemistry (see chapter 8).

Put yourself there now. Imagine fat-fighting cells proliferating and moving throughout your bloodstream. Visualize these cells coming into contact with your adipose tissue and dissolving the excess fat. Imagine the cells continuing day after day, dissolving fat.

This technique works wonders with our patients; it should with you, too. Some report increased energy levels and higher spirits. Some of our most difficult cases showed immediate improvement.

But for it to work, you must believe in it. One patient, for instance, a tough, no-nonsense businessman, was doing everything our program asked for—but lost only a little each week. He appeared to have no success with the visualization of the fat-fighting cells.

Then one day he returned to Dr. Lipton's office and wanted to go over the visualization technique again. His renewed interest was the result of a conversation with another patient who had found success with it.

Dr. Lipton helped him and soon he was losing weight at a much faster rate.

If you remember from our earlier description, people with $PS^2$ are creative, intuitive, and emotionally reactive. This means they are usually better able to visualize the scene described and get results fast!

### Step Six: Exercise

Exercise, as described in chapter 6, is an important part of weight loss. It goes hand in hand with that most important step, cutting back on your caloric intake.

Aerobic exercise will increase your body's oxygenation, thus helping enzyme action in your body and speeding up the metabolism of fat.

If you have difficulty starting an exercise program, try to adopt a nondefensive attitude of self-examination. If lack of motivation is affecting this area, it is likely affecting others as well.

If you have difficulty sticking to the program, talk to your friends and family and learn what they observe about you and your patterns of eating and coping with life. You may find yourself wanting to contradict them, but before you dismiss their observations as inaccurate, give them some thought. It is not the truth that hurts us but the denial of truth that prevents us from understanding ourselves and effecting change.

As simplistic as it sounds, if you want things to change, you cannot keep everything the same.

## Ten Tips to Help You Reach Your Diet Goals

These tips combine sound behavioral and emotional principles with good old common sense. These are good places to start to help you learn to bring areas of your life into control.

1. *Increase your level of general activity.*

   By taking the stairs instead of the elevator or walking a bit more briskly during the day, you will burn a few extra calories. Become aware of times that you are sedentary and look for ways to be more active.
2. *Sit down, eat slowly, chew food thoroughly, sip drinks.*

   Some people do not "count" food they eat standing up as having relevance to their diets.

   Rushing through a meal shortens the amount of time that food or drink is in your mouth, thereby reducing gratification. Put your fork down between bites. Contemplate each taste and savor it. You will be surprised how much more filling a meal can be simply by slowing down.

   It takes twenty minutes for the stomach to tell the

brain it is full. If you stuff yourself in a few minutes, you will not know how full you are until your stomach starts to hurt twenty minutes after you are through eating.

3. *Eat in front of a mirror.*

   Watching yourself eat, really studying the way you handle silverware, the speed at which you eat, how you chew and your posturing at the table can teach you a great deal about how and why you have developed bad eating habits. Do this during one meal a week while you are dieting.

4. *Serve meals on smaller plates.*

   A sensible meal may look lost on a regular ten-inch dinner plate, whereas it would fill a smaller plate. And a full plate of food should fill you as well.

5. *Eliminate junk food from your house and workplace.*

   If temptations are not there physically, your willpower will be less strained. Everyone's health will benefit from your getting rid of high-fat, high-salt, empty calorie foods.

6. *When it is time to eat, do that and nothing else.*

   Reading, watching TV, or doing paperwork while eating is a distraction that keeps you from being aware of how much you are eating and what you are eating. Gratification is reduced and the meal is over before you know it. You are likely to overeat as a result.

7. *Treat yourself to something special.*

   As you reach certain weight loss or measurement goals, or celebrate other dieting milestones or anniversaries, treat yourself to something special. A trip to the theater, an item of clothing or jewelry, or another reward for a job well done goes a long way toward boosting morale. You will be rewarded for the hard work and encouraged to continue.

8. *Stand nude in front of a full-length mirror every day.*

   This will probably bring you surprise—and some consternation—but it should tell you a great deal. This is one of the most important techniques to employ and one of the most difficult to do.

   For a full sixty seconds each day look at yourself in

a mirror while standing naked. Look from all angles. Hold in your hand a familiar object like a purse or wallet or magazine. This familiar object prevents your mind's eye from distorting your body image, that is, making yourself appear thinner than you really are.

This is a perceptual biofeedback technique. It increases your motivation by forcing you to accept rather than deny the reality of your physical condition. It also provides extremely effective and positive reinforcement as the results of your efforts become visible.

Making an accurate assessment of yourself is a positive, insightful experience and it will encourage you to stick with the program. As you reach your goals, you will be proud of the changes that hard work brings.

9. *Seek a sudden taste explosion.*

   Bite slowly into frozen seedless grapes when you feel the urge to eat, or chew cinnamon-flavored sugar-free gum. The sudden taste sensation is very gratifying.

10. *Put on a favorite album or tape.*

    Rather than looking to gratify your needs with food, bring yourself pleasure by listening to a favorite piece of music. Soon you will learn to substitute one type of gratification for another. Sing along if that helps. Or stand back and conduct the orchestra, or dance.

Many people who have been having trouble losing weight for most of their lives feel that it is no use, that they cannot change and will never change. That is simply not the case. We have many, many patients who have thought this way at first, but proved themselves wrong.

Your commitment to change is absolutely essential and the most important factor in achieving results. You *can* do it.

12

# Control Your Pain

Physical pain can be debilitating. Perhaps you know all too well that this is true. It is estimated that as many as 85 million Americans suffer from one of the three major categories—headache, arthritis, or back pain—at any given time!

We spend some $1 billion a year on over-the-counter anti-pain products, not to mention the millions of prescriptions written annually for pain relievers.

But pain does not have to rule your life. You can combat it. In fact, you have already learned the essential elements of the fight against pain.

In this chapter Dr. Lipton and I will describe these physical and behavioral techniques for your battle plan and help you win. We will explain the critical importance of an accurate medical diagnosis of the cause of your suffering and how you can help your doctor make it. And we will discuss the vital role muscles play in promoting all types of discomfort, and ways you can control its effects.

Having said this, however, it is important to point out the reason for the sensation of pain in the first place. It is a survival mechanism. Without it, for instance, you would not feel an inflamed appendix about to burst, or tensed muscles in your lower back, or the heat of the stove as it burns your hand. But once that message has been relayed, once you know that your body needs attention, and take appropriate action, you need not suffer with a continuation of that message.

There are some individuals who feel no sensation of pain whatsoever. This is an enormous disadvantage. They are often not aware that they are in danger. There is no warning system to alert them to the fact that their internal organs are not functioning properly, for instance.

Then there are individuals who feel intense pain when there is no real physical cause. This happens, for example, when an amputee suffers excruciating pain in a foot he or she has lost. The "phantom" hurting is just as real as when the foot was still part of the body. The person suffers further by not being able to make contact with the foot, such as to rub it or soak it.

These two extremes in pain detection tell us something important about its relation to the mind-body connection. In short, it helps us understand how the perception of pain is solely in the mind. Though you and I feel pain at the place we are hurt, that burned hand, for instance, it is because the mind has ordered it to be so.

When your hand touches a hot stove, the heat stimulates pain cells. These trigger a release of biochemicals, such as prostaglandins, bradykinin, and histamine, which lower your pain threshold in the injured area. The signal travels up strings of nerve fibers to the spinal cord and from there into two major pain pathways to the brain. As a result you pull your hand away from the stove before you realize it hurts.

One pathway carries information on the location and severity of the pain to the thalamus and then to the cerebral cortex. The other tells the brain's limbic system that adrenaline is needed for quick movement. Thus, the nervous and endocrine systems are alerted to release their flood of biochemicals and you are ready for "fight or flight."

The cause of the acute pain in this instance is easy to identify. This is not always the case. Most of the patients that Dr. Lipton and I treat have what is known as chronic pain, which is present in some form for anywhere from six months to a lifetime.

Generally involved is one of three types of pain mentioned

earlier—headache, arthritis, or back pain. These are caused or made worse by disease or injury, or by emotional or psychological trauma. Whatever the cause, there is one clear and simple result: pain. Thus, the headache brought on by anxiety can be just as excruciating as a headache caused by a blow to the skull.

Understanding the mind-body connection is aiding us more and more to help patients identify the reason for their suffering and ways they can deal with it. It also shows us that some common methods of treatment—painkillers, avoiding exercise, having unnecessary surgery, and grimly enduring it—may make you hurt more in the long run.

Since the mind perceives pain, we believe it should also be able to control it. If emotions and ways of thinking can make pain worse, they can be turned around to alleviate pain. Particularly where $PS^2$ is concerned, changing your point of view and attitudes can change your experience of ill health—in this case, pain.

This approach to pain relief is now being explored by a growing number of health practitioners. It has been found to offer substantial relief to those who have not been helped by other methods. This is true of our patients as well. They are finding that they can change their minds' perception of pain and, as a result, actually feel less pain!

*Cindy's Headaches.* Cindy, for instance, was an overworked, underpaid secretary. She hated her job and her boss and, at first, looked forward to Fridays the way a prisoner awaits parole. Then, gradually, she began to dread the weekends even more than the weekdays.

It was about this time that she came to see me and described "the nightmare" that began every Friday night.

"It starts as if my head is all full of cotton," she said. "After that I get a dazed feeling and a throbbing on one side of my head and neck. I can't bear to have the lights on and I start feeling sick to my stomach. It usually lasts until I fall asleep from exhaustion. Then I wake up with it the next morning. Here I am," she added, "living for the weekends and I just wind up in bed and miserable."

Cindy was confused by something that puzzles many migraine sufferers. A tension headache generally arrives during or directly after some kind of stress. The curious thing about migraine headaches is that they often appear when a person expects to be relaxing, such as on weekends and holidays.

I believed that Cindy was actually feeling the peak of her weekday tension after work was all over. Her job provided a distraction from her unhappiness with her life; she had to function Monday through Friday. On the weekend, however, she had time to think about her problems and that was when the real stress set in. You could almost say that she then had the luxury of getting a full-blown, incapacitating migraine headache. For this reason I sometimes refer to the migraine as the "layaway headache," though not all migraines behave in this way.

After a thorough medical examination to rule out any medical problems we might have been overlooking, I asked Cindy if she would keep a "pain notebook," which I will describe in a moment. I also prescribed some medication. I asked her not to think of the medicine as a "cure" for her headache problem. I also recommended she see Dr. Lipton to try to relieve some of the built-up tension and to figure out why the headaches had started when they did.

It was a month before I saw Cindy again. She said that the medication and the behavioral techniques were helping, but that the headaches were still troubling her.

Her pain diary revealed a great deal about the onset of her headaches. She said she had gotten "carried away" and probably had written much more than she needed to. I assured her it would be helpful; and, indeed, we saw a pattern emerging clearly. Before every attack she thought, among other things, about a job that was supposed to open up in the communications department of her company.

She had not realized it had so consumed her thoughts, although Dr. Lipton had encouraged her as a writer and suggested she apply for the job.

"It was Dr. Lipton's idea first that you apply for the job?" I asked, trying to help her understand her thoughts.

"Well, actually, I guess I said that I wished I had that job instead of what I'm doing now."

"Tell Dr. Lipton what you just told me," I said. "Though it appears that he has already picked up one of the main reasons you have been getting these headaches."

She nodded.

"Tell me, Cindy, did you ever figure out what first brought on the headaches?"

"No. I tried and tried to come up with something but all I could remember was hearing the rumor that the communications job might be opening up. I'm sorry, I just—"

She stopped in mid-sentence.

"Are you beginning to get the picture?" I asked.

"In technicolor."

When I next saw Cindy she had good news for me. "No more headaches, Dr. Solomon. At least not for the past six weeks."

I was delighted and suggested that she try going off the medication.

As we talked, she said, "I guess I was the last to figure out that I began feeling a lot of added nervousness when the rumor started about the job. On the weekends I knew I should be working on my resumé and trying for it, only I didn't admit it to myself consciously."

"And where did the headaches go?"

"Well, I guess this is going to sound silly, but I applied for the job and the headaches disappeared."

Of course, nothing is quite that easy. When Cindy did not get the job her headaches returned. Not in full force—she only got them about once a month and they were not quite as severe. But with further counseling, Cindy learned to be more assertive and to keep trying for other jobs. As she did this, while continuing the relaxation techniques, the headaches finally went away for good. Then she landed a position as an entry-level copywriter in an advertising agency—work for which she felt much better suited.

It seemed that Cindy's shyness and lack of self-control were the real culprits behind her migraines. As soon as she started acting on her wishes the headaches faded away.

Migraines, like most headaches, reflect the particular problems of each individual. A patient with migraines from caffeine, for instance, may require only a caffeine-free diet. Cindy's case required the combined efforts of Cindy, Dr. Lipton, and myself. In a way, Cindy's migraines had provided clues for her; she had become a more confident person, better able to make her way in the world.

As stated previously, Cindy's pain notebook was a great resource in pinpointing her particular problem. Here are some guidelines to help you, too, keep a pain notebook. They are based on questions I ask my patients.

## Pain Notebook

The object is to keep track of your pain. If you purchase a notebook-type appointment calendar and fill it in appropriately, you will have a good record to share with your physician. Here are the things to note:

- Precisely where is the center of your pain? Examine yourself while you hurt, not after the pain has gone away. Try to place your hand in the place where the pain seems most intense and ignore the tentacles that radiate outward from that location.
- When do you hurt? What time of day? After or before eating? After or just before sleeping? After exercise? How much exercise does it take before pain begins? After drinking alcoholic beverages? After smoking? During tense moments?

- How often do you experience pain? Once a day? Once a month? Make a note each time you feel pain.
- How much pain do you feel? Try to gauge your pain on a scale from one to ten. One might be a nagging ache; ten almost unendurable pain. Any rating over five would indicate severe pain.
- Describe your pain. Is it a stab that seems to cut through you? Do you feel a burning sensation as if part of your body were on fire? Does it throb or is it steady?
- Your diet could be affecting your pain. Record everything you ate during the 24 hours before the pain struck—food, drink, medicines.
- What was your environment just before the pain hit? Were you at work? at home? Who was with you? What were you doing? How did you feel emotionally: angry, sad, tense, happy, excited? Do you see a pattern? Do you usually begin feeling pain on the job or in the company of one person?

Before we look at the three major areas of pain—headaches, back pain, and arthritic pain, and some exercises that, with your doctor's approval, can give you relief—I want to tell you about Brian. This is to emphasize the importance of seeing a doctor about your pain before trying any of the remedies we offer here. Brian is living proof of the importance of accurate medical diagnosis for any chronic or acute pain.

## Locating Your Pain

*Brian's Aneurysm.* Brian first came to me after a friend told him of the success Dr. Lipton and I had had in eliminating her migraine headaches. He told me he had almost constant headache pain, and it was getting worse.

It took a great deal of verbal prompting and probing to put together a picture of the pain, exactly where and when it hurt, how much, and other symptoms that accompanied the headaches.

At the outset it seemed that Brian had many of the classic

symptoms of migraine attacks—throbbing on one side of his head, the appearance of flashing lights, unfocused irritability and depression, at times numbness in his right arm and leg.

But a curious aspect of his headaches kept me from diagnosing migraines: His hearing had changed. It became more acute in a noisy environment and at the peak of the pain he heard what he described as a bass drum beating inside his head. These were not symptoms of migraine headaches.

In my examination of Brian I spent long minutes with my stethoscope pressed tightly against his head and neck. When I detected arterial noise I suspected that Brian had suffered a cerebral aneurysm. This could cause a weakening in the wall of a blood vessel, making it bulge outward and create the "noise" I had heard. It sounded like a bruit, like tiny spurts from a steam valve. If that were the case, it was in danger of rupturing whenever the vessel became engorged with blood.

Brian's brain scan confirmed my diagnosis. Brian had suffered an aneurysm at the place where the internal carotid, the anterior and posterior cerebral arteries, and the anterior and posterior communicating arteries meet. It was precariously close to rupturing and the hemorrhage could have killed him. The aneurysm had undoubtedly been made worse by his increasingly frequent and high levels of tension, generated by pain and fear.

Brian survived the emergency brain surgery to repair the damaged artery. He might not have been so fortunate if he had not sought professional counsel. Today he is a healthy, happy man and uses the techniques taught in this book to reduce unnecessary stress on the repaired cerebral arteries and to regain control over his life and health.

Remember that your doctor needs your help for an accurate diagnosis. The pain notebook can help you be more thorough.

Now let's look at the three major areas of pain—headaches, arthritic pain, and back pain—and some exercises that, used with your doctor's approval, can give you relief.

## Headaches

At least 42 million Americans suffer chronic headaches. Some authorities estimate that anywhere from 50 to 100 million people in this country each year experience recurring tension headaches caused by muscle spasms in the back, neck, and head.

There are many causes for these spasms—tension, inadequate nutrition, Premenstrual Syndrome (PMS), allergies, chemical imbalances.

Knowing the kind of headache pain you have can help point you in the right direction for treatment. Here are several types.

### Tension Headaches

The vast majority of headaches are caused by contraction of the muscles in the neck and head. Tension headaches are a symptom of just that, tension and stress, and may signal that the victim is suffering from Profound Sensitivity Syndrome.

Typically, tension headaches result in a dull pain that encircles the skull, as if a band had been fastened too tightly around your head. They may also be manifest in both sides of your forehead, temples, or neck. They can occur as often as several times a week and can last for several hours or days.

You might suspect you have a tension headache if you are depressed, anxious, or apprehensive. Watch also for poor posture, excessive work or physical activity, and eyestrain.

### Vascular

Vascular headaches include migraines and cluster headaches.

The *migraine* is the most common vascular headache. Two-thirds of my migraine patients are women.

Many neurologists now suspect that migraines may stem from a biological abnormality of nerve cells and chemicals in the brain, notably serotonin. The fact that a large number of migraine sufferers have a family history of headache complaints points further to the possibility that a biochemical disturbance is at work.

Others contend that muscle contractions and the attending change in blood vessels are at fault. This may explain why reactions to stress can trigger the intense pain. During the headache, the temporal artery, the main blood-carrying vessel to the brain, begins to pulsate furiously. Blood rushes into the now-dilated artery and extracranial arteries also dilate and release substances that lower the pain threshold and cause further muscle constriction.

Migraines create a throbbing or piercing agony. They are located generally on one side of the head and may be accompanied by nausea, intolerance of lights or sounds, mood changes, or sleep disturbances. They can last for hours or days and may occur anywhere from daily to monthly.

The *cluster* headache lasts generally from twenty to ninety minutes. It occurs one or more times a day for as long as two months. It may not reappear for a year or more. Cluster headaches produce a drilling or boring pain over or near one eye.

Ninety percent of the four million Americans who suffer from cluster headaches are men. Most of them are smokers and in mid-life. The pain from a cluster is so intense that many doctors call it the "suicide" headache, because its victims sometimes choose to end their lives rather than live with the pain.

Certain foods have been known to cause vascular headaches. You might try this test to see if your headaches are food-related:

1. Eliminate as many of the following foods from your diet as possible for one week:

Monosodium glutamate (MSG is found in many packaged or canned foods, spices, and seasonings); foods that contain nitrates as preservatives such as sandwich meats, cured meats, and hot dogs; caffeine (found also in many soft drinks); fatty foods; aged cheese (not cottage or cream cheese); aged wine; sour cream and yogurt; chocolate; bananas; avocados; organ meats such as liver or kidneys; nuts; citrus fruits; vinegar; canned figs; navy or lima beans.

2. Every four days introduce one of the suspect foods back into your diet. Refrain once more from that food as you test a new one. Note the date and time you added the food on a calendar page.

3. Record the dates and starting times of any vascular headaches.

4. Do the vascular headaches start after eating any particular food? If it appears so, try avoiding that food and see if the attacks subside or become less frequent.

5. Also make note of any drugs you take. Drugs for high blood pressure, for instance, can trigger headaches. If you see a correlation between medication and headaches, consult your doctor.

## Other Headaches

Organic headaches, headaches other than vascular and tension, with a physical cause, account for about two percent of all headache pain. They are usually caused by a medically treatable problem, such as a tumor or high blood pressure.

*Richard's Tumor.* A patient named Richard was under tremendous stress and had trouble relaxing. As his stress mounted, so did the spasms in his neck muscles, resulting in headaches and a tilting of his head toward his right shoulder. An X ray showed a tumor in the soft tissue of his neck. It was removed surgically and he learned the relaxation techniques taught earlier. Within three months he was free of symptoms and has remained so.

*Sinus* headaches are organic in nature. A sinus headache is caused by an infection of the sinuses, which fill and build pressure on the nerves above them causing pain in the forehead or cheek. It may involve aching teeth, fever, a discharge from the nose, or tenderness around the nose area.

Surprisingly few people suffer true sinus headaches. Medical researchers estimate that up to ninety percent of headaches diagnosed as sinus are actually migraines.

*Temporal mandibular joint dysfunction* (TMJ), a headache aggravated by tension, manifests itself in the teeth and jaw. Seventy-five percent of victims are women.

It is aggravated by excessive chewing, bruxism (grinding of the teeth), and clenching the jaw. Muscle spasms in the jaw spread to other nearby muscles, causing them to become tense as well. TMJ headaches begin slowly and ultimately create a dull ache over the entire head that can sometimes go into the ears.

## Arthritis

The two most common types of arthritis are osteoarthritis (OA) and rheumatoid arthritis (RA). They account for about eighty percent of all cases. Some medical authorities estimate that seventy percent of all Americans over the age of fifty have some degree of OA.

Rheumatoid arthritis is an autoimmune disease, meaning that the immune system actually turns on its host body and attacks, in this case, the connective tissue in joints. The subsequent inflammation is the reason for the pain. Evidence that symptoms of this disease are made worse by emotional tension and internal turmoil is overwhelming.

Rheumatoid arthritis, a sign of and aggravated by $PS^2$, occurs when chronic pressure and tension lead to immune malfunction. The immune system then produces RA antibodies that attack the joints. Another occurrence of stress produces another flood of antibodies, and the patient suffers what rheumatologists call a "flare," a sudden, agonizing attack of acute arthritis.

In cases of osteoarthritis cartilage is broken down, allowing bones to bump together. This recurring trauma alerts the body to form calcium deposits at the points of contact as a way of protecting the bones from further damage. Unfortunately, this adds to the problem because those deposits cause additional rubbing and sometimes they can catch or pinch nerves. The result is excruciating pain.

At times the nerves being pinched in one area serve some other part of the body. Thus, a pinched nerve in the cervical spine, just below the skull, can cause pain, tingling, numbness, and even loss of function anywhere from the shoulders to the fingers.

Stress compounds the problems of arthritis because it increases muscle tension, which places additional pressure on already-inflamed joints.

Just as headaches can be related to mounting internal tension, so there appears to be some correlation between arthritis and the stress that comes from the hesitancy to show emotions, particularly anger. We have seen this in a patient who may express the need to "bottle up" her true feelings or "bite her tongue" constantly in order to maintain an appearance of outward placidity.

Does a personal inventory highlight the probability that you, too, may prefer not to express anger, fear, or hurt feelings? Will you do anything to avoid an argument? Do you cling to the motto *Peace at any price*? Do health problems seem to have any relation to these decisions?

If you feel that this might have some validity for you, you might consider talking with someone whose opinion you trust about learning ways to channel your anger and other alternatives to keeping silent. Remember, helplessness is a learned pattern. That means you can unlearn it as well.

Along with gaining a sense of control, some appropriate exercise is vitally important for arthritis sufferers. As previously stated, it helps prevent the joints from becoming stiff and nonfunctional. In some forms of rheumatic disease, such as bursitis, lack of exercise can contribute to loss of mobility because the joints will "freeze." Only surgery restores motion in such cases.

Furthermore, the cartilage that acts as a cushion between bones gets its only nourishment from the synovial fluid created by small sacs surrounding every joint in the body. That fluid also serves as a lubricant in joints. Only physical movement will carry it to the place it is needed. We will give you some samples of exercises to help keep you limber in the upcoming discussion of muscles' role in pain.

Certain foods are believed by some doctors to trigger arthritis pain attacks. You might want to test these in the way suggested earlier. They include red meat, pork, wheat, dairy products, eggs, potatoes, tomatoes, eggplant, peppers, and onions.

*Rebecca's Fibromyalgia.* Rebecca had traveled to see me on a winter's day. "I've been trying to get my husband to agree to move to Florida," she said as she came into my office and removed a heavy coat, two sweaters, two scarves, and a pair of mittens with gloves underneath. "Winter just kills me." She sat tensely, as if she were in a lot of discomfort.

When my nurse had handed me Rebecca's medical records she had remarked that it was the "fattest" chart she had ever seen.

"Rebecca," I said, "I wonder if there's a medical specialist you haven't seen! I see you have been to a neurologist, psychiatrist, rheumatologist, endocrinologist, chiropractor, psychologist, another rheumatologist. . . . What brings you here?"

"Well, about a month ago I met a woman at a potters' convention—that's my work, I make pottery—and we started talking and it turned out that she had been suffering with the same thing I have. But she said you diagnosed her and she's much better."

I knew whom Rebecca was referring to, a vivacious and

talented woman from Alabama who had won prizes for some of her pottery.

"Did this woman tell you what her diagnosis was?" I asked.

"Oh, yes, she told me all about it. Fibromyalgia. And she said she thought I might have it. I had just about given up. Can you tell me if that's what I have?"

I had seen the other diagnoses in Rebecca's chart: neurosis, psychological complaint, as well as multiple sclerosis, acute rheumatoid arthritis, and neuritis. Still, many patients come with their own diagnoses and they are not always correct. I cautioned Rebecca about this.

"I just don't think I can stand it anymore. I used to think I was going to die."

She was almost in tears and I calmed her down enough to proceed with the examination.

Fibromyalgia is actually an illness that has specific, recognizable symptoms, which can be confused for other illnesses. The general symptoms include muscular aches and pains, disturbed sleep, morning fatigue and stiffness, diarrhea, and depression. The aches and pains often intensify during cold weather. Although the muscle aches and pains may seem to be diffuse, or randomly spread throughout the body, there are certain "tender points" that are its signature, so to speak.

These tender points, areas where the greater amount of muscle pain is located, are the bundle of muscles in the back of the neck and shoulders, the sides of the breastbone, the fatty, padded area above the knees, and the bony points of the elbows and hips.

As with her colleague in Alabama, there was no indication of any swelling in her joints or muscles. And she was extremely sensitive to most of the tender points, but showed no abnormal sensitivity elsewhere.

Since she knew the characteristic symptoms of fibromyalgia, I shared this with her but told her I wanted to run some tests before I could say for sure that that was her problem.

The next time I saw her I told her that her tests showed no

abnormalities and, considering the results of her physical exam, I agreed that she did appear to be suffering from fibromyalgia.

She was smiling, but tears gathered in her eyes, too. "Can you help me?"

Though my fibromyalgia patients, like any patients, respond to treatment with varying success, I have never seen a patient who could not be helped substantially. I told her this and together we mapped out her treatment. Because fibromyalgia causes a painful tightening of the muscles, it is especially responsive to treatment with relaxation techniques. Rebecca knew this and agreed eagerly to work to learn all she could to help her condition.

Watching her response to treatment was like watching a tightly coiled spring unwind. Even if she had not told me that the pain was diminishing, I could have seen it in her face and in her movements. Her face lost its taut, pinched expression, and she stopped hunching her shoulders forward. There was still some pain, but it was manageable now.

The Arthritis Foundation has called fibromyalgia "a very common ailment" that is, nonetheless, surrounded by "a great deal of confusion." Still, for this and other arthritic pain, relief can be found in the guidelines offered here.

## Back Pain

As many as 100 million Americans suffer periodic back pain. Only one percent of them have actual damage to vertebrae, discs, or muscles. Muscle tension and misuse of the body are, I believe, responsible for a large portion of the back pain in the rest of those millions who suffer.

Consider the fact that your spine is balancing constantly the equivalent of a ten-pound bowling ball: your own head. Poor posture, poor body management during activities such as bending, squatting, lifting, pushing, or pulling can damage the intricate mechanism of the spine causing you a lifetime of pain.

If the back muscles are weak, tense, or both, they become shorter and less elastic during normal activities. Prolonged periods of inner tension can generate so much tightness in the muscles that something as simple as bending down to tie a shoelace can generate severe back pain. In fact, lower back pain is often caused by chronic muscle tension, which in turn afflicts nerves and the vertebral column.

This is a common complaint of many very athletic male patients. Unfortunately, they seem to think that their bodies can take any kind of punishment they dole out.

*Don's Weight-Lifting Dilemma.* Don, whose muscles were so contracted they felt like knots of rope, had continued his weight-lifting regimen after the pain set in. He said, "I just added more push-ups, more sit-ups. I added some extra pounds on the weights, too, and really worked at getting my back into shape again. I figured I could beat it, but it just got worse."

I almost winced from his description. He had probably started out with a minor sprain from weight lifting and made it worse by pushing even harder.

I took him off his routine and put him on a new set of exercises to help his back, stressing particularly that no one should ever do sit-ups without bending the legs at the knees.

By responding to the pain signals in the right way, Don eased away that painful muscle tension, and so can others who suffer from back pain.

Muscles are intimately involved in the pain process. To help muscles grow stronger, thereby giving you more support and mobility and less likelihood of tensing, we recommend the following "physical" exercises. Following these is a series of "mental" exercises designed to help muscles relax, thereby reducing tension and strain.

## Muscles and Physical Exercises

Check with your physician before doing these or any other exercises. Also remember not to hold your breath while exercising. Do these every day to stay limber. In that way you will help prevent future muscle tension as well as ease any pain you might be experiencing.

### Neck Stretch

*Starting position.* Sit up straight, but not stiffly. Turn only as far as you can without pain. Always move slowly and gently.

1. Turn your head slowly to the right. Hold six counts. Return to center. Repeat stretch to left side.
2. Slowly drop your chin down toward your chest. Hold six counts. Bring your head back to center position.
3. Tilt your head toward your right ear. Hold six counts. Return to center. Repeat on left side. Return to center.

### Neck Press

1. Interlace fingers and press your forehead into your palms. Resist any motion. Hold six counts. Relax.
2. Press your right hand against the right side of your head. Try to bring your ear to your shoulder but resist that movement with your hand. Hold six counts. Relax. Repeat on left side.
3. Interlace your fingers and press both hands against the back of your head. Try to press your head back, but resist any motion. Hold six counts. Relax.
4. Press your right hand against your right temple. Try to turn your chin to your shoulder. Hold six counts. Relax. Repeat on right side.

### The Antipain Stretch

Do not overstretch. If a muscle twitches or quivers you may be overdoing it. Back up, readjust your body position, and resume. Also, do not bounce or force a stretch.

After each set of stretches return to the starting position before going on. Repeat each exercise five times, increasing gradually to ten times. The full stretching session should take between twelve and fifteen minutes. Remember not to do anything that is uncomfortable or painful.

*Starting position.* Lie flat on your back on a mat or firm mattress. Knees are bent and together, feet flat on the floor. Stretch your arms out to the side and firmly press your spine down on the mat.

1. Inhale slowly through your nose and exhale slowly through your mouth. Repeat.
2. Roll your head slowly toward your right shoulder. Hold for a count of two. Return to center. Repeat to the left.

   Remember to keep your head firmly on the floor while rolling it from side to side. Do not lift it. This exercise will loosen neck muscles and strengthen the cervical spine. Return to starting position.
3. Lace your fingers and place your hands behind your head, your elbows pushed outward, away from your body. Take a deep breath and as you exhale lift your head and shoulders, pressing your chin toward your chest. Lower your head back to bed or floor. Return to starting position.

   This also will help strengthen your cervical spine.
4. Lift your right knee and bring it as close as you can to your chest. Hold four counts. Return to starting position. Repeat with left knee.

   This will help you gain better range of motion in your knees and hips.
5. Lift both knees toward your chest and hold four counts. Return to starting position.
6. Lift your right knee toward your chest and hold it there. Slowly stretch your left leg downward on the bed as if you were trying to make it longer. Hold four counts. Return to starting position and repeat by holding your left knee and stretching your right. Return to starting position.
7. Slide your right leg down until it is straight and flat. Flex your foot by pressing down with your heel. Now lift your right leg toward the ceiling and hold it there

four counts. Do not "lock" your knee, keep it bent slightly. Return slowly to starting position. Repeat with left leg.

This exercise will strengthen your ankles as it releases tension in all muscles of the legs.

8. Tense your buttock muscles and lift your hips up slowly. Hold four counts. Return to starting position.

   This is particularly helpful for those with low back pain.
9. Press your knees together. Roll your hips to the left, and turn your head to the right without lifting it. Hold four counts. Return to starting position and reverse the process.

   During the hip swings your feet will roll onto their sides. This exercise brings into play leg muscles as well as muscles up the spine and into your neck.
10. Lift both knees toward your chest. Lower them slowly to your left side as you turn your head to the right. Try to press your left thigh and knee down onto the bed or floor. Hold four counts. Return your knees to your chest. Repeat knee press on the other side.

*Starting position.* For this new starting position you should lie on your left side, your left arm bent with hand under your head. Your knees should be together and bent. Place your right hand flat on the floor in front of you for support. Perform each of these exercises four times.

1. Keep your left knee bent, and slowly straighten your right leg downward. Flex your heel until your toes are pointing outward. Slowly slide right leg up and return to starting position.
2. Slide your right leg downward until it is straight, then slowly lift it toward the ceiling. Hold for four counts. Lower leg to the floor, and return to starting position. Repeat four times.
3. Slide your right leg downward until it is straight. Lift leg toward the ceiling. Lower your leg until it is a few inches above the floor. Hold four counts.

4. Roll over to your right side and resume the starting position. Repeat the exercises using your left leg.

## Muscles and Mental Exercises

The most recommended exercise for relief of muscle pain is relaxation. If you have not yet mastered the techniques taught in chapters 7 and 8, I recommend you take some time to do that now. Relaxation is like a main power switch that turns on all other pain-reducing techniques. The techniques taught in earlier chapters are a good place to start. We have included additional ones here.

Again, it is important that you try to perform these exercises frequently and consistently. Brief frequent practices are more beneficial than longer less-frequent ones.

### The WAIT Technique

For this exercise you will need some type of notification every hour on the hour. I recommend you carry a watch that has an alarm. The WAIT Technique is designed to be done every hour of the day for a period of two minutes each hour. This repeated, hourly practice is an extremely effective behavioral strategy to help your entire psycho-physiology calm down. Carry the watch or hourly beeping device in your pocket or purse to remind you to practice on the hour. This is a particularly helpful technique for chronically stressed, highly anxious people.

This exercise incorporates the techniques of biofeedback, abdominal breathing, visualization, and the relaxation of various muscle groups. In fact, WAIT is an acronym for:

Warm, heavy hands
Abdominal breathing
Imagery
Total muscle relaxation

This will help you remember what to do each time you hear the beep, bell, or buzzer.

Sit in a comfortable chair. Begin by breathing abdominally. While focusing on your stomach, say to yourself, "Warm, heavy hands." Close your eyes. Then think about relaxing all the muscle groups in your body: your head; your face; your neck; your shoulders; your arms and hands; your upper and lower back; your chest, abdomen, and pelvis; your legs, feet, and toes. This process so far should only take a few minutes. Now visualize your favorite, most relaxing scene, the sights, sounds, smells, and feel of it. Slowly open your eyes and bring yourself back to your present surroundings.

This is a powerful technique for changing your psychophysiology and takes only a small part of your waking hours. The more you practice the more quickly and more deeply relaxed you will become. It can have major impact on your chronic pain.

## Distraction

Distraction is a powerful tool for reducing the perception of pain. Think of it this way: Attention to pain intensifies pain. This means that you must avoid, as much as possible, concentrating on your pain and expressing that misery to others.

This may mean a drastic change in your life-style because even body language can signal to others the presence of pain. Try not to grimace or walk or move in a way that emphasizes the pain.

It is just as important that your loved ones change their behavior, too. Their intended kindness—running for pillows, aspirins, and heating pads—may only be hindering you from releasing some of the pain. It will be much more helpful for you in the long run if they ignore—as much as is reasonable—calling attention to your pain.

They should, however, show approval and encouragement for any actions on your part that show a willingness to work beyond the pain, such as going for a walk or helping with a particular chore.

This would all sound very unkind were it not for the reward of unpainful behavior: feeling better. It is, in a sense, changing the reward system. Instead of being rewarded for having pain, you are rewarded for overcoming it.

Getting your mind off your pain helps. Think, for instance, of an upsetting, confusing, or scary situation in which you were involved and later realized you had cut yourself or banged your leg or given yourself a black-and-blue mark and had not realized it.

Our brains, under the right conditions, seem to have the capacity to block the messages coming from nerve fibers similarly to the way one would put a telephone call on hold. Pain reduction in this sense is a form of neural rewiring. We simply do not perceive the message of pain coming into our brains.

That pain message, by the way, is not a one-way street. When the brain does perceive pain, it sends messages back to the area in pain, often making the pain significantly worse.

For instance, when we feel pain we tense our muscles automatically. This causes blood flow to the painful area to be reduced and anatomically worsens the pain.

The techniques recommended here achieve a neural rewiring, lessening the perception of pain and, in turn, keeping the brain from sending messages back to the painful area.

There is the possibility that even though you follow these directions, you will not achieve significant relief. You may, however, find your pain is lessened over time.

## Visualization

Associating an image with a feeling can be a powerful way to allow our creative center to pick up some of the burden of attitudinal change.

Imagine your pain as having an identity and a form. Picture it in your mind. Is it a horrible, ugly giant today? Is it a tiny flea biting you?

Then imagine a conqueror charging at the cause of the pain, hacking at it, stepping on it, beating it until it crawls off to hide.

Steady, ongoing visualization exercises can be very useful.

## Focusing

This is a particularly good technique for those who have trouble with visualization. There are a number of varieties. Here are two and you might want to devise your own.

*Focusing on things around you.* Concentrate as much as possible on objects or events surrounding you. What is the pattern of your wallpaper? How many colors are in it? How many TV commercials are shown in an hour-long program? Do they appeal mostly to men or women? What are some of the benefits they promise?

*Focusing with your memory or thoughts.* Recall names, numbers, and so on from memory. For instance, how many phone numbers do you know that have the digit "0" in them? To whom did you send birthday cards last year? If you were to design a house, how many rooms would you build? Sketch the plans mentally. Name all of the state capitals. How many elementary school classmates can you recall?

Keep this one in mind if you wake up during the night and do not want to get up or turn on a light. Or you can use paper and pencil.

## Hypnosis

You can reduce your pain greatly by entering an Enhanced State of Consciousness (ESC) as described in chapter 8 combined with mental imagery designed to combat pain. Here are two techniques you might try:

*Neural reinterpretation.* In this technique you will persuade your mind to believe the pain is actually a pleasant sensation. Here is one example that works well for our patients.

After entering ESC you will focus on the location of the pain, the part of your body that hurts. Let's use low back pain caused by a pinched nerve as an example. This pain usually radiates from the base of the spine downward, through the buttock and thigh and into the calf.

Focus on that pain as you bring to mind the picture of a hand holding a soft feather. Think about that hand. Is it strong and muscular or smooth and delicate? Try to see it as if it were directly in front of your eyes. Look at the feather. Is it long or short, wide or narrow? What color is it?

Now picture that hand pulling the feather downward gently from the base of your spine, along your buttock to your thigh and on to your calf. Try to feel the sensations as the feather tickles your skin. Now bring the feather and hand back up slowly, stimulating your skin as it moves. Repeat this image several times. If a feather feels too ticklish, substitute another pleasant image in its place.

*Georgia and Michael.* Here are some variations. A patient named Georgia suffered from rheumatoid arthritis in her right hand. She visualized the pain as a radio turned up too high and imagined herself turning down the volume control knob on the back of her hand while in an Enhanced State of Consciousness.

Michael had severe arthritic pain in his knees. He taught himself to relive the joy he felt years before when his young daughters would run to him and throw their arms around his legs in a tight hug. Reinterpreting a painful sensation as a happy one was an effective substitution for him.

*Mental anesthesia.* In this technique you will concentrate on numbing the area affected by the pain.

Think of a time when you had a local anesthetic, such as when your dentist gave you a shot of Novocain. Relive that physical experience as vividly as you can, without the anxiety you might have felt. Remember how the numbness began, first at the site of the injection, then spread over your lower jaw all the way up to the center of your lower lip. You knew that your lower jaw and lip were numb without touching them by the slight tingling sensation in the area. Practice this until you can actually sense the numbness in your mouth.

Now, in an Enhanced State of Consciousness experience your pain and visualize an injection of anesthetic into the area. Practice this until you are successful at numbing the entire area of pain.

If you master this technique you will be able to think at any point during the day of that flow of anesthetic to the area of pain and experience amazing relief.

After you master these techniques, performing them just two or three times a week can help keep you more in control of the effects of pain.

The important thing as you approach these exercises is to understand that you can lessen your sense of helplessness where pain is concerned by putting yourself back in control. Pain is an important message that a part of your body needs attention. Once you have gotten that message, however, and taken appropriate medical measures, you can help let go of the lingering pain by using the physical and mental resources at your disposal.

Relief is in sight.

# Afterword

There is often no single event that, in itself, can cause your system to go haywire; it is the way you perceive the situation and the coping strategies you use to deal with it that affect you physically. What you tell yourself about what is happening to you largely determines how you will react.

The experiences Dr. Lipton and I have had with our patients, supported by the research findings of dozens of medical scientists, demonstrate that the body's response to these sensitizers, even a heightened response due to Profound Sensitivity Syndrome, can indeed be controlled consciously. In fact, a sense of control reduces the severity of a hormonal and biochemical explosion, lessening its potential for destruction of immune function.

This is not to say we can cure every disease, overcome every physical ailment, merely by wishing it so. But we can control our minds and many of the messages sent to our bodies' systems. We can make a difference in how our bodies function. And that is an exciting concept.

The purpose of this book is to demonstrate *how you can gain more control over your own health,* just as our patients have learned to do.

Begin by making a conscious decision to take responsibility for your own life. Say to yourself, "I will take control. I will be healthier. I will be happier. I will do these things. I will not leave them to my family, my friends, my doctor. I am in control now. I am calling the shots. I will be healthier because now I know the secret. I understand what is wrong and I know I can do something about it."

If you are determined to believe that, you have already started to win the battle against the effects of Profound Sensitivity Syndrome.

# For Further Reading


Achterberg, J., *et al.* "Rheumatoid Arthritis: A Study of Relaxation and Temperature Biofeedback Training as an Adjunctive Therapy." *Biofeedback Self-Regul.* 6 (1981):207–223.

Ader, Robert. "Behaviorally Conditioned Immunosuppression." *Psychosomatic Medicine* 37 (1975):338.

Ader, Robert, ed. *Psychoneuroimmunology.* New York: Academic Press, 1981.

Anderson, E. "Effect of Hypnotic Instruction on the Nasal Congestion of 24 Hayfever Sufferers." *Diss. Abstr. Int.* 44 (1983):1050.

Atkinson, Holly. *Women and Fatigue.* New York: Pocket Books, 1985.

Baker, G. H. B. "Psychological Factors and Immunity." *J. Psychosom. Res.* 31 (1987):1–10.

Ben-Sira, Z. "Potency: A Stress-Buffering Link in the Coping-Stress-Disease Relationship." *Soc. Sci. Med.* 21 (1985):397–406.

Benson, Herbert, with Proctor, William. *Beyond the Relaxation Response.* New York: Time Books, 1984.

Benson, Herbert. *The Mind/Body Effect.* New York: Simon & Schuster, 1979.

———. *The Relaxation Response.* New York: William Morrow & Co., 1975.

Berne, Eric. *Sex in Human Loving.* New York: Simon & Schuster, 1970.

Borysenko, Joan, with Rothstein, Larry. *Minding the Body, Mending the Mind.* Reading, Mass.: Addison-Wesley Publishing Co., 1987.

Brown, Barbara B. *Stress and the Art of Biofeedback.* New York: Harper & Row, 1977.

Chanowitz, B., and Langer, E. "Knowing More for Less than You Can Show: Understanding Control through the Mindlessness-Mindfulness Distinction." *Human Helplessness: Theory and Application,* edited by J. Garber and M. E. P. Seligman. New York: Academic Press, 1980.

Charlesworth, Edward A., and Nathan, Ronald G. *Stress Management*. New York: Atheneum, 1984.

Clawson, T. A., *et. al.* "The Hypnotic Control of Blood Flow and Pain: The Cure of Warts and the Potential for the Use of Hypnosis in the Treatment of Cancer." *Am. J. Clin. Hypn.* (1975):160–169.

Cousins, Norman. *Anatomy of an Illness as Perceived by the Patient*. New York: W. W. Norton & Co., 1979.

———. *The Healing Heart*. New York: Avon, 1983.

Crasilneck, Harold B., and Hall, James A. *Clinical Hypnosis,* 2nd ed. New York: Grune & Stratton, Inc., 1985.

Emery, Gary, and Campbell, James. *Rapid Relief from Emotional Distress*. New York: Rawson Associates, 1986.

Farquhar, John W. *The American Way of Life Need Not Be Hazardous to Your Health,* rev. ed. Reading, Mass.: Addison-Wesley Publishing Co., 1987.

Frank, Jerome D. *Persuasion and Healing*, rev. ed. New York: Schocken Books, 1974.

Frankl, Viktor. *Man's Search for Meaning*. New York: Pocket Books, 1969.

Freudenberger, Herbert J., and North, Gail. *Situational Anxiety*. New York: Carroll & Graf, 1982.

———. *Women's Burnout*. New York: Doubleday & Co., 1985.

Garrison, F. H. *Introduction to the History of Medicine*. Philadelphia: W. B. Saunders Co., 1913.

Glaser, Ronald; Kiecold-Glaser, Janice K.; Speicher, Carl E.; Holliday, Jane E. "Stress, Loneliness, and Changes in Herpesvirus Latency." *J. Behav. Med.* 8, no. 3 (1985).

Groddeck, G. *The Meaning of Illness* (rev.). Independence, Mo.: International University Press, 1977.

Guillemin, R., Cohn, M., and Melnechyk, T., eds. *Neural Modulation of Immunity*. New York: Raven Press, 1985.

Harman, William, and Rheingold, Howard. *Higher Creativity*. Los Angeles: Jeremy P. Tarcher, Inc., 1984.

Hiroto, D. S., and Seligman, M. E. P. "Generality of Learned Helplessness in Man." *J. Pers. and Soc. Psy.* 31 (1975):311–317.

Hutchison, Michael. *Mega Brain*. New York: William Morrow & Co., 1986.

Kwiterovich, Peter O., Jr., M.D. *Beyond Cholesterol: The Johns Hopkins Complete Guide to Avoiding Heart Disease*. Baltimore: Johns Hopkins University Press, 1989.

Locke, Steven, and Colligan, Douglas. *The Healer Within.* New York: E. P. Dutton, 1986.

Macek, Catherine. "Of Mind and Morbidity: Can Stress and Grief Depress Immunity?" *J. Amer. Med. Assoc.* 248, no. 6 (July 23/30, 1982).

Mandler, George. *Mind and Body.* New York: W. W. Norton & Co., 1984.

Masters, William H. *Human Sexuality.* Boston: Little, Brown & Co., 1985.

Mathews-Simonton, Stephanie; Simonton, O. Carl; and Creighton, James L. *Getting Well Again.* New York: Bantam Books, 1978.

Matje, Sister Diane, R.N., M.S.N. "Stress and Cancer: A Review of the Literature." *Cancer Nursing,* October 1984.

Ornstein, Robert, and Sobel, David. *The Healing Brain.* New York: Simon & Schuster, 1987.

Pearsall, Paul. *Super Immunity.* New York: McGraw-Hill Book Co., 1987.

Pelletier, Kenneth R. *Mind as Healer, Mind as Slayer.* New York: Delacorte Press, 1977.

———. *Holistic Medicine.* New York: Delacorte Press, 1979.

Risenberg, D. E. "Can Mind Affect Body Defenses Against Disease?" *JAMA* (1986):256–313.

Rotter, L. "Generalized Expectancies for Internal versus External Control Reinforcement." *Psych. Monogr.* 80 (1966):28.

Seligman, Martin E. P. *Helplessness.* New York: W. H. Freeman & Co., 1975.

Seligman, Martin E. P., and Garber, Judy, eds. *Human Helplessness.* New York: Academic Press, 1980.

Selye, Hans. *The Stress of Life,* rev. ed. New York: McGraw-Hill Book Co., 1976.

———. *Hormones and Resistance.* New York: Springer-Verlag, 1971.

———. *Stress in Health and Disease.* Stoneham, Mass.: Butterworth Pubs., 1976.

———. *Stress without Distress.* New York: Harper & Row Pubs., Inc., 1974.

Siegel, Bernie S. *Love, Medicine & Miracles.* New York: Harper & Row Pubs., Inc., 1986.

Stevens, Anita. *Your Mind Can Cure.* New York: Hawthorne Books, 1974.

Turk, Dennis C., Meichenbaum, Donald, and Genest, Myles. *Pain and Behavioral Medicine.* New York: The Guilford Press, 1983.

Udelman, Harold D., M.D., and Udelman, Donna Lou, Ph.D. "Current Explorations in Psychoimmunology," *Amer. J. Psychother.* XXXVII, no. 2 (April 1983).

Van Dyke, Craig, and Temoshok, Lydia, and Zegan S., eds. *Emotions in Health and Illness.* New York: Grune & Stratton, 1983.

Wallston, B. S.; Wallston, K. A.; Kaplan, G. D.; and Maides, S. A. "Development and Validation of the Health Locus of Control Scale." *J. Cons. Clin. Psych.* 44 (1976):580–585.

Weitzenhoffer, Andre M. *Gen. Tech. Hypn.* New York: Grune & Stratton, 1957.

Winick, Myron. *Your Personalized Health Profile.* New York: Ballantine Books, 1985.

Wurtman, Judith J., with Danbrot, Margaret. *Managing Your Mind and Mood through Food.* New York: Rawson Associates, 1986.

Zilbergeld, Bernie, and Lazarus, Arnold A. *Mind Power.* Boston: Little, Brown & Co., 1987.

# Glossary

**Addison's disease:** a destructive disease of the adrenal gland resulting in adrenal insufficiency.

**Adenosine triphosphate (ATP):** high-energy phosphate groups produced by the metabolism of foods.

**Adipose tissue:** fatty tissue.

**Adrenal glands:** endocrine organs that produce steroids, metabolic hormones, and adrenaline.

**Adrenaline:** epinephrine; a blood pressure-raising hormone that also effects metabolism; secreted by the adrenal glands.

**Aerobic exercise:** physical conditioning aimed at increasing oxygen consumption and making the heart and lungs work harder.

**Aldosterone:** a steroid hormone secreted by the adrenal gland that regulates the body's balance of salt and water.

**Alpha interferon:** a biotherapeutic that acts against hairy cell leukemia and fights off infections.

**Aneurysm:** a blood-filled expansion of a weakened blood vessel wall.

**Angina pectoris:** chest pain precipitated by an inadequate oxygen supply to the heart muscles.

**Anorexia nervosa:** an eating disorder characterized by a pathological fear of weight gain leading to faulty eating habits, malnutrition, and excessive weight loss.

**Antibodies:** highly specific defense forces formed in response to individual antigens to protect the body against future attacks by the same antigen.

**Antigen:** an alien substance that has invaded the body.

**Anxiety disorders:** chronic fear, panic, worry, or avoidance behaviors.

**Arrhythmia:** irregular heartbeat.

**Arterioles:** tiny artery branches.

**Arteriosclerosis:** hardening of the arteries.

**Atherosclerosis:** arteriosclerosis characterized by fatty deposits.

**Attention-deficit disorder:** inability to concentrate for a determined period of time.

**Autoimmune disease:** damage to one's own body caused by lymphocytes and antibodies mistaking body organs for antigens.

**Autonomic nervous system:** the part of the nervous system that functions automatically and includes brain, spinal cord, and nerves.

**B-cells:** lymphocytes from the bone marrow that deal with antigens in the bloodstream.

**Beta endorphins:** opiatelike proteins secreted by the brain and other body organs that have pain-relieving effect.

**Biofeedback:** a training procedure by which people can learn voluntary control over their internal physiological systems.

**Biotherapeutics:** disease-fighting substances found naturally in the body.

**Bradykinin:** a polypeptide hormone that slows intestinal contractions and lowers blood pressure.

**Brain stem:** the part of the brain that connects the base of the brain with the spinal cord.

**Bulimia:** an eating disorder characterized by binge eating followed by self-induced vomiting.

**Bursitis:** inflammation of a bursa, a fluid-containing sac that surrounds a joint reducing friction, as between a tendon and a bone.

**Candidiasis:** an overgrowth of the yeast *Candida albicans,* which normally lives in the human gastrointestinal tract.

**Catecholamine:** adrenal gland secretions, including norepinephrine, that affect the sympathetic nervous system.

**Central nervous system:** the brain and spinal cord.

**Cholecystokinin:** a hormone that promotes satiation from lower food intake, and affects bile release.

**Cholesterol:** a steroid abundant in animal tissues, important in physiological processes, and implicated in atherosclerosis.

**Chronic Epstein-Barr virus (CEBV):** a virus that causes debilitating fatigue and numerous other symptoms.

**Chronic fatigue syndrome:** debilitating fatigue for which other medical diagnoses have been excluded.

**Chronic mucocutaneous candidiasis:** infection of the mucous membrane and skin with *Candida* yeast organisms.

**Clinical hypnosis:** an induced mental state for psychotherapeutic purposes.

**Clinical psychologist:** a psychologist who works directly with people who have problems, as opposed to experimental or laboratory psychologists; a psychologist trained in the psychopathology of human interactions.

**Cognitive:** having to do with thinking.

**Cognitive distortion:** an irrational thought pattern.

**Colitis:** inflammation of the large intestine.

**Corticosteroids:** adrenal steroids such as corticosterone, cortisone, and aldosterone.

**Corticosterone:** an adrenal steroid hormone that is important in protein and carbohydrate metabolism and affects sodium reabsorption.

**Cortisol:** an adrenal secretion that helps regulate carbohydrates and is used to treat various inflammatory and allergic diseases.

**Cortisone:** an adrenal steroid biotherapeutic that counteracts inflammation, allergies, and arthritis.

**Diabetes mellitus:** a major carbohydrate metabolism disorder but also a metabolic protein and fat disorder characterized by inadequate secretion or utilization of insulin.

**Electromyography:** a test used for the measurement of the electrical activity in muscles.

**Endocrine system:** the glands that produce internal secretions, such as the pituitary and thyroid.

**Endocrinologist:** a specialist in dealing with the endocrine glands.

**Endorphins:** the body's natural painkillers.

**Enhanced State of Consciousness:** hypnotic state achieved through self-hypnosis.

**Epidemiology:** the study of the incidence, distribution, and control of disease in a population.

**Epinephrine:** adrenaline; a blood-pressure raising hormone secreted by the adrenal glands.

**Etiology:** identifiable cause.

**Existentialism:** a school of philosophy and psychotherapy that emphasizes man's existence with regard to mortality and choice.

**Fibromyalgia:** an illness featuring muscle pain.

**Fight-or-flight response:** a defense mechanism that causes one to attack or run away from a stress-provoking situation.

**Gastroenterologist:** a specialist in the diseases of the stomach and the intestine.

**Glucagon:** a hormone produced by the pancreas that raises the concentration of sugar in the blood.

**Herpes simplex II:** a genital disease caused by a virus.

**Histamine:** a biochemical substance released by the body in allergic reactions.

**Hormones:** substances formed by one body organ and carried by a body fluid to a tissue or another organ, where it has a specific effect.

**Hyperarousal:** excessive physiological readiness for activity.

**Hyperplastic hypertrophic obesity:** increase of fat cells in size and number.

**Hyperthyroidism:** excessive functional activity of the thyroid gland resulting in an increased metabolic rate, rapid heart rate, and high blood pressure.

**Hypertrophic obesity:** increase of fat cells in size but not in number.

**Hyperventilation:** extremely rapid breathing that drops the carbon-dioxide levels in the blood and causes dizziness and fainting.

**Hypnotherapy:** psychotherapy that facilitates suggestion, reeducation, or analysis by means of hypnosis.

**Hypoglycemia:** an abnormally low concentration of sugar in the blood.

**Hypothalamus:** a brain center controlling glands such as the pituitary and affecting other endocrine organs.

**Hypothyroidism:** deficient activity of the thyroid gland, resulting in a retarded rate of metabolism, sluggishness, and puffiness.

**Immune system:** specific parts of the body that protect against infectious disease.

**Immunoglobulins:** disease fighters, and antibodies in allergic reactions.

**Insulin:** a biotherapeutic that helps regulate normal carbohydrate metabolism and prevents diabetes.

**Intermittent claudication:** severe leg cramps caused by inadequate blood supply.

**Irritable bowel syndrome:** a disorder of the small intestine and large bowel that causes abdominal pain and constipation or diarrhea.

**Limbic:** pertaining to brain structures, such as the hippocampus and the amygdala, that act upon the endocrine system and affect emotion and motivation.

**Limbic-hypothalamic system:** the limbic system, the hypothalamus, and the connections between them.

**Lymphocytes:** white blood cells formed in lymph tissue.

**Mast cells:** large cells found in connective tissue, and involved in allergic reactions.

**Meditation:** a focused state of mind aimed at reducing the tension (stressors) of the outside world.

**Metabolism:** the chemical changes in living cells by which energy is provided for vital processes and new material is assimilated.

**Migraine:** a common type of intense vascular headache.

**Mononucleosis:** an acute infectious disease characterized by fever, swollen lymph nodes, sore throat, and abnormally large lymphocytes.

**MRI (magnetic resonance imaging):** a noninvasive diagnostic procedure.

**Myasthenia gravis:** a neurological degenerative disease of faulty nerve conduction characterized by weakness and quick fatigue of muscles.

**Myocardial infarction:** heart attack.

**Neuritis:** inflammation of a nerve causing pain, sensory disturbance, and reflex impairment.

**Neuro-immuno-modulation:** psycho-neuro-immunology.

**Neurological:** having to do with the nervous system, its structures, and its diseases.

**Neurons:** nerve cells.

**Neuropathy:** any disease of the nervous system.

**Neuropeptides:** amino acids produced in the brain and by immune cells.

**Norepinephrine:** an adrenal hormone that assists in transmitting nerve impulses and is used medically to constrict blood vessels and stop bleeding.

**Pathology:** the structural and functional changes caused by disease processes.

**Peripheral nervous system:** the nerves running from the brain and spinal cord to and from all parts of the body.

**Pernicious anemia:** a severe, progressive decrease in the number of red blood cells, characterized by paleness, weakness, and gastrointestinal and nervous disturbances.

**Phenol:** a poisonous acid in coal tar and wood tar used in disinfectants, explosives, and plastics.

**Phlebitis:** inflammation of a vein.

**Physiologist:** a specialist in the normal functions and vital processes of living organisms.

**Pituitary gland:** an endocrine gland that secretes hormones that affect body growth, metabolism, and the activity of other endocrine glands.

**Placebo:** an inert preparation given as a medicine either to humor a patient or to test the effects of another substance in a controlled experiment.

**Placebo effect:** a set of assumptions that triggers emotional impact and biochemical change.

**Platelet:** a blood cell that assists in clotting.

**Premenstrual Syndrome (PMS):** physical symptoms caused by the impending onset of menstruation.

**Procaine:** a local anesthetic.

**Profound Sensitivity Syndrome:** hyperreactivity of the body to any stressor or sensitizer.

**Progesterone:** a hormone that prepares the uterus for pregnancy.

**Prophylactic:** preventive or protective against disease.

**Prostaglandins:** hormonelike substances in the body involved in blood pressure control and intestinal smooth-muscle stimulation.

**Protozoa:** single-celled microscopic organisms that thrive on specific vitamins.

**PS$^2$:** Profound Sensitivity Syndrome.

**Psychogenic:** of mental origin.

**Psycho-neuro-immunology:** the close interaction between mind and body as the source of health and well-being.

**Psycho-physiology:** psycho-neuro-immunology.

**Psychotherapy:** treatment of emotional or behavioral disorders by verbal communication with the patient.

**Pulmonary:** having to do with the lungs.

**Raynaud's Syndrome:** spasm of arterioles such as of the finger arteries with blanching and numbness of the fingers.

**Reserpine:** a drug extracted from the rauwolfia tree and used to treat hypertension and mental disorders.

**Rheumatoid arthritis (RA):** an autoimmune disease manifested in joint inflammation and pain.

**Rheumatologist:** specialist in the diagnosis and treatment of muscle and joint disease.

**Sensitizer:** chemical or emotional factor that can elicit a stress response.

**Serotonin:** a hormone found in the blood and the brain that constricts blood vessels, contracts smooth muscles, and inhibits gastric secretion.

**Somnambulism:** literally means sleepwalking, but also refers to a deep level of hypnotic trance state.

**Steroids:** a large family of chemical substances including hormones, vitamins, and drugs.

**Subarachnoid:** the area between two of the brain membranes that contains cerebrospinal fluid and all the large blood vessels supplying the brain and the spinal cord.

**Subclinical:** prior to the appearance of symptoms in the evolution of a disease.

**Sudden Death Syndrome (SDS):** a fatal heart attack or sudden inability to breathe suffered by one who has never shown signs or symptoms of heart or lung disease.

**Synovial fluid:** a clear fluid that lubricates joints, tendon sheaths, and bursae.

**Systemic lupus erythematosus (SLE):** an autoimmune inflammatory connective tissue disease.

**T-cells:** lymphocytes from the thymus gland that reject foreign tissue, regulate cellular immunity, and control the production of antibodies in the presence of an antigen.

**Temporal mandibular joint dysfunction (TMJ):** a tension-aggravated condition manifested by the grinding of teeth and painful chewing, and/or headache.

**Testosterone:** a hormone that induces and maintains male secondary sex characteristics.

**Thermal biofeedback:** biofeedback directed toward warming one's hands and feet.

**Thymus:** a glandlike organ inside the neck that functions in the development of the body's immune system.

**Thyrotropin-releasing hormone (TRH):** a biochemical that stimulates the production of thyroid-stimulating hormone and also causes the flood of gastric acids that can cause stomach ulcers.

**Tinnitus:** ringing in the ears.

**Triglycerides:** fatty acids commonly called fats.

**Vasculitis:** inflammation of the blood vessels.

# Index

# About the Authors

**Dr. Neil Solomon** specializes in internal medicine, including selected aspects of endocrinology and metabolism, environmental illness, and allergy. He received his M.D. from Case Western Reserve University with Alpha Omega Alpha honors, and his Ph.D. in physiology from the University of Maryland. He did his internship and residency on the Osler Medical Service of the Johns Hopkins Hospital where he received the coveted Schwentker award for his outstanding medical research.

Dr. Solomon has held the following academic positions: Assistant Professor of Psychiatry and Behavioral Sciences, Johns Hopkins University School of Medicine; Associate Professor of Physiology and Assistant Professor of Medicine, University of Maryland School of Medicine; and Clinical Professor of Pharmacology, University of Miami School of Medicine.

For almost a decade, he also headed the health and mental health programs for the State of Maryland, serving in the Governor's cabinet.

A best-selling author, he maintains a private practice in Baltimore; writes an internationally syndicted medical column for the Los Angeles Times Syndicate; is a consultant to corporations and governments, and frequently appears on national television and radio.

**Dr. Marc Lipton,** a clinical psychologist practicing in Baltimore, specializes in the treatment of stress-related disorders. He received his Ph.D. from the State University of New York at Buffalo and M.P.A. from Cornell University in Health Care Administration. Dr. Lipton has held faculty appointments at Johns Hopkins University and the University of Maryland, and has designed many specialized programs for the treatment of emotional, alcohol, and drug-related problems.